They are descended from the patriarchs
and from their flesh and blood came Christ
who is above all, God for ever blessed!

ROMANS 9:5 JB

It is one and the same Son of God Who exists
in both natures, taking what is ours to Himself
without losing what is His own.

POPE LEO THE GREAT

Without the cross there is no christology,
nor is there any feature of christology which
can escape justifying itself by the cross.

MARTIN KÄHLER

Christ not only exercises the judgment of God on us,
He absorbs it, so that we are judged not only
by Him but in Him. And so in Him we are
judged unto salvation.

P. T. FORSYTH

Christian Foundations

A THEOLOGY OF WORD & SPIRIT
HOLY SCRIPTURE
GOD THE ALMIGHTY
JESUS CHRIST
THE HOLY SPIRIT
THE CHURCH
THE LAST THINGS

CHRISTIAN
FOUNDATIONS

JESUS CHRIST

Savior & Lord

DONALD G. BLOESCH

IVP Academic

An imprint of InterVarsity Press
Downers Grove, Illinois

InterVarsity Press
P.O. Box 1400, Downers Grove, IL 60515-1426
World Wide Web: www.ivpress.com
E-mail: mail@ivpress.com

InterVarsity Press® *is the book-publishing division of InterVarsity Christian Fellowship/USA*® *, a student movement active on campus at hundreds of universities, colleges and schools of nursing in the United States of America, and a member movement of the International Fellowship of Evangelical Students. For information about local and regional activities, write Public Relations Dept., InterVarsity Christian Fellowship/USA, 6400 Schroeder Rd., P.O. Box 7895, Madison, WI 53707-7895, or visit the IVCF website at <www.intervarsity.org>.*

The Scripture quotations quoted herein are from the Revised Standard Version of the Bible, *copyright 1946, 1952, 1971 by the Division of Christian Education of the National Council of the Churches of Christ in the U.S.A. Used by permission. All rights reserved.*

Design: Cindy Kiple

Images: Guy Wolek

ISBN-10: 0-8308-2754-4
ISBN-13: 978-0-8308-2754-1

Printed in the United States of America ∞

Library of Congress Cataloging-in-Publication Data
Bloesch, Donald G., 1928-
  Jesus Christ: Savior & Lord / Donald G. Bloesch.
     p. cm.—(Christian foundations)
  Originally published: c1997.
  Includes bibliographical references and indexes.
  ISBN 0-8308-1414-0 (cloth: alk. paper)—ISBN 0-8308-2754-4 (pbk.: alk. paper)
     1. Jesus Christ—Person and offices. I. Title.
  BT203.B56 2006
  232.8—dc22

                                                                                    2005052141

P	20	19	18	17	16	15	14	13	12	11	10	9	8	7	6	5	4	3	2	1
Y	20	19	18	17	16	15	14	13	12	11	10	09	08	07	06	05					

*Dedicated to the
memory of
Peter T. Forsyth*

Acknowledgments

I acknowledge my indebtedness to the following: my wife, Brenda, for her painstaking labor in editing and proofreading; Debbie Lovett for her careful typing of this manuscript; Joel Samuels, Shannon Franzen-Lau and Mary Anne Knefel of the Dubuque Seminary library for helping me to locate needed references; and Arthur C. Cochrane for encouraging me to formulate a biblical doctrine of the preexistence of Jesus Christ. I thank Bradley Nassif for inviting me to lecture on the evangelical doctrine of salvation at the Evangelical-Orthodox conference held at the Billy Graham Center, Wheaton College, September 24, 1993. A revised version of this lecture is found in chapter seven. I am grateful to Southwestern Baptist Seminary for allowing the republication of the article "The Lordship of Christ in Theological History," which appeared in *Southwestern Journal of Theology* 33, no. 2 (1991):26-34. I am also grateful to *Touchstone* magazine for permission to include the article "The Finality of Christ and Religious Pluralism," which first appeared in the summer 1991 issue (vol. 4, no. 3, pp. 5-9) and was republished in abridged form in *Cross Point* (vol. 4, no. 4) and *Mission and Ministry* (vol. 9, no. 2). Chapter ten in this volume represents an expansion and updating of the original version.

Abbreviations for Biblical Translations

DRV   Douay Rheims Version
GNB   Good News Bible
JB   Jerusalem Bible
KJV   King James Version
NASB   New American Standard Bible
NEB   New English Bible
NIV   New International Version
NJB   New Jerusalem Bible
NKJ   New King James Version
NRSV   New Revised Standard Version
REB   Revised English Bible

(Note: Bible references not otherwise indicated are from the Revised Standard Version.)

Preface

The aim of my Christian Foundations series is to set forth a theology of Word and Spirit, which seeks to do justice to both the objective and subjective poles of revelation and salvation. A theology of Word and Spirit will be at the same time a theology of the Christian life, since the truth revealed in the Bible must be appropriated through the power of the Spirit in a life of obedience and piety. When I affirm the pivotal role of the Christian life I am calling not for a new form of the imitation of Christ but instead for a deepening recognition that the risen Christ lives within us, empowering us to realize our divinely given vocation under the cross. The Christian life is not simply the fruit and consequence of a past salvation accomplished in the cross and resurrection of Christ but the arena in which Christ's salvation is carried forward to fulfillment by his Spirit. The Pauline and Reformation doctrine of salvation by free grace must be united with the call to holiness and discipleship, a theme found in Catholic mysticism and Protestant Pietism. The law of God must be united with the gospel, just as faith must be supplemented by obedience. Jesus must be followed as Lord as well as confessed as Savior.

My goal is to spell out a centrist evangelical theology, not in the sense of occupying a middle-of-the-road position but in the sense of reclaiming the dynamic center of biblical and apostolic faith—God's self-revelation in Jesus Christ. It is a theology that draws upon sacred tradition without accepting everything in this tradition uncritically. It is alert to what the Spirit of God is doing in the culture without trying to accommodate the claims of the gospel to cultural ideologies. It holds both Holy Scripture and holy mother Church in high esteem, but it is always careful to distinguish between form and content, the sign and the thing signified. It does not absolutize what is relative, yet recognizes that the absolute comes to us in the form of the relative. It does not confound the infinite and the finite but firmly maintains that the finite can be a bearer of the infinite, though this is a divine, not a human, possibility.

I hope that my theology will appeal to two groups: those coming out of fundamentalism in search of a biblical alternative to liberalism, and those who have become disillusioned with liberalism and sense the need to recover the transcendent truth of the gospel kept alive in church tradition by the Spirit of the living God. Holy Scripture must be reclaimed as our infallible standard for faith and practice, but it is always Scripture illumined by the Spirit and applied by the Spirit to the existential and cultural situation in which we find ourselves.

I seek not a refurbished Pietism but instead an ecumenical orthodoxy that unites doctrine and life, faith and experience. Such a stance must be contrasted with a sectarian orthodoxy that is characterized by a narrow one-sidedness as opposed to a many-sidedness, the mark of an evangelical catholicity. Particular claims to truth must be informed by a comprehensive vision of the whole truth if they are to serve the cause of the holy catholic church. We must continue to affirm *sola gratia* (grace alone) and *sola fide* (faith alone) while remembering that though we are justified only *by* grace and only *through* faith we are justified *for* holiness, and this means that a holy life is not an appendage to our salvation but the sign and evidence of the authenticity of our salvation. Likewise we should continue to uphold *solus Christus* (Christ alone), albeit not in the sense that Christ stands alone or works alone, for he employs his people as earthen vessels and agents to communicate his saving grace to the world.

Today the finality of Christ is being called into question, whereas in a past age the relation of the two natures in Christ was the overriding issue. The latter continues to be of crucial importance and must therefore still be addressed, though it is not where the heart of the battle is.

Under the impact of the new theology the church is now trying to be inclusive rather than exclusive, global rather than provincial, universal rather than particular. While we need to affirm the inclusive outreach of the gospel, it is imperative that we stand firm for the exclusive claims of the gospel. The battle today is between a global theology that seeks to uncover continuity with the culture and a theology of crisis that signals a break with the goals and self-understanding of the culture. Our mandate is to combat the universalist strand in modern Christian thought that postulates the Spirit of God working redemptively in all cultures and religions. A corollary notion is that people can be saved while remaining true to the highest expressions of their own faiths. We should strive for a genuinely Christian universalism that heralds the coming reign of Christ over the whole world but that correlates the salvation that he brings with faith in his word as revealed in the New Testament. He is Lord of all but Savior only of some—of those who believe and trust in his name, those who take up the cross and follow him in faith and obedience.[1]

We are living at the end of an era in which denominational loyalties were still important and the church still had a common understanding of its mission. With the transition from modernism to postmodernism the mainline churches have succumbed to the beguilements of relativism and have thereby become reluctant to uphold a particular claim to truth. The mainline denominations are no longer custodians of revealed truth but loose coalitions tied together by a social agenda that bears the marks of ideological commitment. I contend that the age of the denominations is over and that what we are already beginning to see are confessional communities intent on biblical fidelity that cross all denominational lines and that may provide the basis for a revitalized Christianity in the future. It is my hope that the Spirit of God will use my theology to prepare the way for a confessing church for our time.

---

[1]Christ is Savior of the whole world in that his salvation is offered to all and intended for all, but it comes to completion only in those who believe.

·ONE·

CHRIST IN DISPUTE

If Christ has not been raised,
your faith is futile and you are still in your sins.
1 CORINTHIANS 15:17

A Christ that differs from the rest of men only in saintly degree
and not in redeeming kind is not the Christ of the New Testament.
P. T. FORSYTH

The christological debate that has persisted since the dawn
of the modern age has not yet been resolved.
HANS KÜNG

Virtually all modern theology has abandoned the idea
of sudden irruptions from outside
(the old supernaturalism) and sees things
happening as gradual processes,
though not without critical moments.
JOHN MACQUARRIE

Christology constitutes the heart of theology, since it focuses on God's work of salvation in the historical figure Jesus of Nazareth and the bearing that this has on the history of humankind. To know the nature of God we must see his face in Jesus Christ. To know the plan of God for the world we must see this plan realized in the cross of Christ and fulfilled in his resurrection and second advent. Whereas philosophy ponders the nature of God in the abstract, theology reflects on the divine-human encounter in history as we find this in Jesus Christ. The way to knowledge of God is through knowledge of Christ, and the way to knowledge of Christ is by faith in his promises as revealed in the Bible.

The Pivotal Issues

The identity of Jesus is a key issue in current biblical and theological scholarship. Some portray Jesus as a guru, a sage or a visionary. For Ralph Waldo Emerson, who has had an enormous impact on the shaping of American spirituality, the kingdom is inward and spiritual, and the role of Jesus is to make people aware of this fact. Burton Mack contends that the Gospels must be seen as "the result of early Christian mythmaking."[1] According to Pheme Perkins, Mack views Jesus as "a sage in the asocial, iconoclastic tradition of the ancient Cynics."[2] Similarly, John Dominic Crossan depicts Jesus as an itinerant teacher, a "peasant Jewish Cynic."[3] For Geza Vermes Jesus was a "charismatic holy man" or "charismatic prophet."[4] Marcus Borg presents Jesus as a charismatic healer, who was both deeply political and deeply spiritual.[5]

Others view Jesus as principally an eschatological prophet with apocalyptic expectations. This tradition was given academic respectability in the modern world by Johannes Weiss and Albert Schweitzer, both of whom depicted the kingdom of God as a radically new reality breaking into present history from the outside and bringing the world as we know it to an end.[6] More recent scholars who envision the kingdom as an apocalyptic denouement rather than an immanent-historical reality are Rudolf Bultmann, Martin Dibelius, the early Karl Barth, Emil Brunner and John P. Meier.[7]

Biblical scholars who regard Jesus as an epiphany of God or God in human flesh include Ben Witherington III,[8] William R. Farmer[9] and N. T. Wright.[10] Some, such as Marcus Borg, are willing to use the language of epiphany but refuse to embrace the traditional understanding of the incarnation of God in Christ. According to Witherington Jesus' divinity was upheld in Palestinian Jewish Christianity no later than "within the first twenty years after Jesus' death."[11] Farmer contends that the New Testament gives ample vindication to those who uphold

Jesus as a heavenly or divine Savior.[12] N. T. Wright exposes the shallowness of the Jesus Seminar, which calls into radical question the authenticity of the words attributed to Jesus in the New Testament; he maintains convincingly that the whole New Testament corpus presupposes the miracle of Jesus' resurrection from the grave.[13]

A closely related critical issue in christology today is theological method. Do we affirm a christology from above, in which we begin with a supernatural Christ before history, or a christology from below, in which we begin with a historical analysis of Jesus as presented in the New Testament? Wolfhart Pannenberg, John Macquarrie, Karl Adam, Hans Küng and Stanley Grenz are among those who call into question the momentous task of unearthing the mystery of Christ by beginning with an abstract concept of his deity. They strongly contend for a historical approach that may indeed culminate in a confession of his deity.[14] If I read Karl Barth correctly, he would have us eschew both these methods and instead focus our attention on the living God incarnate in Christ—discernible only to the eyes of faith.

The meaning of the cross of Christ has also divided theology—in the past and the present. Whereas traditional theology upheld Jesus' death as an atoning sacrifice or payment for sin, the new mood is to treat Jesus as a vicarious sufferer who identifies with the human condition. Is the death of Christ on the cross substitutionary or exemplary? For many liberationist and feminist theologians the cross is a symbol of the battle against oppression rather than a substitutionary atonement.

Equally controversial is the doctrine of sin, which is being drastically revised in current theology. While classical theology conceived of sin as rebellion against God and transgression of God's law, the new theologies view sin in terms of failure and brokenness. Sin is refusing to measure up to one's highest potential or shirking responsibility rather than deliberately breaking God's commandments. The remedy for sin, it is said, lies in a new understanding of ourselves rather than in faith in a divine Savior.

Still another issue that engrosses contemporary theologians is the language of faith. Are the statements about God and his works in

Scripture univocal or symbolic, propositional or narrational? If we allow for the element of legend or myth in the biblical accounts, does this undermine the historical claims of the faith? John Hick presciently maintains that "there will be a growing awareness of the mythological character of this language, as the hyperbole of the heart, most naturally at home in hymns and anthems and oratorios and other artistic expressions of the poetry of devotion."[15] Hick can be faulted for not giving adequate recognition to the fact that language can be poetic or figurative and yet describe concrete, objective historical realities rather than simply inner longings of the soul.[16]

Are the miracles in the Bible facts, legends or myth? John Macquarrie contends that miracles are simply signs of the impact of creative forces within nature that excite wonder.[17] Many scholars of the liberal persuasion give a psychosomatic explanation for many of Jesus' healings but relegate the nature miracles to creative fiction.[18] In the view of John Dominic Crossan Jesus' miracles were really "liberating declarations that sick people were fully acceptable members of society." The miracles are not so much physical changes as changes in social perception.[19] Evangelical theology continues to maintain the classical definition of miracles as acts or events that defy natural explanation and that can be attributed only to God's decisive intervention in human history.[20]

Theological differences also come to light in the discussion of models of salvation. Whereas the Reformation understood salvation as basically justification and sanctification and mystical theology as purgation and deification, liberationist and feminist theologies uphold the models of empowerment and freedom. In the newer theologies justification is equated with liberation from the bonds of deception, sanctification with resoluteness against the powers of oppression.[21]

Another festering issue in soteriology is the complex relation between the law and the gospel.[22] At the time of the Reformation this issue was very prominent especially in the conflicts between Lutherans and Calvinists, but it continues to be a source of aggravation today, particularly in light of Karl Barth's thesis that the gospel has priority over the law. In liberationist theology the gospel is virtually transmuted into a new law. In process theology the gospel becomes the vision of a new future rather than the good news of an accomplished reconciliation in the past.

Christologies in Conflict

The contemporary religious scene is marked by a radical pluralism reflected in disparate and often opposing christologies. Although increasingly adapted to a postmodern agenda, the older liberal theology still exerts a potent influence. Its underlying motif has been the continuity between the human and the divine and the capacity of the human to ascend to the divine. According to Schleiermacher, "As certainly as Christ was a man, there must reside in human nature the possibility of taking up the divine into itself, just as did happen in Christ."[23] Joseph Bracken restates the liberal creed with the aid of a process conceptuality: "Human personhood is basically continuous with divine personhood, although clearly only an imperfect realization of the latter. A divine person, then, presumably can unite himself with a human person in such a way as progressively to open up that human being to the fullness of what it means to be a person, i.e., one able to know and love everything that exists."[24] The experiential cast of the older liberalism was conspicuous in Henry Ward Beecher, a transitional figure in that he still retained a Calvinist heart:

It is the Christ *in them*—so far as he *is* in them—that they are to preach. It is not the theological Christ, necessarily, it is not necessarily the Christ of the Gospel, it is not even the Gospel, alone, that is to be taught. Your specialty in teaching is *Christ in you the hope of glory*. How much has been turned into personal experience, how much God has manifested himself as able to save you from sin—this is the Christ, this is the Gospel, that you need to preach.[25]

Existentialist theology, a variant of neoliberalism, continues the emphasis on personal experience over objective truth. Rudolf

Bultmann's interest was in the function of Christ rather than his ontology. What is of crucial importance is whether the message of the church directs us to the redeeming power of the cross.[26] For Paul Tillich the goal of christology is to lead us to participate in the power of the New Being actualized in the historical Jesus. In his view Jesus was adopted as the Christ, but he refused to say that Jesus was born as the Christ. Existentialist theology generally takes issue with the metaphysics of the Council of Chalcedon (451), which affirmed the inseparability and indivisibility of the divine and human natures of Christ. John Macquarrie accepts Chalcedon's "governing intention" while advocating a change of language into more dynamic categories.[27]

Chalcedonian christology has also been vigorously challenged by the theology of hope. Jürgen Moltmann upholds a "christology of history" over an "eternal christology."[28] Jesus is the victorious representative of humankind, a "revealer of God in a godless and godforsaken world."[29] No longer an expiation for sin that satisfies the demands of the law, the cross of Christ is now seen as enabling us to make contact with the power of liberating love. Moltmann anticipates the liberationist emphasis on praxis over logos: "To know Jesus does not simply mean learning the facts of christological dogma. It means learning to know him in the praxis of discipleship."[30] The doctrine of the two natures of Christ has also been criticized by Pannenberg, who combines a theology of hope with a theology of universal history. In this perspective Jesus gains his identity as a person not before or outside history but in the unfolding of his historical life on earth.[31]

Liberationist theology celebrates Jesus as a pioneer in a social revolution that looks forward to a kingdom of justice here on earth. Jesus does not turn us away from the world but motivates us to change social structures in a spirit of love. Jesus, says Jon Sobrino, "advocates a political love, a love that is situated in history and that has visible repercussions for human beings."[32] According to Leonardo Boff, "The salvation proclaimed by Christianity is an all-embracing one. It is not restricted to economic, political, social and ideological emancipation, but neither can it be realized without them."[33] John Howard Yoder, who speaks out of the Anabaptist tradition but whose work resonates with liberationist themes, describes Jesus as "the bearer of a new possibility of human, social, and . . . political relationships."[34]

In feminist theology, which reflects and converges with liberationism at many points, Jesus is a motherly figure who nurtures and sustains his people rather than commands and oversees. He also has brotherly and sisterly qualities as he works alongside us in creating a better world. He is "Mentor and Friend" rather than "Savior and Lord."[35] In the words of Virginia Ramey Mollenkott,

> Many of us would understand Jesus to be our elder brother, the trailblazer and constant companion for us who are here in time and space but ultimately one among many brothers and sisters in an eternally, equally worthy siblinghood. [He was] firstborn only in the sense that he was the first to show us that it is possible to live in oneness with the divine source while we are here on this planet.[36]

Process theology is inclined to separate the two natures of Christ, giving precedence to the Christ ideal over the earthly or human Jesus. Pierre Teilhard de Chardin, one of the luminaries of this movement, refers to the "living" and indomitable idea of "the universal-Christ."[37] Our goal is to seek union with "the Eucharistic Cosmic Christ."[38] Joseph Bracken contends that the incarnation took place "primarily to give new direction and focus to the collective power of good in the world."[39] But Jesus could not have accomplished this task by himself. He had to enlist others to preach the good news, viz., "that God is a loving Father and that one can, accordingly, turn the direction of one's life over to such a Father in the confident expectation that others will do the same and that thereby the Kingdom of God on earth will truly be established."[40] For Bracken, as for Adolf von Harnack earlier, Jesus' original message was "the Fatherhood of God, the need for all men and women to live together in peace and love as the Father's most dear children, the universal character of the Kingdom."[41]

Peter C. Hodgson, a synthetic thinker who blends insights from both Hegelian and Whiteheadian process philosophies with liberationist themes, believes that openness to God is constitutive of true humanity, and Jesus is the one who manifests this openness par excellence. As "the radically free person" Jesus embodies "the fulfillment of human potentiality."[42] Hodgson regards Jesus as "the representative human being," and therefore as the "son of God" but not as God.[43] Jesus' ministry focused "not on humanity's guilt-ridden disobedience of God," which would require substitutionary atonement, but rather "on humanity's wounding of itself, its self-imposed and self-destructive bondage," and this requires "liberating power and redemptive healing."[44]

The theology of religions reduces Jesus to the role of a pathfinder who opens up new dimensions of experience for seekers after truth. No longer the unique embodiment of the presence of God, he is comparable to the prophets and mystics in the other great world religions. These theologians generally favor a theocentric perspective, in which God reveals himself equally in all religions, over a christocentric or what some prefer to call an ethnocentric perspective, which absolutizes a particular revelation in history. Paul Knitter recommends that we go even beyond theocentrism to soteriocentrism, where the absolute is no longer the church or Christ or even God but rather "the kingdom and its justice."[45] John Hick regards the story of Jesus Christ in the New Testament as "mythologically true" but not "literally true."[46] This approach makes it possible to draw from other stories in other religions in order to arrive at a global or multicultural vision that celebrates the world and its religions in their diversity. In our investigation of the multiple forms of religion, we will at the same time maintain the bonds that tie all religions together—the universal quest for union with "the Real."[47] While still trying to hold on to the unique role of Jesus Christ in God's self-manifestation in human history, Jacques Dupuis advocates "a comprehensive, universal perspective" capable of integrating in their many differences all religious experiences.[48]

Orthodox or traditionalist thought continues to retain a significant following especially in the circles of traditional Catholicism, Eastern Orthodoxy and conservative evangelicalism.[49] Neo-orthodox theologians like Karl Barth and Dietrich Bonhoeffer strongly affirmed the Chalcedonian definition, though Emil Brunner and Reinhold Niebuhr treated it with considerable reserve. Barth gave orthodox christology a new slant as he questioned the suitability of the idea of propitiating a vengeful God and stressed the fact that God vicariously identifies with our suffering and shame and absorbs this suffering into his own life.

The Road Ahead

The mood today is pluralistic and inclusivistic, and any claims to absolute truth are peremptorily dismissed by the academic elite. Those who would reaffirm orthodox christology must take into serious consideration the radical relativism and historicism that pervade the intellectual life of the West. In light of the breakdown of the legacy of the Enlightenment we should not be beguiled into absolutizing the relative, but we should also protest against the postmodern penchant for relativizing the absolute. Even in the midst of change God remains ever the same, though God is always free to relate himself to mortals in ever new ways. While truth invariably comes to us in a particular context, it is not limited to any particular context. Although the Bible itself is culturally shaped and conditioned, this does not imply that the message of the Bible is the product of history or culture. It is possible and indeed mandatory to affirm the transhistorical dimension of biblical revelation even while trying to do justice to the historicity of any particular passage or claim. We should treat every text in terms of its place in history *(Sitz im Leben)* but always look beyond the text to the reality to which it points—the living Word of God. The absolute breaks into the relative, and we therefore have the absolute only in the form of the relative. But we are not to conclude that our grasp of what is revealed to us is therefore untrustworthy or out of harmony with the truth disclosed by God in history.

We must strive to be faithful to what has been revealed by the Spirit of God to his church, but we should never be arrogant or condescending, for we see this truth only dimly, we have this truth only partially (1 Cor 13:12). Now we walk by faith, not by sight (2 Cor 5:7). We are called to be witnesses to the truth and seekers after the truth at the same time. We should not hide the light given to us (Mt 5:14-16), but manifest this light in our lives and words, though always in a spirit of humility, knowing that this light is God's, not our own, and that we are at the most only instruments of and reflectors of his grace.

·TWO·

THE PLIGHT
OF HUMANITY

And this is the judgment, that the light has come into the world,
and people loved darkness rather than light
because their deeds were evil.
JOHN 3:19 NRSV

None is righteous, no, not one; no one understands,
no one seeks for God.
ROMANS 3:10

This, then, was the plight of men . . . turning from eternal things
to things corruptible, by counsel of the devil,
they had become the cause of their own corruption in death.
ATHANASIUS

The anomalous thing is then not the outer tragedy of fate
but the inner tragedy of guilt,
and man's chief end is to be forgiven and redeemed.
P. T. FORSYTH

Sin kills by perverting, polluting and dividing,
breaking down persons and their vital relationships.
CORNELIUS PLANTINGA JR.

One cannot fully appreciate the significance of the cross and resurrection of Jesus Christ as well as his incarnation apart from a keen perception of the plight of a humanity corrupted by sin. Scripture plainly teaches that all humans—male and female—are created in the image of God, but this image has been blurred and defaced by our willful contumacy and rebellion against our Creator.

The imago Dei is probably best understood as an asymmetrical relationship between God and the human creature, a relationship in which the latter reflects the glory, goodness and wisdom of the former. Even in sin we are still inescapably related to God, though now we fail to comprehend the truth of our origin as creatures of God. Now we are entangled in a web of deceit that signifies a rupture in our relationship to God. The awareness that we presently have of God judges us and confirms us in our guilt. Yet God will not let us go, even in our prideful folly, and he continues to sustain us even in the depths of our depravity (cf. Mt 5:45; Acts 17:25-28). God has made us for himself (Augustine); we come from God, and we are destined to give glory to God, whether as believers or as unbelievers.

In an era when education and social reform are so readily upheld as antidotes to fractured human relationships, evangelical Christianity teaches that the expansion of human knowledge and human welfare in and of themselves simply create new opportunities for greed, corruption and the lust for power. Behind social conflict lies personal depravity that infects all people, severely undermining their search for happiness and security. Both theology and philosophy have labored to construct elaborate explanations of the presence of radical evil within the human heart, but more often than not they end either by denying this evil or by proposing too simple a solution, such as a resolution to do the good. The question is: Can we do the good if we are prone toward evil even from our inception?

Part of the conflict in theology today revolves around anthropology. Are we mortals basically good, kind and honest, as possibility thinkers blithely assure us? Or are we wicked or corrupt in our innermost being and therefore basically helpless to help ourselves—either morally or spiritually? One's answer to this question cannot be made to fit easily under any theological label, since conservatives as well as liberals today betray an unwarranted confidence in human capability and freedom. The spell of the Enlightenment is as pervasive in revivalist or evangelical Protestantism as it is in liberal Protestantism and neo-Catholicism.[1]

When we proffer too facile explanations of sin and evil, we show that we have failed to understand the gravity of the problem. I agree wholeheartedly with Emil Brunner: "The more deeply we become aware of the reality of evil, the less we can explain it. Sin is something which we cannot explain, something which will not fit into any reasonable scheme at all."[2] It can be said that nearly every philosophy is seriously flawed because of its failure to take into consideration the hidden depths of human depravity.[3]

Sin indeed is a rare concept in philosophy and even in much modern theology. We either summarily deny it or assiduously work to dilute it in order to make sense of this abysmal, sinister reality that casts a perduring pall over human existence. We see the hope of humanity in the remnant of goodness within human nature, but invariably this hope is crushed when radical evil proves more powerful than human determination to mold a better self or build a better world.

Even in his earlier writings Reinhold Niebuhr maintained a keen insight into the two-sidedness of human nature. He acknowledged proclivities toward good and evil within the human creature but rightly discerned that the proclivity toward evil is stronger. Therefore humanity needs redemption, not simply education or enlightenment. "The real religious spirit has no illusions about human nature. It knows the heart of man to be sinful. It is . . . not subject to the cynical disillusion into which sentimentality degenerates when it comes into contact with the disappointing facts of human history."[4] One can justly raise the question whether Niebuhr gave proper recognition to the victory over sin through the resurrection of Christ and the outpouring of the Holy Spirit, but he did perceive the human dilemma possibly more profoundly than any other theologian in recent American history.

Classical and Modern Views

The great thinkers of classical Western culture were keenly aware that something is radically wrong in the human condition, but their answers differ drastically from those of Hebraic religion. They had no real conception of sin in the biblical sense, only an intimation of human error and negligence. They had no thought of enmity against God, only of defect and ignorance. They did have a sense of human guilt, but this was associated with human limitation and was posited by life itself.[5] In the classical view guilt had to be accepted and confessed not in order to get in the right before God but in order to come to terms with one's self and thus be reconciled with one's fate.

For Plato sin is privation, not opposition. The Fall signifies separation from the ground of our being, and salvation means reunion with being. No one is willfully bad. Evil can be traced to some faulty habit of the body or to a stupid upbringing.[6] No one does wrong voluntarily. If we know the right we will do it.[7] The solution to human ills lies in education and self-mastery.

For Aristotle the principal impediment to human well-being is untoward desire. The irrational precedes the rational. Anger, will and desire are implanted in children at birth. Reason and understanding develop as we grow older. We can make ourselves good by consciously and methodically practicing the virtues of courage, wisdom, temperance and justice.[8]

Similarly the Stoic philosophers located the source of evil in the passions. The hope of humanity lies in rational discipline, bringing the passions into subordination to rational thought. The good life is a life in conformity to our rational nature. The Stoic ideal was to affirm oneself in spite of fate and death. In the Christian view it is "to affirm oneself in spite of sin and guilt."[9]

The Greek tragedians saw the source of evil in the perduring conflict between vitality and form. Evil lies in immoderation—the tendency to exceed the bounds that fate has allotted one. The tragic flaw is hubris—defying the limitations assigned to mortal humanity. It is also fate, since every attempt to rise above the human condition is doomed to failure by the structures that govern life and history. Ignorance too plays a major role, for it is through our ignorance of the factors that shape human life and destiny that we are led to transgress the boundaries that circumscribe human existence.

The modern view ushered in by the Renaissance in the fourteenth century and elucidated further in the Enlightenment (eighteenth century) and Romanticism (nineteenth century) derives partly from classical notions and partly from the heritage of Christian faith (especially the mystical side). It also encompasses some distinctly new motifs such as progress and evolution. In the modern view the tragic flaw is sickness, instability, resistance to change, stubbornness or intransigence in the face of new challenges. It is no longer self-assertiveness but the failure to rise to new occasions. It is cowardice and weakness rather than heroic defiance, which is now a virtue rather than a flaw. Sin is the inertia of nature (Leibniz, Whitehead) rather than the aggrandizement of the self over nature. It is lack of harmony with the universe (as in the early Schleiermacher) rather than a rift within ourselves.[10] Evil is now a steppingstone to the good rather than a deficiency in being. Salvation is a breakthrough into freedom rather than deliverance from the prison of the body (as in the Platonic view). The focus is no longer on the fatefulness of human existence (the classical view) or the depravity of the human heart (the biblical view) but on the infinite possibilities of the human spirit.

Sin in the Non-Christian Religions

All the leading world religions have an insightful recognition that something is amiss with the human race, but they differ considerably on exactly what has gone wrong. There is no universal consensus on human turpitude, and this is why a phenomenological analysis of world religions cannot serve as a viable point of departure for the doctrine of sin. At the same time, as Christians we can surely learn from the insights of the seers and prophets of the great world religions when these insights are deepened and expanded and in the process remolded by the revelation of God in Jesus Christ. One can say that the non-Christian religions are both negated and fulfilled by the Christ revelation, which constitutes the center of world history.

In Hinduism sin is defined as *avidya*—ignorance of the truth. It is also associated with *maya,* in which reality is falsely attributed to empirical human personhood, and with *mala,* a heightened awareness of one's individuality.[11] The practical violation of caste rules is a sign of our entrapment in sinful illusion. In the Hindu worldview all human beings are destined to work out their karma—the fateful consequences of human action—through repeated reincarnations. We can escape the law of sin and retribution only through a practical and theoretical real-ization of our essential oneness with the Absolute (Brahma).

In Buddhism, which grew out of Hinduism, the source of human mis-ery lies in a deep inner craving or unfulfilled desire, which is ultimate-ly rooted in ignorance. The way to rise above the pain of desire is through inner enlightenment, which is reached by way of methodical detachment from the world of illusion and emptiness. The earnest seeker after truth cannot rely on the help of any god. The source of one's hope and confidence instead lies in the teaching of the Buddha and in the resolution of the human will. In the words of the Buddha, "Be lamps unto yourselves. Betake yourselves to no external refuge. Hold fast as a refuge to the Truth. Work out your own salvation with diligence."[12] Correspondingly, "By oneself the evil is done, by oneself one suffers; by oneself evil is left undone, by oneself one is purified."[13] In contrast to Hinduism, Buddhism does not posit any permanent self or ego but instead a consciousness that is reactivated in every newly arising human being. In later (Mahayana) Buddhism the concept of the bodhisattva emerged—one who realizes inner peace in this life but who lingers on in order to point others to the way of Nirvana.

Whereas Hinduism gravitates toward monism and original Buddhism is in fact atheistic, Zoroastrianism, which was made the state religion in Persia late in the third century B.C., is a form of prophetic monotheism. Its worldview is dualistic: history becomes the battlefield between the cosmic forces of righteousness and perfidy. Ahura Mazda, the one good god, is challenged by an evil spirit, Angra

Mainyu, who is sometimes depicted as coeternal with the former, though Ahura Mazda alone has ultimate power and emerges triumphant. Human beings are fundamentally good, though again and again they are enticed into sin. Their hope lies in right belief and ritual purification.

Confucianism, which has left an indelible mark not only on China but also on Japan and Korea, emphasizes the inherent goodness of human beings and their innate ability to do the good. Evil is due not to one's nature but to a bad environment, lack of education and "casting oneself away." According to Mencius, the eminent Confucian philosopher (d. 289 B.C.), "Man's nature is good, as water flows down."[14] Just as water can flow uphill only by force, so the human being can do evil only by going against human nature. The foundation of happiness is virtue, so by doing right we can ensure our own happiness. The existence of a Supreme Being is presupposed as a sanction for human conduct. Confucianism was admired by Voltaire and indeed has underlying affinities to the Western Enlightenment.

Much closer to the Christian perspective is Islam, founded by the prophet Muhammad (d. 632). The essence of religion is obedience to the law revealed in the holy book, the Qur'an. Sin is straying from the straight path, and salvation lies in making reparation through penance. In the words of one Muslim scholar, "There are sins, but there is no Sin that has come into the world. There is no 'mystery of iniquity'; there are just wrong decisions."[15] Adam's fall was not really a fall but a blunder. "There is no redemption in this system, and Muhammad does not intercede for anyone."[16] "For Muslims the framework of faith is not sin and salvation but error and guidance."[17] In contrast to orthodox Christianity, Muslims believe that human beings are born innocent but weak. Their weakness makes them vulnerable to sin, but there is no idea of a universal disposition to sin. It is even held that true prophets may indeed be sinless throughout their lives.

Like Islam, Judaism is a nomistic religion. Sin is regarded basically as transgression of the law or missing the mark, and salvation lies in keeping the commandments. Rabbinic Judaism acknowledges an inclination toward evil in human nature, but also sees an inclination toward good, and it is therefore up to individuals to chart their own destiny. Reparation for sin is made through repentance and sacrifices. "Divine-human reconciliation is not solely a matter of repentant return to covenantal requirements; it requires the agency of sacrifices. Some of these were for guilt and transgressions, but others were made in thanksgiving, or to honor God, or in celebration."[18] Rabbinic Judaism does not eschew the notion of grace but sees grace as enabling us to remain true to the Torah and the ceremonies. On the Day of Atonement believers cleanse themselves by "fearless self-examination, open confession, and the resolve not to repeat the transgressions of the past year."[19] In contrast to evangelical Christianity and in harmony with liberal Protestantism, rabbinic Judaism stresses original virtue and righteousness rather than original sin.

In Christian perspective Judaism is unique among the world religions, since it is the mother religion of the church of Jesus Christ. Christianity was originally a sect within Judaism, but the break came already in the first century when Christians hailed Jesus as the Messiah of Israel and proclaimed salvation through divine grace alone rather than through keeping the law. In Pauline theology the law was not the source of salvation but the catalyst for the knowledge of sin and thereby a preparation for salvation. It reminds us of our need for God but does not provide the power to meet this need. Jews and Christians have the Old Testament in common, but only the latter read it in light of God's self-revelation in Jesus Christ and therefore view it essentially as a testimony to unmerited divine grace rather than a code for moral living.

Sin in the History of Theology

Contrary to what one might expect, theology in the history of the church does not conform to any one model of sin. Although Scripture is the principal criterion—for conservative theology especially—it allows for various views and emphases, though within certain parameters.

Particularly interesting among the church fathers is Irenaeus's (c. 130-200) conception of the fall of Adam—not as a damnable revolt against God but instead as a miscalculation due to immaturity and weakness. The sin of our first parents elicits God's compassion because of their vulnerability. The Fall occurred in the childhood of the race and indeed prepares the way for growth toward a perfection that represents the fulfillment of God's promises for humanity. The Fall sets us on the way to redemption and finally to deification.[20]

Significantly different was Augustine's (354-430) doctrine of sin, in which he postulated on the basis of Romans 5:12 that the whole human race sins in Adam, its seminal and natural head. All are guilty because of Adam's sin, and all therefore stand in need of redemption even from birth.[21] In keeping with his rootage in Hellenistic philosophy, Augustine interpreted sin basically as privation—yet not in the sense of mere negation but including the element of assault and rebellion against the good. The essence of sin is inordinate self-love, and the cure for sin is an infusion of grace given through faith in Jesus Christ.

In his conflict with Pelagius, Augustine insisted that through sin the human race has lost the capacity to do the good required by God and therefore is incapable of taking even the first steps toward salvation. We are still free, but our freedom has been impaired and needs to be reconstituted. Whereas Pelagius held that the sin of Adam belongs to him alone and that each individual may choose whether to follow Adam or Christ, Augustine believed that the Adamic fall had left the whole human race in bondage to sin. For Pelagius death is a natural event; for Augustine death is the painful consequence and evidence of original sin. While Pelagius saw grace as the condition for moral advance provided by God in creation, Augustine understood grace as the internal operation of the Holy Spirit given in baptism and conversion. Pelagius's views were condemned at the Council of Carthage (416), and semi-Pelagianism, which allowed for grace as an aid to natural human effort, was condemned at the Second Council of Orange (529).[22]

Thomas Aquinas followed Augustine in stressing the priority of grace in Christian salvation, but he tended to underplay the noetic effects of the Fall. Sin not only impairs the human will but also dulls human reasoning; yet it is possible to reason toward faith because we are created in the image of God. What perished in the Fall were the supernatural virtues, whereas the natural virtues survived, though weakened by sin. Supernatural insight was lost, but natural law remains. Thomas distinguished between mortal sins, which imperil salvation, and venial sins, which do not completely sever one from the state of grace. Disordered desire (concupiscence) is the soil out of which sin emerges.[23]

Martin Luther strenuously attacked the opinion, especially prominent in late Catholic scholasticism, that the human will on its own can move toward grace and that human reason on its own can know something about grace. Luther saw the imago Dei as wholly defaced by sin, and although fallen human beings still reflect some of the light and truth of God, they are completely incapable of doing the good that God requires for their salvation. Luther emphasized the bondage of the will and the helplessness of sinners to save themselves.[24] In order to be free we must be made free by regeneration through the power of the Holy Spirit and faith in the atoning work of Jesus Christ. Luther held the root and source of sin to be unbelief, just as the root and source of righteousness is faith.[25] The chief manifestation of sin is pride, which is particularly evident in the spiritual aspiration to godlikeness so prevalent in the Catholic mystical tradition. Luther was emphatic that sin continues even in the Christian, and this is why even the most sanctified still stand in need of the medicine of the Word and sacraments.

John Calvin followed Luther in accentuating the depravity and help-lessness of the person in sin and the divine initiative in moving the sin-ner into the kingdom of grace. For Calvin the source of sin is faith-lessness conjoined with pride. The antidote to sin is free, unmerited grace made available through the atoning sacrifice of Christ and the outpouring of the Holy Spirit on the church. Original sin is inherited and is transmitted through procreation. The tinder of sin (concupiscence) is also sin and merits eternal death. In the Fall the supernatural gifts were lost and the natural gifts were corrupted. Calvin perceived that not all sin is due to deliberate malice, for ignorance also plays a role in the fall of humanity. We are responsible for sin because we freely assent to it, but sin is inevitable because we are born with a proclivity toward it that cannot be effectively resisted apart from divine grace. With Luther, Calvin believed that even the Christian is hampered by sin, but Calvin was adamant that under the impact of grace the Christian could make real progress toward holiness.

Marking a new departure in the Reformed understanding of sin, Friedrich Schleiermacher (d. 1834) saw the original human being as existing in a state of imperfection in which sin becomes virtually inevitable in the struggle to achieve maturity. Sin occurs as a preparation for grace rather than grace occurring to repair the damage caused by sin.[26] Sin is not so much moral rebellion against God's will as the arresting of the God-consciousness within us. To Schleiermacher's credit he was keenly aware of the social character of sin. Sin is both individual and organic. It is "in each the work of all, and in all the work of each."[27] Sin is stored in humanity and kept in circulation by social influence. He located sin in the social solidarity of the race rather than in biological unity. The antithesis is not between the sinner and the holy God but between spirit and nature. Redemption signifies the mastery of nature by spirit.[28]

A more biblically based doctrine of sin is found in Søren Kierkegaard (1813-1855), who unearthed dimensions of the human psyche that had been lost sight of by the intelligentsia of his day.[29] According to Kierkegaard sin is universal and inevitable but not a necessity of human nature. It is presupposed by anxiety or dread, which generates a sense of uneasiness in the human subject, who stands at the juncture of spirit and nature. Because humanity is a synthesis of the finite and the infinite, the temporal and the eternal, we are susceptible to being pulled in one direction or another and thereby los-

ing our equilibrium. Sin is a leap into the abyss of despair, which undermines human hope and vitality. The story of the fall of Adam is neither
myth nor literal history but a historical exemplification of what happens
to all humanity. We are guilty not because of Adam's sin but because of
our own. Sin is not only occasioned by dread but brings dread with it. In
the state of sin dread is heightened. The essence of sin is despair, what
Kierkegaard called the "sickness unto death."[30] The consciousness of
despair sires hope, however, for it can be used by the Spirit of God to
induce the leap of faith, thereby bringing meaning and purpose to a lost
humanity. All people have a consciousness of guilt, but only some are
graced by the consciousness of sin—the first step in our redemption by
which we are converted from despair to faith in the living Christ.

In a similar vein Emil Brunner (d. 1966) endeavored to present a
viable alternative to both the liberal theology that emphasized the
environmental matrix of sin (esp. Ritschl) and Augustinian theology,
which perceived sin as an enduring stain on human nature. Brunner
staunchly held to the paradox of the universality of sin and personal
responsibility.[31] Sin is not a defect in human nature, nor is it ignorance
of our status as children of God. It is an act, not a quality or substance
that can be inherited. The sinful act has its roots in a disposition to sin
that is part of the human condition. The primal sin is not the fall of our
first parents from an original paradise but the fall of the emergent
human being as it becomes aware of itself in the world. The relation
of the primal sin to particular sins is not the relation of cause to effect
but "a relation *sui generis,* which has absolutely no analogies at all."[32]
Brunner criticized Augustine for viewing sin as a fatality due to natural causes. Sin in its essence is disobedience to God, not a weakness in
human character. The most malignant form of sin is pride; doubt is the
intellectual form of sin. Religiosity is the most subtle form of sin. Even
in our worship of God we seek our own salvation, even in surrender
to God we are intent on finding our own security. Only demonic sin is
sheer rebellion; human sin is always a mixture of defiance and weakness. Sin involves disruption in the social fabric, but it arises out of a

heart that is turned inward upon itself.

A more open attitude toward philosophy in shaping the Christian doctrine of sin is evident in Paul Tillich (d. 1965), who freely drew on Plato, Plotinus, Hegel and Kierkegaard, among others. He defined sin as estrangement or alienation from the ground of our being. In keeping with the Platonic tradition he affirmed an ontological fall before any historical fall, signifying the transition from essence to existence. The condition of being finite means being separated from the eternal source of our being and therefore subject to anxiety and temptation. The quest to discover or regain our essential unity with God constitutes salvation. In contrast to Augustine he did not see the essence of sin as sexual concupiscence. Also in opposition to Augustine he did not regard sin as the physical cause of death. Sin is the cause of the horror of death but not of the fact of death, which belongs to human mortality. Sin "gives to death the power which is conquered only in participation in the eternal."[33] Sin is a matter of human freedom, but freedom is embedded in "the universal destiny of estrangement in such a way that in every free act the destiny of estrangement is involved."[34] Adam before the Fall is a symbol of "the dreaming innocence of undecided potentialities."[35] Like Hegel, Tillich saw the transition from innocence to maturity and responsibility as necessary for human civilization and progress.

Reflecting a more biblical, personalistic stance, Reinhold Niebuhr (d. 1971) conceived of sin as a refusal to acknowledge our dependence on the living God. Similarly to Kierkegaard, he viewed anxiety as the precursor of sin. The condition of being both free and finite tempts us either to deny our finitude in prideful self-affirmation or to escape from our finitude into sensuality. The story of Adam and Eve refers not to a specific fall in prehistory but to existential realities that pertain to every human being. With Kierkegaard, Niebuhr contended that sin posits itself. We are driven into sin not by anxiety in and of itself but by anxiety plus sin. Before every actual sin there is an inclination to sin that makes sin inevitable, though it is not necessary. Sin is both an abuse of our freedom and an impairment of our freedom, which casts a shadow over all human activity.[36] The chief manifestations of sin are the pride of power, the pride of knowledge and the pride of virtue (moral pride). Out of moral pride comes religious pride when sin manifests itself in the pretension to a higher form of spirituality.

Karl Barth (d. 1968) called sin an ontological impossibility, since we are created in the image of God, and this means we are created for freedom in service to God. The possibility of sin does not lie in human nature but intrudes into humanity from the outside and induces humans to fall away from their freedom. Sin is committed not out of freedom but out of the denial of our freedom. It signifies a fall into unfreedom. Its basis is in folly rather than in deliberate rational strategy, though it employs strategies for self-aggrandizement and therefore for evil. "There is no reason for it. It derives directly from that which is not, and it consists in a movement toward it. . . . To try to find a reason for it is simply to show that we do not realize that we are talking of the evil which is simply evil."[37] It is "an impossible possibility and unreal reality." Barth saw the two chief forms of sin as pride and sloth, the first heroic, the second unheroic and trivial.[38] It is interesting to note the prominence Barth assigned to sloth, which involves stupidity, inhumanity and dissipation. Salvation means the restoration of freedom and the mastery of untoward passions that lead to anarchy and lawlessness.

A colleague of Barth's in the Confessing Church movement, Dietrich Bonhoeffer paved the way for a distinctly new understanding of sin. His indebtedness to classical Reformation orthodoxy is apparent in his *Creation and the Fall, The Cost of Discipleship* and *Life Together*, but he began moving in another direction in his later works *Ethics* and *Letters and Papers from Prison*.[39] While in the earlier and middle stages of his career he saw the world as irrevocably subverted by the ravages of sin, he now began to discern signs of promise in the natural order.[40] In a break with the mystical heritage of the church, Bonhoeffer maintained that Christianity involves not the negation of earthly desires but their celebration and sanctification. Sin is not the natural but the unnatural, not the human but the inhuman. Whereas in his earlier writings he portrayed the things on earth as temptations and snares leading us to forgetfulness of God, he now regarded them as welcome gifts from God, since they serve human preservation and happiness.[41] He even claimed that God can be found in earthly bliss as well as in the church. He affirmed natural human goodness as well as the spiritual righteousness of the kingdom of God. These are not antithetical, though they must never be confounded. Natural goodness does not justify us, but it may prepare the way for faith in God's justification. While he did not repudiate the Reformation understanding of sin as rebellion against a holy God, he expanded the idea of sin to include contempt for humanity. Sin is not only an affront to God but a putting down of humanity. Sin is in the last analysis inhumanity, and salvation is the realization of true humanity. Sin is what diminishes humanity and undermines the human quest for hope and happiness not only in the world to come but in this world as well. Although still convinced of the universality of sin, he contended that there is an elemental humanness and decency that sin can obscure but not obliterate—at least not in humanity as a whole. Bonhoeffer's new insights did much to free Christian anthropology from its Manichaean and Neoplatonic cast.

Finally, we need to give serious consideration to Wolfhart Pannenberg's reappraisal of the Christian doctrine of sin. With Brunner, Niebuhr, Tillich and many others, Pannenberg rejects the traditional notion of Adam as the historical ancestor of the race, for this claim cannot be substantiated on scientific grounds.[42] Instead the story of the Adamic fall is better understood as a mythical prototype of the human condition; his history "manifests what is repeated in the history of each individual human being."[43] Yet Pannenberg maintains that the mythical elements in this story are transcended by virtue of the fact that biblical history is oriented toward the future rather than the past. Human self-realization was not achieved in the past but is still to come in the future when all of humankind will be included in the eschatological reign of Christ. The Adamic story is the antitype of the unity of human destiny in Jesus Christ. It is in the light of Christ that we can see ourselves as sinners standing in need of redemption. Our fulfillment lies not behind us "in an irretrievable past"[44] but ahead of us in the absolute future toward which all history moves. Pannenberg sees sin as universal in its penetration of humanity, but it is not inherited from a primeval couple. It has its roots not in created human nature but in the "immoderation of concupiscence,"[45] which is part of the human condition. Sin is "not a fate that comes upon human beings as an alien power against which they are helpless."[46] He is insistent that the biblical concept of sin is inseparable from the ideas of responsibility and guilt. He affirms both the universality of sin and human responsibility in assenting to sin. The essence of sin is unrestrained egoism and the failure of selfhood—the failure to relate to others in a manner that respects their dignity and personhood.[47] In a way reminiscent of Hegel's idea of a fall upward, Pannenberg regards the consciousness of the failure of the self as "a necessary phase in the process whereby human beings are liberated to become themselves."[48] The universal rule of sin is given empirical validation in the universal corruption associated with death.[49]

Many other eminent theologians could have been included in this section, but I have limited myself to those thinkers who have played a formative role in shaping my own understanding of this problem. I might have given a more comprehensive analysis of Kierkegaard, though I have already appraised his general position in an earlier volume,[50] and his seminal insights have been preserved in Reinhold Niebuhr, Brunner and Tillich. Feminist and liberationist thinkers have made a signal contribution to the ongoing discussion on sin, and I have sought to embody some of their insights in the following section of this chapter (see pp. 45, 51).

A Biblical Perspective

In delineating a biblical perspective on this issue I am by no means implying that the theological positions that I have discussed thus far are lacking in biblical content. I simply wish to share my own thoughts on the plight of humanity, appealing to biblical wisdom and also to the wisdom of the fathers and mothers of the church through the ages. There is no one biblical perspective on sin, but there is an underlying unity of perception shared by the prophets and apostles. I do not claim to be able to give an exhaustive treatment of biblical truth, but it is my intention to be faithful to the biblical record as much as possible.

First of all it should be noted that the presence of sin in the world is depicted as a "mystery" (2 Thess 2:7), since its origin in the human race is inexplicable. The Bible is insistent that humanity is created good (Gen 1:27, 31); at the same time "all have sinned and fall short of the glory of God" (Rom 3:23). There is nothing in our created nature that would dispose us to sin, yet we invariably fall into sin as we make our own way in the world. It is an "impossible possibility" that defies human comprehension. Its essence is irrationality and absurdity. This is why it cannot be neatly fitted into any conceptual scheme.

We need to do justice to the paradoxical biblical affirmation that sin is universal and that the human person is fully responsible. Sin is a predisposition to evil antecedent to particular sins. It is not innate in human nature but alien to human nature. It is a spiritual contagion that is communicated through both procreation and the environmental or social nexus in which we are nurtured. Its origin lies in an inexplicable deviation of the human will from its divinely appointed destiny. It is not a necessity of nature but an inevitability of existing in a world fraught with peril. It has penetrated human nature and corrupted the essence of humanity.

The Platonic tradition of the church has portrayed sin as a privation of being *(privatio)*. It is that but it is more—a corruption of being *(depravatio)*. It includes both weakness and iniquity. Sometimes sin is depicted in the Bible as an objective power seeking to master us (Gen 4:6-7; 2 Thess 2:7). It is one of the powers that hold the self in bondage.[51]

The act of sin brings about the loss of human freedom. We are still free in the things "below," but not in the things "above" (Luther). We are free from outward compulsion but not from interior disharmony. Even in sin we are free from metaphysical necessity, but we have lost the freedom to do the good or come to God. We can do relative goods, but we cannot do the good that God demands—perfect love of God and of our neighbor. Sin is a condition of unfreedom from which we are powerless to extricate ourselves. To sin is to fall into captivity, but we are willing accomplices in this tragic state of affairs.

New Testament scholar Peter Stuhlmacher astutely describes sin as both an act and a fate. We sin not only because we freely choose to sin but also because the circumstances of life move us in this downward direction. Sin is both a "conscious offense" against God's will and an "involuntary transgression of this will, both of which cause an individual or a group of people to be guilty."[52]

It has been fashionable since Kierkegaard to see anxiety as the precondition of sin.[53] Yet the fuller biblical view (and Kierkegaard would agree) is that sin posits itself. The crux of the human dilemma is not anxiety by itself but a bias toward sin that converts our natural anxiety into something pathological. Sin is preceded by temptation, yet paradoxically we could not be tempted unless we had already sinned (Reinhold Niebuhr).[54]

With some cogency Pannenberg maintains that anxiety is not simply a condition for sin but a prime manifestation of sin, since anxiety is rooted in self-fixation.[55] He acknowledges that anxiety feeds into sin but contends that sin is already present in anxiety. Perhaps we should distinguish between the anxiety that belongs to finitude, which is purely natural and indeed one of the sources of creativity, and the anxiety that drives one deeper into the self. Sinful anxiety is not simply awareness of the uncertainty of the future but dread of the future. It is not a sense of our limitations but a gnawing uneasiness over our limitations. It is well to note that anxiety in sinful humankind is always destructive; it does not merely create the possibility for sin but is itself a catalyst for sin.[56] There is always something of the pathological in existential anxiety—anxiety that is experienced in concrete human existence as we know it under the shadow of sin. Pannenberg rightly reminds us that Jesus warns against being anxious about the morrow (Mt 6:25-27; Lk 12:22-26).[57]

Sin could not find a lodging within us unless we already had a predisposition to sin. Yet this predisposition does not compel us to sin but tempts us to sin. We are lured into sin rather than forced into sin. Sin comes to reside within the self when we allow it entry into our lives. Sin is not a defect in human nature (this would be Manichaeism) but a corruption of human nature by a force outside the self. Even so, this corruption could not take place unless we freely assented to it. The blame for sin must be assigned neither to biological inheritance nor to environmental upbringing but to the misuse of our freedom.

Many theologians have seized upon the biblical story of the fall of Adam (Gen 3) to explain the corrosive presence of sin in the human race. This story must be taken with the utmost seriousness, since it belongs to the written Word of God and indeed throws much light on the human condition. At the same time it plays little role in the depiction of sin in biblical history, and if it were not for Paul's allusions to the Adamic fall it would not have had the significance it has in theology. While the details in the story are figurative, it has both a universal and a historical locus, for it depicts a fall in primeval history that is repeated in the life histories of all humans. This story describes not simply the fall of an original couple but the fall of the human race. It depicts a transition from communion with God to a break in this communion (Ellul). It should not be taken to refer to the passage from innocence to interdependence (Hegel), or from innocence to sin (Ricoeur), or even from anxiety to prideful self-affirmation (as in Niebuhr). It does not pertain to the childhood of the race from which we are evolving toward greater maturity; instead its focus is on a fall in primeval history from a paradisal state of fellowship with the divine Creator. How this fall is related to the universal fall into sin throughout history is simply inexplicable. The text in Romans to which Augustine often appealed (5:12) does not tell us how Adamic sin is related to general human sin and therefore cannot be used to argue for inherited sin or guilt; it simply informs us that death pervaded the whole human race "inasmuch as all have sinned" (REB). According to the Catholic biblical scholar Joseph A. Fitzmyer, Paul is ascribing death to two causes not unrelated: "to Adam and to all human sinners."[58] First Corinthians 15:22 suggests a solidarity of humanity with the Adam of prehistory, but this may be not because we sin in Adam but because of the sin unleashed into the world through our first parents and other baleful acts in primeval history *(Urgeschichte).*[59]

The Genesis story also alludes to prehuman sin. Before the Adamic fall there was an angelic fall, and it is the devil symbolized by the serpent that tempted Eve to defy the divine warning against eating of the tree of the knowledge of good and evil (Gen 3:1-5; cf. Is 14:12-15; 2 Pet 2:4; Jude 6; Rev 12:7-9). The devil and his hosts are not gods, but they pretend to be so. They are really "feeble and bankrupt elemental spirits" (Gal 4:9 REB), and their power is that of the lie (Jn 8:44).

In biblical perspective the essence of sin is unbelief or hardness of heart.[60] Its chief manifestations are pride, sloth and fear. Pride can take the form of self-adulation, self-righteousness and supercilious condescension toward others. It is also associated with idolatry, for it involves the vainglorious attempt to reshape God in our own image. Sloth includes sensuality, intemperance and laziness. Fear is the passion to secure oneself in the face of real or imagined danger.[61] Other and related manifestations of sin are hatred, greed, deceit, doubt, envy, cowardice, selfishness, ignorance and depression.

From another angle one can say that sin can appear as either self-deprecation, which is born out of cowardice and weakness, or self-exaltation, which has its roots in pride and conceit. When we unduly deprecate ourselves we retreat from our responsibility as people called by God to subdue the earth and herald the coming of the kingdom of God. We use our failings to justify our refusal to rise to the challenges of life. We sedulously try to avoid the command of God to do battle for his kingdom. When we exalt ourselves we likewise eschew the divine imperative to serve others rather than to gain power over others. In both cases we deny our God-given responsibilities by seeking to be autonomous individuals, blithely independent of God and of our neighbor.[62]

It is important to recognize that sin has social as well as personal dimensions. It can appear in the form of racism, sexism, ethnocentricism, classism, ageism, religious bigotry, ecological pollution and genocide.[63] Feminist and liberationist theologies rightly remind us that sin can poison the structures of a society as well as the hearts of individuals.[64] It is therefore permissible to speak of unjust social structures, but changing the social structure does not effect a real change in the human condition. This is why personal transformation must accompany and indeed undergird social reformation.

The dreaded consequences of sin are guilt, shame, death, despair and hell.[65] These might also be said to constitute the punishment for sin. Guilt is the state of being in the wrong before a holy God. Shame is the pain born of the realization that one has failed God. Despair is the state of being overcome by a sense of futility and defeat. Hell denotes the enduring rupture in our relationship with God—extending into the life to come.

A special word should be said about death as a punishment for sin.[66] When Paul teaches that the wages of sin is death (Rom 6:23) or that death came into the world through sin (Rom 5:12), is he referring to physical death or spiritual death? Does mortality include death, or is death an alien power that brings an end to human life? I agree with Stuhlmacher that death in this context means "exclusion from eternal life" and not simply "a matter of the mortality which belongs to being a creature."[67] In Romans 7 the "body of death" signifies our "fleshly existence under the reign of sin."[68] According to Fitzmyer death for Paul "is not merely physical, bodily death (separation of body and soul), but includes spiritual death (the definitive separation of human beings from God, the unique source of life)."[69] In my view man and woman were created as mortals, meaning subject to the possibility of death. This view of the human creation does not disallow the fact that death was already in the world prior to Adam and Eve—in the plant and animal creation. Nor does it deny the fact that the world was already open to intrusion by demonic powers before the human creation. Spiritual death is indeed the only meaning in Ephesians 2:1: "You once were dead because of your sins and wickedness" (cf. 2:5 REB). We cannot assume on the basis of the Genesis account that Adam and Eve were created as immortals and then became subject to death because of the Fall. A better interpretation is that the reality of death is now forced into human consciousness and that the fallen human being "must let this knowledge overshadow his entire life."[70]

The magisterial Reformation was adamant that sin infects the whole human being. The imago Dei is not eradicated, but it is defaced and needs to be restored. Sin not only binds the human will but also blinds human reason. This blinding is not equal in all areas, however; Brunner was right that in the personal area where our ultimate destiny is concerned sin is much more conspicuous than in the area of abstract reasoning.[71] Sin does have noetic effects, which makes any appeal to a universal, natural law suspect.[72] There is sin not only in action but also in thought. Niebuhr poignantly described this as the ideological taint in human reasoning. The principal problem in the church at the present time is that ideology rather than theology is setting the agenda.[73]

The Reformers did not hesitate to speak of total depravity, meaning that every part of human existence bears the taint of sin. Total depravity is total inability—the helplessness of human beings to extricate themselves from the power of sin. The Reformation view was that sin is thoroughly pervasive in human life and existence; yet one should not infer that human beings even in their fallen condition do not reflect in any way the goodness and glory of the Creator. Total depravity too often was taken to mean that humanity contains no vestige of original righteousness, but this is to exaggerate the power of sin and undermine human dignity.[74] For this reason I believe it more felicitous in our day to speak of the radical pervasiveness of sin rather than total depravity.

We become guilty of sin through our personal transgression, and must not assign our guilt either to Adam or to the devil. The Bible is clear that human beings are fully responsible for their sin, and this is why they stand under the condemnation of God. We cannot escape from responsibility by claiming that "I was born this way," or "the devil made me do it." Although even from conception we are under the influence of sin, we become personally accountable when we freely assent to this bias toward sin, which theology calls concupiscence.[75] We are by nature "children of wrath" (Eph 2:3) because the virus of sin has corrupted our inner being, but our lack of resistance to this virus is what renders us culpable before God. Our essential nature is good, for we are created in God's image; our existential nature is evil, for we have allowed the proclivity to sin to gain mastery over us. Guilt is not inherited, but the weakness that leads to sin is part of our human inheritance.

The knowledge of sin is included in the knowledge of faith. We do not have any reliable knowledge of our sin apart from God's self-revelation in Jesus Christ. Pannenberg is critical of this position because it seems to ignore the fact that sin is something more universal than the Christ revelation and indeed precedes the revelation.[76] Pannenberg agrees that we can identify the root of sin as unbelief only in the light of an encounter with the God of historical revelation.[77] Yet to claim that we can know of our sin only through Christ does not of itself deny the universality of sin apart from Christ. It was fashionable in Reformation theology (especially Lutheran theology) to contend that the knowledge of sin comes through the law and the knowledge of grace comes through the gospel. The law indeed gives us a "sense of sin" but not "the true picture" of our condition (Heb 10:1-2 REB). The law engenders a consciousness of guilt but not the power that convicts us of our sin. When Peter preached his Pentecost sermon his hearers "were cut to the heart" and asked, "Brethren, what shall we do?" Peter replied, "Repent, and be baptized every one of you in the name of Jesus Christ for the forgiveness of your sins" (Acts 2:37-38). They heard the gospel and then the commandment to repent, and this is indeed the biblical pattern. The law does bring knowledge of sin when united with the gospel, but by itself it simply drives people deeper into sin (1 Cor 15:56). When united with the gospel it becomes the "law of the Spirit of life" (Rom 8:2) and brings liberation as well as admonition. The mystery of iniquity cannot be comprehended apart from the mystery of grace.

It is interesting to note that the new Catholic Catechism echoes many of the things I am saying here. In order to know Adam as "the source of sin" we must first know Christ as "the source of grace."[78]

Only the light of divine Revelation clarifies the reality of sin and particularly of the sin committed at mankind's origins. Without the knowledge Revelation gives of God we cannot recognize sin clearly and are tempted to explain it as merely a developmental flaw, a psychological weakness, a mistake, or the necessary consequence of an inadequate social structure, etc.[79]

The wide differences between Christianity and other perspectives on life and the world are brought to light when we consider the antidote to sin. In Christian Science and kindred neotranscendentalist movements the way to combat sin is to deny its reality. Such denial allegedly brings inner peace, but it is peace at the price of living in a world of illusion. In gnosticism and Platonism the key to countering inner misery is the discovery of the true self—the self in its unity with God. Education, which is designed to draw out the wisdom latent within us, supposedly assures a life of virtue and happiness. Plato contended that when we know the good we will do it. Spinoza held a similar view: "To understand something is to be delivered of it."[80] Then there is the way of escape followed by hermits and other solitaries in all the great religions. The biblical basis is the story of Lot fleeing from Sodom and being warned never to look back (Gen 19). While it is true that the Spirit of God may counsel disengagement and withdrawal for some people in certain periods of history, the overall biblical antidote to sin is repentance and forgiveness. Sin can be overcome only by radical love, which forgives and forbears. But this radical love is not a simple human possibility. It has to become incarnate in history in order to reach us. In the life, death and resurrection of Jesus Christ the power of sin is overcome through the vicarious and atoning love of the Creator for the creature. The guilt of sin is removed by God's justifying grace; the pollution of sin is expelled by God's sanctifying grace. God's grace liberates us to do battle with the entrenched powers of sin in society. The Christian response to the problem of sin is neither fright nor flight but fight!

One area of divergence between evangelical Protestantism and Catholic tradition is the former's resistance to the common distinction between mortal and venial sins. In the Catholic view not all sins have the same gravity. While some sins indicate a slight falling away from grace, others precipitate a falling out of grace and therefore necessitate a new act of conversion; this takes place ordinarily in the sacrament of penance. Love to God can still exist when venial sins are committed, for they only offend and wound charity.[81] For a sin to be mortal requires full knowledge and complete consent. Although it is true that this distinction has some basis in Scripture (1 Jn 5:16-17), the Reformers contended that Catholic theology misinterpreted the intent of Scripture by viewing sin in a legalistic framework. For the Reformers sin is not fundamentally a misdeed or a breaking of the moral code but a whole life orientation that is in the wrong. All sin is mortal if it is not repented of, and no sin requires further reparation if it is covered by the grace of God in faith.

At the same time, Protestant theology has not always given adequate recognition to the relative distinctions among sins, distinctions that are also found in the Bible. Reinhold Niebuhr rightly perceived that though there is an equality of sin, there is an inequality of guilt—the objective consequences of sin.[82] While even the smallest sin merits the damnation of God, God considers some sins more heinous than others and therefore meriting a more severe judgment. Paul gave special warning against the sins of idolatry and sexual perversion (Rom 1:18-32). The epistle to the Hebrews tells us that the sin of apostasy even places one beyond the pale of forgiveness (Heb 10:26-31). Bonhoeffer noted: "There are heavier sins and lighter sins. A falling away is of infinitely greater weight than a falling down. The most shining virtues of him who has fallen away are as black as night in comparison with the darkest lapses of the steadfast."[83] Every sin will damn us unless we forsake it in repentance and obedience, but some sins will keep us in darkness when the help offered by the Holy Spirit is deliberately spurned (Mk 3:28-29).

Pitfalls to Avoid

Finally, we need to note the false roads in the treatment of sin that constitute not only theological but also spiritual dangers. Among these is moral defeatism, the attitude that sin is such an integral part of human nature that it is useless to expend efforts to overcome it and that one should simply live in the hope that all will be forgiven. Far from counseling retreat from the battle against sin, a more authentic evangelical position insists that sin, any sin, can be overcome through the sanctifying grace of God and that it is possible to live in victory over sin, even though one can never be free of temptation and the pervasive presence of sin.[84]

Sometimes moral defeatism takes the form of a triumphalism of grace in which grace is construed as simply the divine covering over of sin without requiring the forsaking of sin in daily life. It is occasionally said that because we are saved by grace alone, we need not struggle against sin, since we are now perfectly righteous in the sight of God through our faith. Some draw the erroneous conclusion that if God promises always to forgive, we should feel free to sin boldly so that grace may abound.[85] But this undermines the biblical imperative that though grace is free, it is not cheap and demands a life of obedience under the cross.[86]

An opposite error is perfectionism, in which the vain hope is entertained that we can make ourselves acceptable to God by cultivating the virtues and living above sin. While perfectionists generally recognize that the assistance of grace is necessary on life's pilgrimage, the focus is on what we can do through our own efforts to guarantee a place in the kingdom of heaven. Such persons lose sight of the central truth of the gospel that God justifies us while we are still sinners, that the ground of our acceptability before God is the alien righteousness of Jesus Christ that is imputed to us through faith but in which we also participate by grace. Perfectionists only dimly see that sin persists even in the most sanctified Christian, that even the righteous must come before God with empty hands, making no claim on his mercy. The call to holiness must be sounded, but this call must be based on the gospel message that we are saved by free grace. Yet this grace does not leave us in our sins but awakens within us a hunger for the perfect love that is dramatically embodied and revealed in the person of Jesus Christ.

Still another danger is reductionism, which focuses on only one kind of sin—for example, sexual indiscretion or social injustice—and loses sight of sin in its fuller dimensions. If we warn exclusively or primarily against sexual concupiscence, we neglect the demands for social justice and the need to counter the spiritual sins of idolatry and rebellion of the human spirit against its Creator. If we neglect or downplay the gravity of sexual sin and portray all sin as social in nature, we then fail to recognize that sex, which is part of original creation and therefore good, is now exposed to the infection of sin and can itself become a crucible for sin. Our sexual life needs to be redeemed just as much as every other part of human existence. We must avoid both a Manichaeism that depreciates the bodily passions and a libertinism that celebrates bodily appetites without realizing that they finally lead to self-destruction unless they are curbed and regulated by a self-discipline made possible only by the continuous assistance of the Holy Spirit. The Christian mandate is not to eradicate our natural impulses but to subdue them and channel them for the glory of God and the service of his kingdom.

Furthermore we must not be seduced into redefining sin so that its rough edges are blurred and its horror is mitigated. Sin is not a mishap that can be easily covered over but a curse that casts a shadow over all human activity and that can be removed only by a new creation. Likewise sin is not a mistake that can routinely be taken care of by an apology, however sincere, but a willful transgression that calls for confession and absolution. We should heed Bonhoeffer's trenchant admonition: "It is part of the Church's office of guardianship that she shall call sin by its name and that she shall warn . . . against sin; for 'righteousness exalteth a nation,' both in time and in eternity, 'but sin is perdition for the people,' both temporal and eternal perdition."[87]

Sin can be overcome only by being exposed and confessed. With the assistance of grace we can come to an honest admission of our sins, but we cannot wipe our slate clean in the sight of God. The condemnation that sin carries can be dealt with only by Christ, who alone has made adequate satisfaction and reparation for sin. Our task is to battle against sin in our lives by daily repentance and obedience under the cross. But our works of penitence and obedience are to no avail unless they rest on faith in the mercy of God manifested in Jesus Christ. The final answer to sin lies in its expiation by Christ's atoning sacrifice and its expulsion by the Spirit of Christ in the awakening to faith.

·THREE·

THE MYSTERY

OF THE

INCARNATION

And the Word became flesh and dwelt among us,
full of grace and truth.
JOHN 1:14

Jesus Christ, in His infinite love, has become what we are,
in order that He may make us entirely what He is.
IRENAEUS

The meaning of the Word being made flesh
is not that the divine nature was changed into flesh,
but that the divine nature assumed our flesh.
AUGUSTINE

The simple faith that Jesus was God and man in one person
can be easily accepted as plain and vital truth,
but the moment you *deny* personality in the man
Christ Jesus you run into a thousand difficulties and errors.
JOHN NELSON DARBY

The Son did not unite himself with an
independently existing human being but with the human nature,
and that in a most mysterious manner.
Hence there can be no two Sons or two persons.
G. C. BERKOUWER

The church is founded on the incarnation of the preexistent
Word of God in Jesus Christ. This is an event that happened in
past history—at a particular time and place. It is a mystery that

surpasses human understanding, yet it can be described in various ways. John's Gospel speaks of the Word becoming flesh (Jn 1:14). Paul contends that God was "born in human likeness" (Phil 2:7 NRSV). The Nicene Creed confesses that "God became man." For Kierkegaard God became history, Eternity entered into time. Karl Barth put it this way: "In Jesus Christ it comes about that God takes time to Himself, that He Himself, the eternal One, becomes temporal."[1]

A still more dramatic way of articulating this mystery is to affirm that God became sin, thereby linking the incarnation to the atonement. Among theologians who occasionally employed such language were Paul, Ambrose, John Chrysostom, Augustine, Luther, Forsyth and Barth. In Paul's words, "For our sake he made him to be sin who knew no sin" (2 Cor 5:21; cf. Rom 8:3). Ambrose confessed: "Having become the sin of all men, He washed away the sins of the human race."[2] Luther could say, "He became the worst sinner of all." Barth went so far as to describe Jesus Christ as "the reprobate" and "the rejected." What these scholars meant was not that God or Christ actually succumbed to sin but that God took our sinful nature upon himself in that he carried the burden of our sin. He did not become a sinner in fact, as Nels Ferré and some others have held, but he identified with our sin and overcame it through the power of vicarious love.[3]

When the church affirms that God became man, it does not mean that God changed into a man, as in ancient mythology. The flesh was not "changed into the nature of Godhead nor was the ineffable nature of the Word of God transformed into the nature of flesh."[4] Orthodox Christianity holds neither to an appearance of God in a man nor a metamorphosis of God into a man. As the Athanasian Creed put it, he is one "not by conversion of the Godhead into flesh, but by taking of the manhood into God" (art. 35).[5] In the words of Augustine, "Christ added to himself that which he was not; he did not lose what he was."[6]

Heretical theology has often reduced the mystery of the incarnation to a manifestation of God's presence in a human life rather than a real incarnation in human flesh. The theologians who drew up the Leiden

Synopsis (1625) warned: "When he is said to have become flesh, not a phantasm of it is meant, but a true body consisting of flesh and bones and blood."[7] Yet as orthodox Christians we must insist that divinity was not transmuted into bodily flesh but that it assumed flesh while still remaining divine.

True Humanity and True Divinity

The church has always affirmed that the Jesus Christ of history was at the same time truly God. Paul proclaimed that "Christ . . . who is over all" is "God blessed for ever" (Rom 9:3, 5 NRSV).[8] And in Colossians 2:9: "In him the whole fulness of deity dwells bodily" (cf. Col 1:15). In 2 Corinthians Paul speaks of "the power of the Lord who is the Spirit" (3:18 REB) and "the glory of Christ, who is the image of God" (4:4 REB; cf. 4:6). In 1 Corinthians 2:8 Paul describes Jesus as "the Lord of glory," which is tantamount to acknowledging his deity.[9] John confesses, "The Word became flesh; he came to dwell among us, and we saw his glory, such glory as befits the Father's only Son, full of grace and truth" (Jn 1:14 NEB). In 1 John Christ is described as "the true God and eternal life" (5:20 NIV). And in Revelation he is exalted as the "King of kings and Lord of lords" (19:16). Other texts that explicitly refer to Jesus Christ as God include Matthew 4:7; Luke 4:12; John 20:28; Titus 2:13; Hebrews 1:8 and 2 Peter 1:1.

While the New Testament indeed teaches the divinity of Christ, it also insists on his true humanity. According to Paul, Jesus was "born of woman, born under the law" (Gal 4:4). God sent his Son "in the likeness of sinful flesh" (Rom 8:3; Phil 2:7). The author of Hebrews refers to Christ as "one who in every respect has been tempted as we are, yet without sin" (4:15). The sinlessness of Jesus is pictured as a result of conscious decision and intense struggle rather than being a formal consequence of his divine nature (Heb 4:15; 5:7-9; 12:2-4). He "became obedient unto death, even death on a cross" (Phil 2:8). In the words of the Apostles' Creed, he "was crucified, dead and buried." Christ is not only our glorious Savior but also our "Elder Brother" (cf.

Rom 8:29; Col 1:15; Mt 28:10). He is not only representative God but also representative humanity.

Jesus Christ is not a divine being less than God who mediates between God and humanity but God in humanity. In Calvin's thought God and humanity sometimes appear to be so far apart that the Mediator becomes virtually a tertium quid, a thing neither fully true God nor true humanity but "a degree midway between God and us."[10] God was in humanity in a unique and incomparable way. This is why the church was led to affirm two natures in one person. The one person is the preexistent Christ, and the two natures are the divine and the human. The fathers and teachers of the church further held that there is a full and free cooperation of the two natures without conflict and confusion. Jesus Christ is visible as "true man" and invisible as "true God" (Karl Barth). He is both the God who has become human and the human who is exalted to God (Barth).

What we have in Jesus Christ is an irreversible union between the Word as God and Jesus as man.[11] This is a personal or hypostatic union and cannot be duplicated or repeated. It is not a mystical union in which Jesus is one with God only in the core of his personality. Nor is it an essential union in which the being of Jesus blends into the being of God. Neither is it a moral union in which Jesus is united with God only in his will. The hypostatic union means that Jesus is one with the Logos, the preexistent Word who was with God in the beginning and who was God (Jn 1:1, 2). Jesus therefore differs from other human beings in kind, not simply in degree. He is more than a great teacher, a spiritual master or a pathfinder; he is a divine Savior, "very God and very man" in one person.

Following a long tradition in the church I affirm both the *anhypostasia* (impersonal humanity) and *enhypostasia* (personality in God). Jesus has no independent human personality: he has his personality in God. These terms as originally used do not mean that Christ's human nature lacks personality (as we understand it today).[12] Instead, it has no independent existence or being. "His manhood is only the predicate of His

Godhead."[13] Jesus is not autonomous or self-existent. God is the acting Subject in Jesus.

We should begin not with an abstract concept of deity (as in many christologies from above) nor with the historical Jesus (a christology from below) but with the living God incarnate in Jesus the man. I see Jesus not simply as a historical figure accessible to historical and scientific research but as the Word made flesh, the paradox of Eternity entering time at a particular point and place in history. This Jesus Christ is accessible—not to the probings of the historian nor to the speculations of the theologian but to the petitionings of the humble and penitent, who simply believe even as they try to understand. Those who pretend to see will be made blind; those who confess that they are in and of themselves blind will be made to see (Jn 9:39).

Theologians in the history of the church have used illustrations to clarify the enigmatic relationship between the two natures of Jesus Christ. John of Damascus taught that the two natures interpenetrate one another like fire and iron. The iron in the fire takes on the coloring of the fire, but it remains iron. One danger in this illustration is that it can imply an altering or transfiguring of the human nature.[14] Calvin compared the two natures of Christ to the two eyes of the human person: "Each eye can have its vision separately; but when we are looking at anything . . . our vision, which in itself is divided, joins up and unites in order to give itself as a whole to the object that is put before it."[15] Drawing upon modern physics, one might say that just as light can have the characteristics of both waves and particles, so Jesus embodies both humanity and divinity in his one person.

Christological Heresies

Whereas the trinitarian heresies concern the relation between Christ and God, the christological heresies pertain to the relation between the historical Jesus and the eternal Christ. Both types of heresy represent imbalances in the expression of faith with the result that certain truths are either underplayed or denied.

The Ebionites, an early Jewish sect or sects that acknowledged Jesus as the Messiah, began with the humanity of Jesus and then tried to relate this to his divinity. While some of them affirmed the miraculous birth of Jesus, they treated Jesus as exclusively human. Jesus was permeated by the presence of God, but he was not quite divine. A striking example of ebionitism in the sixteenth century was Faustus Socinus, who taught that Jesus differed from other mortals only by his extraordinary affinity to God. Like many of the Ebionites in the early church, Socinus believed in the virgin birth of Christ and his miracles but not in his preexistence. He also accepted the resurrection of Christ, but he reduced baptism to an interior experience. Ebionitism can be detected in the Enlightenment and the modern period in general. For example, Johann Herder (d. 1803) hailed Jesus as a supreme religious genius who proclaims and embodies "what is most divine in man."[16]

Much more of a threat to the integrity of the Christian faith in the early church was docetism, which held that Jesus Christ only appeared to be flesh. It posited a divine life in a human body. Early docetists like Valentinus and Apelles taught that the body of Christ was not born of humanity. It was a heavenly or ethereal body that simply passed through Mary. Docetists tended to deny that Jesus really died. The Marcionites decried the picture of Christ as a man with a "material, suffering body."[17] In the eighth and ninth centuries the Paulicians maintained that the body of Christ was human only in appearance. Mary was not the mother of Christ but "a mere conduit who had assisted the disguise of the holy spirit, worthy of no special reverence."[18] In the later nineteenth century Mary Baker Eddy held that Jesus did not really die but went through "what seemed to be death."[19] For Carl Jung (d. 1961) Jesus Christ is but one expression of the universal process of the creativity of the unconscious. Jung's fidelity was to the Christ archetype of which Jesus is one historical expression. Edgar Cayce declared, "Christ is not a man! Jesus was the man."[20] The Maharishi Mahesh Yogi, founder of Transcendental Meditation, ruminated: "I don't think Christ ever suffered or Christ could suffer. . . . It's a pity that

Christ is talked of in terms of suffering."[21]

Considerably closer to classical orthodoxy was Monophysitism, which asserted that Jesus Christ has only one nature—the divine. His form is human, but his true being is divine. Gregory of Nazianzus (d. 389) held that in the incarnation the humanity of Christ had by a process of mixing completely disappeared in the divinity. Gregory of Nyssa (died c. 395) likened the human nature of Christ to a drop of vinegar that is completely absorbed into the vastness of the ocean. Eutyches (died c. 455) held that Christ was *of* two natures but not *in* two natures. Some Monophysites said that Christ's flesh was not of the same nature as ours, for it was incorruptible and impassible. This would mean that Jesus could no longer be our Elder Brother or even our example. In later Roman Catholicism some of the Marian maximalists have argued that Mary provides the human side of salvation while Christ provides the divine side. There was certainly a docetic or monophysite strand in Gabriel Biel, who contended that Christ's ascension did not speak to people as directly as Mary's assumption, for Mary was *only* human.[22]

Closely related is Apollinarianism, named after Apollinarius (c. 310-390). This theologian held that Christ had a human body but a divine soul. The Logos took the place of the human soul of Jesus. Christ was primarily divine, and the human was no more than a passive instrument. Apollinarius went so far as to assert that Christ was not a complete man. While Christ had human flesh and a lower animal soul, the rational soul, which knows and chooses, was wanting, and its place was supplied by the eternal Word. Jesus had only a divine, not a human intelligence. In this heresy God takes on a temporary human disguise. Apollinarius's doctrines were condemned at the First Council of Constantinople (381).

The Monothelites acknowledged that Jesus had two natures, but the human nature was no longer capable of its own distinctive natural acts. Jesus had only one will—the divine. If we affirm that the divine will totally dominated the human life of Jesus, we may be veering toward monothelitism.[23] One of those who led the battle against monothelitism was Maximus the Confessor, who had his tongue torn out because he would not retract his accusations. Monothelitism was condemned at the Third Council of Constantinople (681).

Nestorianism was a more subtle heresy, for it preserved a veneer of orthodoxy. Nestorius (died c. 451) taught that Jesus is linked to God by means of a moral union or voluntary union, not a substantial union. His position allowed for Jesus being like God but called into question the affirmation that Jesus *is* God. Nestorianism stands in the tradition of dynamic monarchianism, which subordinated Jesus Christ to God. For Nestorius there are two natures and two wills, but the divine will gives direction to the human will. The two natures are loosely associated, not organically related. It is consequently no longer possible to speak seriously of a real incarnation because of the separation of the two natures and the two wills. The logic of his position was that there are "two persons," but he generally refrained from drawing this conclusion. Nevertheless, it seems that there are two personalities. Nestorius called the human nature the vesture or temple of the Godhead and drew a sharp distinction between the acts of the human nature and the acts of the divine person. Orthodoxy holds that there are two natures but only one person. Nestorius could not support the *theotokos* (Mary as the Mother of God), which was affirmed at the Council of Ephesus (431) amid much acclamation from the populace. The Council of Chalcedon (451) stated against Nestorius that the two natures coexist "without division and without separation."

The conflict between Nestorius and his opponent Cyril of Alexandria should be seen as a conflict between two types of christology. The christology of the indwelling Logos was associated with Nestorius and the school of Antioch. The theology of the hypostatic union was associated with Cyril and the Alexandrian school. Nestorius emphasized the distinction of the two natures and Cyril their indivisible unity. The problem with the theology of the indwelling Logos is that it tended to make the Logos one person and the man assumed by him another person.[24]

The Protestant Reformation generally adhered to the Alexandrian christology. Luther declared: "You should point to the whole man Jesus and say, 'That is God.'"[25] Luther, Zwingli and Karl Barth all accepted the *theotokos*, although Calvin deemed it more appropriate to refer to Mary as the Mother of Christ.

A heresy that belongs to the modern age is kenoticism, based principally on two texts: Philippians 2:6-7 and 2 Corinthians 8:9. The kenotic theory holds that "Christ voluntarily emptied himself" of "the relative attributes of omnipotence, omniscience and omnipresence while retaining the essential attributes of holiness and love."[26] This view, developed by the Lutheran Gottfried Thomasius (1802-1875), was anticipated by Count Nicholas Ludwig von Zinzendorf. The Calvinist W. F. Gess (d. 1891) argued that Christ laid aside *all* his attributes, and the Logos became a human soul. The divine consciousness was totally absent at the incarnation, but Christ regained it in the course of time. British kenoticists include A. M. Fairbairn, Bishop Gore, H. R. Mackintosh and P. T. Forsyth. Forsyth saw the divine attributes "not as renounced at the Incarnation but as retracted from the actual to the potential." The kenosis "is accompanied by a plerosis, a process of gradual reintegration through which, by genuine moral effort, Christ regained the mode of being that He had voluntarily laid aside."[27] One could legitimately argue that there is an orthodox form of kenoticism and a heretical form. It is possible to maintain that Christ emptied himself of his divine power but not of his divine nature. His power was always available to him, but he did not choose to draw upon it.

Kenoticism is able to uphold the true humanity of Jesus but not his deity. It affirms not that Jesus is both God and man but that Jesus is first God and then man. It is well to note that in 1 Corinthians 2:8 Paul refers to Jesus even in his humiliation as the "Lord of glory," reflecting Psalm 24:10, where God himself is described as "the Lord of hosts" and "the King of glory" (cf. Jas 2:1). Against the kenoticists I contend that the exalted one and the humiliated one are the same. The divine attributes are not renounced by Christ but are concealed in the humiliated Christ.

Tensions Between the Churches

The churches of the magisterial Reformation were united in their affirmation that Jesus Christ is at the same time fully human and fully divine. But as they began reflecting on the mystery of the hypostatic union, some divergences in understanding became apparent. On the one hand, the Lutheran emphasis was on *finitum capax infiniti*—the human Jesus is able to receive and bear the infinite, and this includes the properties of the divine nature. For Luther the two natures came together and are mingled in one person, but there is no confusion of natures. Lutheran doctrine contends that after the union the two natures can be thought of as not apart from each other but wholly together without giving rise to a mixture. The Lutherans held to *communicatio idiomatum*—the mutual participation and exchange of the properties of the individual natures.

On the other hand, Reformed theology favored *finitum non capax infiniti*—the finite in and of itself cannot receive or bear the infinite. In this view the Word assumes flesh rather than literally becomes flesh. (This emphasis is also apparent in Karl Barth.) The divine Logos remains God even while dwelling in human flesh—the earthen vessel of the Logos. The Word while being in the flesh also exists "outside the flesh." The humanity or the flesh is grounded in and dependent on the deity, but there is no merging of natures. The unity is in the person of Christ, not in the natures.

In Reformed christology the unity between the two natures is indirect—through the person or the Spirit who unites Jesus and Christ. Reformed christology has been criticized for holding to two planks united by glue at one end. In Lutheran christology the divine nature governs the human nature. Lutheran christology tends toward monophysitism and docetism, despite concerted efforts to guard against this. The danger in Reformed theology is Nestorianism. According to Herman Bavinck Reformed theology eluded or circumvented Nestorianism by holding that the union of the two natures is embedded in the unity of the person of Christ.[28]

The tensions between Reformed christology and Roman Catholic christology are much more substantial. Catholicism tends to underplay if not deny the real temptations of Jesus. While affirming the humanity of Christ, John Cassian insisted that Jesus Christ was not capable of experiencing genuine temptation, ignorance or fear. Catholic theologians have also questioned whether Jesus had real faith in God. In traditional Catholic thought Jesus had the vision of God from his birth or at least from his early years. For Thomas Aquinas Christ experienced neither faith nor hope, since both are excluded by his perfect vision of God. Even in the Virgin's womb Christ possessed omniscience. Modern Roman Catholic theology has sought to do more justice to the true humanity of Jesus. For example, Karl Rahner speaks of an evolving messianic consciousness.

Reformed theology has always affirmed the reality of faith and hope in Jesus. One of the early Puritans described Jesus as "the greatest and best Believer that ever lived."[29] In the words of Abraham Kuyper:

With our Reformed Church we confess that according to His human nature our Mediator has really and factually *believed*. Faith is that expression of the soul which clearly seizes hold of God's Word and through this Word again possesses its God, while human nature lies in the midst of death and in misery and under the curse and so has nothing to look forward to but perdition.—Well, of such a faith we now say that it was also in Jesus.[30]

Reformed and Catholic christologies also diverge in their understanding of the incarnation. Roman Catholic theologians tend to see the incarnation as a cosmic principle working from the union of God and humanity apart from the cross of humiliation. Reformed theology subordinates the incarnation to the atonement and stresses its historical particularity. Some Roman Catholic scholars envision the incarnation as a universal process of the divinizing of humanity of which Jesus is the revelation or the chief exemplification. For Thomas O'Meara the incarnation means "God's attempt to become flesh and blood in each of us."[31]

Roman Catholic theology is prone to speak of the church as the continuing incarnation of Christ. Or the church is seen as a prolongation of the incarnation. For Reformed theology such a position divinizes the church or elevates the church unduly. Whereas Greek, Roman Catholic and Anglo-Catholic theologians are open to the concept of "progressive incarnation," Reformed theologians identify the incarnation exclusively with the historical Jesus Christ. In their view the church is not an extension of the living Word of God but a divinely ordained channel of the Word. The church is the temple of the Spirit of God or the historical bearer or vessel of God's Spirit.

Roman Catholic theology speaks of the interpenetration of the two natures of Christ: the human nature is elevated to its culmination point. It sees Christ's human nature as an elevated and glorified human nature—a transfigured humanity. Reformed theology to the contrary emphasizes that Christ took on our weakened humanity in all its imperfections and limitations. Barth even says that Christ assumed our fallen human nature.

Regarding the purpose or goal of the incarnation, Catholic and Eastern Orthodox theology look forward to the deification or divinization of humanity. This is not the only purpose, but it is very prominent, especially in the writings of the Christian mystics.[32] In Reformed theology, by contrast, God incarnated himself in Christ in order to deliver humanity from the penalty of guilt and its bondage to the powers of darkness. The emphasis is on reconciliation with God over reunion with God. The final goal is fellowship with God in the holy community of the saints rather than the beatific vision of God. The latter is not denied but reinterpreted as a divine-human encounter rather than a mystical return to unity with God.

Modern Restatements of Christology

Friedrich Schleiermacher (1768-1834) gave a significant restatement of christology by replacing the two-nature doctrine with a doctrine of divine-human relation. Jesus Christ is not a divine being who assumed human nature but a prophetic figure who fully realizes the divine nature that is in all mortals. Christ does not intervene in creation but instead completes creation. He is not the Word made flesh but the exemplar of perfected human nature, the essence of elevated humanity. Jesus is not the arrival of something new in the sensible world but rather a clue to the divinity inherent in us all. The incarnation happens in order to advance an evolutionary pattern. "He alone is destined gradually to quicken the whole human race into higher life."[33] Christ is the Quickener of the higher self-consciousness. He saves by awakening the God-consciousness within us. Christ's ideal humanity includes both the realization of spiritual sensibility and the power to communicate this heightened spiritual awareness to others. Christ is the model of the redeemed life, a model that evokes admiration and commitment. In his *On Religion: Speeches to Its Cultured Despisers*, Schleiermacher considers Jesus Christ not the only mediator nor is Christianity the absolute or final religion.[34]

One can discern a marked docetic strand in Schleiermacher's theology. It is not the person of Christ but the idea he actualized that is critical for human salvation. Central to his thought is the *Urbild* or image of Christ as the "essential man" rather than Jesus Christ, the incarnate God-Man. His ruling norm is not the Christ who breaks into history but the original teachings of Jesus. Schleiermacher asserted both the sinlessness and the inerrancy of Jesus. Jesus is the perfected man who stands unmoved above the conflicts of the human soul, just as God stands above the polarities of the world. Thus Jesus is superior to emotion and invulnerable to temptation.

Albrecht Ritschl (d. 1889) proffered a christology in which the ethical more than the mystical element dominates. Jesus was one with God in will, not in essence. Through his obedience he procured justification for all peoples. Jesus made justification accessible to mortals by revealing it. His sacrifice was one of obedience, not a penal sacrifice. Jesus is celebrated as the revelation of the love of God to humanity. He was not a divine Savior but the founder of the kingdom of God.

His vocation was a moral rather than a priestly one involving a sacrifice for sin. Ritschl began with the historical Christ, not the dogma of the God-Man. At the same time his theology has a docetic thrust: faith is made to center in ideas or value judgments, and for Ritschl these ideas must be clear and concise.[35]

Emil Brunner (1889-1966) also disputed the doctrine of the two natures of Christ but still tried to maintain continuity with orthodoxy. Brunner dismissed Chalcedonian christology as an intrusion of Greek metaphysics into biblical faith and the Virgin Birth as a mythological trapping. For Brunner it is enough to assert that Jesus is true God and true Man. In his early work *The Mediator* he spoke of the humanity of Christ as a "historical mask" in which the divine Word clothes himself.[36] He also made a distinction between the "personality" of Jesus as an observable historical phenomenon and his "Person," which is a hidden suprahistorical mystery. The former is purely human; the latter is divine.[37] He tried to correct this docetic tendency in his *Dogmatics* but never wholly succeeded.

Much closer to classical orthodoxy was Karl Barth, who held that the essential origin of Jesus was in heaven. Barth defended the *anhypostasia* or impersonal humanity of Christ affirmed at Chalcedon. Its meaning is not that Jesus had no personality but that he had no independent personality. Barth interpreted the Word becoming flesh in terms of assuming flesh, for the Word of God remains God even in the incarnation.[38] For Barth the Word became not merely a human but also a particular man. He stoutly maintained this position against the view of some sectarian Christians, including the German Christians, that Christ was not a Jew but the "universal man." Barth also contended that Jesus Christ does not take on simply human nature but fallen human nature. He identifies fully with our sinful predicament even though he never succumbs to sin, thereby becoming a sinner. Against Nestorianism Barth strongly affirmed the *theotokos*—Mary as God-bearer or Mother of God. That is, he refused to separate the human and divine natures.

In an attempt to circumvent the metaphysics of the two natures of

Christ, Donald Baillie reinterpreted the incarnation in terms of the paradox of grace and freedom.[39] In Jesus Christ we see the coincidence of perfect freedom and divine predestination. The incarnation involved both free human choice and the initiative of God's grace. The incarnation of the divine Word in Jesus was conditioned by his continual response. Jesus had a fully human personality because it was completely centered in God. All those who are in Christ also experience the reality of the incarnation because the paradox of grace and freedom is present in their lives as well. The sinlessness of Jesus consisted in his renouncing all claim to ethical heroism. For Baillie it seems that it was necessary for Christ to die only as the revelation of God's incomparable love, not to pay the penalty for sin that would satisfy God's holiness. My main criticism of Baillie is that he appears to regard the union between the eternal Christ and Jesus as only a moral one, and he was therefore unable to affirm the preexistent Jesus Christ.[40]

J. A. T. Robinson also tried to do justice to the humanity of Jesus.[41] Jesus is critical for our salvation because in him we see the human face of God (though there are other faces of God in other religions). Jesus is normative for us because he represents God to humanity. He does what God commands. Robinson affirmed the full humanity of Jesus but not his deity except in a functional sense. He described the incarnation as "a breakthrough of cosmic consciousness."[42] Jesus is a product of human evolution rather than the transcendent Word breaking into human history from the beyond. The incarnation signifies not the condescension of the holy God but "the maturation of the human spirit."[43] Jesus is God not in a metaphysical sense but in a personal-ethical sense. He is one with the will of God. The Jesus of history is now dead, but the eternal Christ lives on in his members. Jesus is a man with a kingly role, representing God to humanity and humanity to God. Robinson contrasted his own functional christology with the mythological and metaphysical types. In his view Jesus' divinity signals a mutation in the evolutionary process, one that can be described as life in pure, unbounded love. For him "Jesus is but the clue, the parable, the sign by which it is possible to recognize the Christ in others."[44] Robinson was deeply influenced by Teilhard de Chardin and process philosophy as well as by the experiential theology of Schleiermacher and Tillich.

The separation between Christ and Jesus is also glaringly apparent in Paul Tillich. Tillich acknowledged Jesus as the Christ but would not uphold Jesus Christ as God. His criterion was not the Jesus of history but the biblical picture of Christ that would continue to be valid even if Jesus had not existed. He declared, "The assertion that Jesus as the Christ is the personal unity of a divine and a human nature must be replaced by the assertion that in Jesus as the Christ the eternal unity of God and man has become historical reality."[45] Here we see the influence of Hegel, for whom the incarnation symbolizes the ideal of divine-human unity that all mortals approximate. For Tillich what is pivotal is the power of the New Being manifest in Jesus but also in other holy personalities throughout history. The key to christology is not "to turn backward to an unknown historical past or to exert oneself about the applicability of questionable mythical categories to an unknown historical personality."[46] Instead it is to grasp the reality of divine-human unity that is exemplified in Jesus but that lies embedded in the depths of our own interior being. To discover the true self is to discover God, and an acquaintance with the historical Jesus can help us in this task.

In our day Wolfhart Pannenberg tends to deny or radically qualify the two-nature doctrine. He prefers to speak of the "revelatory presence of God in Jesus" and the "revelatory identity of Jesus with God" rather than of a divine and a human nature in one person.[47] Because the old Logos christology is tied to an outmoded philosophy, we are obliged to draw upon modern evolutionary philosophy—Hegel, Teilhard, Bergson—in order to communicate the mysteries of divine revelation.[48] Our point of departure should be not the preexistent Logos who assumes human flesh but "the new eschatological man," the Jesus of history, whose unity with God can be discerned only in the light of the revelatory event of the resurrection. For Pannenberg Jesus was a real man who lived completely in and for the future—that is, in and for God. Jesus is both functionally one with God in his will and mystically united with God in the depths of his being. He represents the fulfillment of humanity in complete openness to God. Pannenberg contrasts this christology "from below" with one "from above." He begins with the humanity of Jesus or the history of Jesus as man and then tries to relate this to divinity. Jesus' messianic identity is fulfilled in his resurrection, an event open to reason. The knowledge of revelation is not supernatural but humanly rational.

Although Pannenberg appeals to the catholic tradition of the church and is especially appreciative, though not uncritical, of the patristic fathers, the influence of the Enlightenment and of Hegel is very pronounced in his theological reflection. One critic complains that Jesus' nature proves to be the Hegelian one of finite spirit participating in infinite Spirit but unable to represent the latter until the course of history "incarnates" Absolute Spirit in its full series of manifestations (Kenneth Hamilton).[49] The incarnation becomes the self-actualizing of God in human history.[50] In the eschatological history of Jesus we see the anticipatory revelation of God, though the whole revelation is still ahead of us. In fairness to Pannenberg, he does recognize the dangers of a too heavy reliance on philosophy in order to explicate theological truth, and he rightly reminds us that every bona fide theology needs to be in dialogue with the great minds of the age if the truth of redemption is to be correlated with the truth of creation.

A Reaffirmation of Orthodox Christology

Even while acknowledging that Greek philosophical categories were used to produce the Chalcedonian formula, I unashamedly stand by Chalcedon as an enduring expression of the faith once delivered to the saints. With the church fathers I affirm that Jesus was consubstantial with the Father, according to his divinity, and consubstantial with us mortals (except for sin) according to his humanity. I agree with

Dietrich Bonhoeffer: "The Chalcedonian Definition is an objective, but living, statement which bursts through all thought-forms."[51] Chalcedon is an extraordinary witness to the biblical truth that revelation comes to us veiled in mystery. Chalcedon does not explain away the paradox of the incarnate Christ in human flesh but lets it stand as a depiction of mystery at the outer limits of human reason.

The heresies of the church all have their source in the often well-meaning attempt to rationalize or resolve the christological paradox. They generally constitute an effort to exalt one nature to the detriment of the other. By contrast, orthodoxy exercises reason in order to safeguard the mystery of faith. It recognizes in humility that the full depth and breadth of what God has done for us in Jesus Christ far surpasses human comprehension, though it still throws much light on the human predicament and on the divine solution to this predicament.

In my christology I choose to begin neither with an abstract concept of God or Christ removed from history nor with the historical man Jesus. Instead my point of departure is the paradox of God himself entering world history at a particular place and time, in a particular historical figure—Jesus of Nazareth. I wish to begin with the Word made flesh rather than with the preexistent Logos or with the historical Jesus. My focus is not on the human personality of Jesus or the Jesus of history, nor is it on the Christ principle, the Spirit of Christ or the eternal Christ. It is dangerous to make the human personality of Christ the pivotal center of theology, for this tends to deny that Christ is a divine person, though in human form.

A christology from below is apparent in the ebionitic type of heresy, which ends in the divinization or apotheosis of man. Here we begin with Jesus' humanity and then try to relate it to his divinity. This heresy is reflected in adoptionism, Arianism, Nestorianism and subordinationism.

A christology from above often becomes a variant of the docetic type of heresy. Here we begin with the eternal Word or an abstract concept of God, which we then try to relate to Jesus' humanity. We end either in the materialization of divinity or in the humanization of an idea. The docetic type of heresy has an affinity with modalism, monophysitism and Apollinarianism. The Word becomes a timeless truth rather than a living address. Docetism has an affinity with Sabellianism just as ebionitism has with Arianism. Nestorianism could lend itself to either type. In docetism the God-Man has the nature and essence of humanity but not human individuality.

Most theologians agree that docetism has always represented the dominant threat to the integrity of Christian faith. In our efforts to uphold Christ's divinity we are first of all tempted to begin with his divinity and then ascertain how this is reflected in the Jesus of history. The eternal becomes more important than the historical, ideas become more pivotal than deeds. Modern theologians who veer toward the docetic type of heresy include Schleiermacher, Tillich, Bultmann, Brunner, Ritschl[52] and Nels Ferré. Their christologies are docetic in that they tend to separate the Jesus of history from the Christ of faith. The Word only appears in the flesh, or the Word was manifested in Jesus. Or the power of the Logos is reflected in Jesus' humanity.

Moderns who tend toward ebionitism include Unitarians, social gospelers, death of God theologians, and secular and political theologians. Jesus becomes a religious genius, the greatest of the prophets, the authentic saint, a spiritual master or guru, or the original liberator. He is portrayed as a divinized man, a "man for others," a prophetic or servant figure. Tolstoy regarded Jesus as the greatest of all ethical teachers, the flower of humanity. For Walter Rauschenbusch Jesus was "a perfect religious personality."[53] In H. Richard Niebuhr's theology Jesus was the prototypical faithful human being. Glenn Bucher acclaimed Christ as "the full historical exemplar" of the human potential for liberation or as "the human expression of life lived in radical human freedom."[54] Ellen Flesseman, a Dutch theologian, argued that "the Son Jesus Christ is not God, but a man who was so one with God that in Him I meet God."[55] According to Thomas O'Meara Jesus is "the climax of man," the culminating point in human evolution.[56] Piet

Schoonenberg held that there is only one person in Jesus Christ and that is the human person. Other theologians who tend toward the ebionitic type of heresy include William Hamilton, Paul van Buren, Harvey Cox, J. A. T. Robinson, John Dominic Crossan and Juan Segundo.

Our faith is not in the Jesus of history or in the eternal Christ but in the historical Jesus Christ, who was both fully divine and fully human at the same time. We must not say that Jesus *becomes* the Christ but that he *is* the Christ, that he has been united with the Christ, the eternal Word of God, from his very conception. The content of our message is not the ideals that Jesus expressed in his personal life or the teachings that he proclaimed to his disciples and others. What makes him significant for faith and life is his messianic identity as the Son of God in human flesh and his redeeming work in human history.

The union of divinity and humanity in Jesus Christ is a unique, incomparable union. It is both personal and ontological. This is why the church calls it a "hypostatic union" (from the Greek *hypostasis* or person). As I have stated earlier, it should be sharply distinguished from other forms of union—essential, mystical and sacramental.[57]

We need to confess that Jesus Christ was both fully God and fully human at the same time. Barth phrases it well: "He is the Lord humbled for communion with man and likewise the Servant exalted to communion with God."[58] Kierkegaard described the incarnation as the paradox of Eternity entering into time. Yet this is not a paradox to God. There was no cleft in God's nature. His humiliation was consonant with his nature (Barth). The paradox of grace and freedom, which Baillie upholds, allows more room for human cooperation, but the mystery is not simply a merger of wills but a union of being. It is a mystery that can be described but only inadequately explained.

The church affirms not the identity of God and Jesus as man but the coinherence of God and humanity in Jesus Christ (see Jn 14:11). There is no identity between the manhood of Jesus and his deity, for he has two natures that must never be confounded, though they are inseparable. Nor do I hold to a mingling or synthesis of humanity and divinity in Jesus. Then Jesus would simply be a phantasmal appearance of God. Nor do I affirm an essential union, for this would mean that Jesus is overwhelmingly and exclusively divine. Instead the church teaches the identity of the person of Jesus and the eternal Christ. There is one person—the Son of God—and two natures—the divine and the human. The divine person is not alongside the human personality of Jesus (this is Nestorianism). Rather the divine person relates to us in and through the human personhood of Jesus. The perfect manhood of Jesus is not to be equated with deity but is the garment or vessel of deity. There is a direct identity between the Word of God and the personhood of Jesus but only an indirect identity between the living Word of God and the Bible or the sermon.

The human nature of Jesus is subordinate to his divine nature. This subordination does not mean the cancellation of humanity but the realization of true humanity. True freedom lies in perfect submission (Rom 6). God dwells and acts not in the appearance of a man but in a man with real flesh and blood. It is God himself who acts and speaks in and through this earthen vessel. Quoting Isaiah 63:9, Cyril of Alexandria insisted that "it was not an elder, nor an angel, but the Lord himself who saved us, not by an alien death or by the mediation of an ordinary man, but by his very own blood."[59]

I affirm the sinlessness of Jesus because he was filled with the Holy Spirit from his conception. True humanity is the humanity as designed and created by God—the humanity that lives in perfect conformity with the will of God. Fallen humanity represents a corruption of humanity, a spurious humanity. Christ took upon himself human corruption though he lived as a person victorious over sin and corruption (cf. Heb 4:15). He experienced temptation but always rose above it. Because of the purity of his commitment, temptation could find no lodging in his being (as in the case of sinful mortals).[60]

To be truly human does imply being limited, and Jesus was limited as a human being. He could have erred because of his kenosis or self-emptying, but he never swerved from the truth because of his union with divinity. He was vulnerable to error, but he did not stumble into error.

We do not yet exist in communion with Christ simply by the knowledge that God was present in the historical Jesus. We must be awakened to faith in the living Christ if his incarnation is to be salvific for us. In Luther's words, "You do not yet have Christ, even though you know that he is God and man. You truly have Him only when you believe that this altogether pure and innocent Person has been granted to you by the Father as your High Priest and Redeemer."[61]

The incarnation was not limited to the earthly life of Jesus, but Christ continues to exist in incarnate form because his humanity was resurrected. This is why we can speak of a permanent incarnation. As Baillie says, "If we believe in the Incarnation, we cannot possibly say that Jesus ceased to be human when He departed from this world."[62] This belief in the continuing or permanent incarnation is reflected in the Westminster Shorter Catechism: He "being the eternal Son of God, became man, and so was, and continueth to be, God and man in two distinct natures and one person forever."[63]

We may speak of an extension of the incarnation not in the sense that the church is the incarnation but that all members of the church are related mystically to its Head, who alone is the Incarnate One. Through the power of the Spirit of God we who believe participate in the one incarnation, but we do not replicate the incarnation. We are indwelt by the Spirit of Christ, but we do not ourselves become the Christ. We are servants and emissaries of the Word but not re-presentations of the Word.

The relation of the incarnation and the atonement has continued to be a subject of theological dissension. Protestant or Reformation theology has underlined the centrality of the atoning death of Christ, since this belongs to the essence of the gospel. Catholic theology has emphasized the priority of the incarnation over the atonement. While it is true that who Jesus was determined what Jesus did, his divine identity becomes visible only in light of his atoning work. We come to recognize Jesus as the Son of God only when we experience the efficacy of his atoning work for our salvation. Forsyth put it well: "The doctrine of Redemption is signally absent from the creeds, yet the Church has a more direct connection with Redemption than with Incarnation. Only by experience of Redemption has it a religious knowledge of what Incarnation means."[64] Forsyth was quite firm that "Christ did not become incarnate *and* redeem; He became incarnate *to* redeem. His Redemption is both the crown and the key of His Incarnation."[65] Yet when he says that "the incarnation has no religious value but as the background of the atonement," he opens himself to criticism.[66] Melanchthon put a similar emphasis on the work of Christ when he declared that to know Christ is to know his benefits. Yet this is only part of the truth. When we experience his benefits we come to understand his messianic identity as the preexistent Son of God. The truth of his person and work is not simply ontological but transformational. Not until we are transformed by his grace through an encounter with the cross can we come to appreciate his status as the eternal Word of God who existed with the Father and the Spirit from all eternity.

Appendix A: Implications of Gender-Inclusive Language for Christology

The ideological movement of feminism is having a resounding impact on christology. When gender-inclusive language is mandated for the persons of the Godhead and even for Jesus Christ, a theological shift of major proportions is taking place. If we say that God became "a human person" rather than "a man," we are veering toward Nestorianism, for orthodoxy contends there is only one person in the incarnation—the divine person. If we say that God became a human being, we are not speaking an untruth, but the implication is that there was a metamorphosis rather than an incarnation. The church confesses not that the Word turned into flesh but that the Word took human flesh unto himself. God became man while still remaining God. If we aver only that God became human, this could imply that God simply assumed human qualities or that God became humane. A similar difficulty confronts us when we confess that God became humanity, thereby blurring the particularity of the incarnation. God did not become generic humanity or generic man but a particular historical individual.[67] We can affirm that God assumed human flesh or that God entered the stream of humanity in the historical figure of Jesus Christ. We cannot substitute the "personhood" of Jesus Christ for his "manhood," since there is one person but two natures in the incarnate Christ.

In the ideological climate today we are also witnessing the expurgation of personal pronouns for God. It is alleged that simply to repeat the word *God* instead of using a personal pronoun avoids the implication that God is male or masculine. To refer to Christ as "he" but to God as "God" reflects a subordinationist mentality. To use the neologism "Godself" rather than "himself" creates an ambiguity in how we conceive of God.[68] Such usage could imply polytheism, since in some formulations a disjunction is inferred between God and "Godself." For example, to say that "God made Godself vulnerable to suffering" creates a different picture of the Godhead from the traditional formulation "God made himself vulnerable to suffering." To substitute "God's only Son, our Lord" for "his only Son, our Lord" in the Apostles' Creed indicates a shift away from trinitarianism. The Lutheran theologian Robert Jenson regards this substitution as "strictly heretical." "The creed does not confess that God generically has a Son; it confesses that the antecedent of 'his,' 'the Father' of the previous article, has a Son. With the pronominal relation deleted, the creed's trinitarian confession is undone."[69]

Some advocate an "expansive language" over the gender specific language of the trinitarian legacy. They claim that given the wealth of metaphors for God in the Bible, choosing only the masculine ones betrays a patriarchal bias. While there are indeed many metaphors applied to God in the Bible, there is only one proper name for God— "I AM WHO I AM" in the old dispensation and "Father, Son and Holy

Spirit" in the new. We are not allowed to name or reimage God by drawing upon the myriad metaphors in the Bible and in culture, for God names himself by revealing himself as Father, Son and Spirit (cf. Mt 28:19).[70] Our task is to acknowledge his name rather than to rename him in our image. This is not to deny that the Christian may use metaphors in order to bring out the infinite depth and breadth of God's self-revelation in Jesus Christ, so long as these metaphors are not substitutes for the personal designations in biblical faith and history. Expansive language for God must be subordinated to the specific language of biblical revelation, and then it may have a place in the Christian story. The Bible itself describes God by such metaphors as "rock," "fortress," "wind" and "river," but these are never proper names for God.[71]

To refer to Christ as "Child" instead of "Son" (as does the new NCC Lectionary) is another subversion of trinitarian religion. "Child" indicates immaturity; "Son" indicates an abiding filial relationship to God as Father. Christ was a child in his personal history, but from all eternity he is the Son of the Father, equal to the Father.

Feminist ideology is unwilling to tolerate not only masculine designations for God but also hierarchical ones. It is commonly said that God is not above us or over us but beside us and within us. Words like *Lord, King* and *Master* derive from an outmoded patriarchal culture. In a democratic or egalitarian cultural milieu, preference should be given to *Friend* or *Companion*. The Bible does at times speak of God in this manner, but not at the sacrifice of the language of hierarchy. Christ is Lord before he is Friend; he is Master before he is Companion.

I do not deny that the Bible was composed in a patriarchal context and that the language of patriarchy is pervasive in Scripture and in church tradition. But we need to realize that patriarchy is also overturned in the Bible. God is not a father in the sense of one who is domineering or tyrannical but in the sense of a caring and nurturing parent. Christ is Lord not in the sense of domination but in the sense of servanthood (Mt 20:25-28; Jn 13:13-14). His lordship is demonstrated in his servanthood; his kingship is manifested in his condescension to our weakness and misery. He overcomes not through sheer coercion but through the power of the powerlessness of love. Patriarchal language has revelational sanction because it retains the abiding distinctions between "an above and a below," "a first and a second," and "a before and an after." But new meaning is poured into these distinctions, a fact that is sometimes lost in both sides of the debate.[72]

Inclusive metaphors may have a place in our depiction of God, but not at the price of compromising the biblical witness. Our haste to accommodate to the latest theological fashions too often results in a subtle dilution of the biblical scandal of particularity. God not only identifies with us, but he also stands over against us. He is not only the Infinitely Near but also the Wholly Other. His fatherhood is not so much a reflection of universal fatherhood as a revolutionary alteration of the very concept of fatherhood. Similarly his lordship stands not in continuity but in disparity with cultural conceptions of lordship. His love goes out to all peoples, male and female, white and black, slave and free, and so on; but his revelation occurs only in one person, Jesus Christ, and in one particular people, the Jews. His promises are intended for all, but they are revealed only in one event or series of events in history. We are called to renounce not only other ways to salvation but also all images of God intended as substitutes for God's revealed name. We are commanded to call on only one name for God, for there is no other name given by which we must be saved (Acts 4:12). In our passion for an inclusive religion and liturgy we must not deny the historical particularity of divine revelation. The object of our faith is not a universal Christ-consciousness or an all-encompassing Primal Matrix but the living, personal God who revealed himself only at one point in history and whose sacrifice is adequate to regenerate the entire human race.

The New Inclusive Version of the Bible, recently published by Oxford University Press, reveals an almost total capitulation to the ideology of political correctness, which threatens to tear the church apart as we move toward the end of a century.[73] In this Bible Jesus is referred to as "the Human One" rather than "the Son of God" for fear of insulting women. God is referred to as "Father-Mother" because "Father" is allegedly tied to a hopelessly patriarchal, repressive cultural ethos. In an effort to avoid anti-Semitism, the editors are sometimes led to deny the Jews their Jewish identity, referring to them as simply "the people," without regard to their religious or ethnic origin. This reminds one of the beguiling attempt of the so-called German Christians in the 1930s to expurgate from the canon all references to the Jewish roots of the Christian church in order to build a more culturally cohesive religion.[74] Even more absurd, verses that refer to Jesus' being on the right hand of God are changed in order not to discriminate against left-handed people. With translations like this it is no longer possible to uphold the inerrancy of Scripture, even when we are thinking primarily of its teaching or doctrine.[75]

FOUR

THE VIRGIN BIRTH

All this happened in order to fulfill what the Lord declared through
the prophet: "A virgin will conceive and bear a son, and he shall
be called Emmanuel," a name which means "God is with us."
MATTHEW 1:22-23 REB

Had it not been for the Virgin Birth it is highly improbable that the
Doctrine of the Incarnation would have ever gained a
prominent lodging in the human mind.
DOUGLAS EDWARDS

The virgin birth is not a necessity created by the integrity and
infallibility of the Bible; it is a necessity created (if at all)
by the solidarity of the Gospel, and by the requirements of grace.
P. T. FORSYTH

Supernatural conception is a most credible and befitting
preface to a life consummated by rising from the dead.
H. R. MACKINTOSH

T he doctrine of the virgin birth of Christ has been contested in
the church, particularly since the Enlightenment of the eighteenth century, which called into question the supernatural
claims of the faith. In the early church the virgin birth was a powerful
witness to the true humanity of Jesus, since it asserted that the Word
was really made flesh in the historical figure of Jesus of Nazareth. In
the modern period the virgin birth is important in the church's affirmation of the divinity of Christ in the face of a corrosive naturalism.
Under the impact of docetism and gnosticism many Christians have

been tempted to create a cleavage between the spiritual and the material to the point of affirming that the Son of God is not born in history but simply appears in history or at the boundary of history.

The Current Controversy

In the nineteenth and twentieth centuries the virgin birth has had some worthy defenders as well as notable opponents. It is presently receiving considerable support from a revitalized evangelicalism and a resurgent traditionalist Catholicism.[1]

In liberal theology the fashion has been to treat the virgin birth as a mythological expression of an abiding truth or of an enduring experience. David Strauss viewed it as a nonhistorical myth that reflected the hopes and expectations of the early disciples.[2] Similarly Rudolf Bultmann regarded it as a mythological attempt to reinforce the church's faith in the divinity of Jesus. John Hick also reflects this mindset: "As the stories . . . of the six day creation of the world and the fall of Adam and Eve after their temptation by the serpent in the Garden of Eden are now seen as profound religious myths, illuminating our human situation, so the story of the Son of God coming down from heaven and being born as a human baby will be seen as a mythological expression of the immense significance of our encounter with one in whose presence we have found ourselves to be at the same time in the presence of God."[3] Episcopal Bishop John Spong is convinced that "in time the virgin birth account will join Adam and Eve and the story of the cosmic ascension as clearly recognized mythological elements in our faith tradition whose purpose was not to describe a literal event but to capture the transcendent dimensions of God in the earthbound words and concepts of first-century human beings."[4]

The tradition of Protestant orthodoxy and fundamentalism has been vigorous in its defense of the historicity of the virgin birth of Christ, often to the extent of elevating it into an essential of the faith indispensable for salvation. The older Lutheran orthodoxy could describe the virginal conception of Christ as "the corner-stone on which all wisdom of this world will shatter."[5] Indeed, according to John R. Rice, "All Christianity stands or falls with the doctrine of the virgin birth. If Jesus had a human father, then the Bible is not true."[6] And in the words of Robert Glenn Gromacki: "To confess the virgin birth is to confess the deity of Christ; to confess the deity of Christ is to confess the virgin birth."[7]

Karl Barth, who characterized the infancy narratives in Matthew and Luke as saga or legend, nevertheless affirmed the virgin birth of Christ as the sign of the mystery of God's self-condescension in human flesh.[8] It is not an idea in mythological garb but an event that is given a theological interpretation in the poetic language of narrative. The virgin birth testifies to the breadth and wonder of God's grace rather than to the creativity of human imagination, though the latter is not excluded. As a supernaturalist, Barth insisted that the fact of the virgin birth does not have its roots in the causal sequence that composes the natural order.

Another stalwart defender of the virgin birth was Anglican theologian Alan Richardson, who like Barth did not cursorily dismiss the historical and critical study of the Bible. He maintained that "reluctance on the part of some modern Christians to believe in the Virgin Birth of Christ has been due to a failure to understand the Bible and the nature of its testimony; ignorance of scriptural meaning always results in failure to perceive the wonderful activity of God."[9] Richardson skillfully refuted the allegation that the virgin birth stories in the New Testament are analogous to virgin birth stories in the pagan world, showing that the latter were focused on the birth of heroes through intercourse between gods and mortals. He also took issue with the criticism that belief in the virgin birth of Christ springs from an unwholesome asceticism that regards sexuality as sinful. "This morbid notion of sexuality is totally absent from the Jewish mind in general and from the birth narratives of the Gospels in particular."[10]

A mediating position is taken by the Reformed theologian Thomas Boslooper, who affirms the importance of the virgin birth narratives to the faith of the church in the true humanity and full deity of Jesus

Christ. He contends that "the Christian story of the virgin birth is as different from pagan 'analogies' as monotheism is from polytheism, as different as Biblical ideas of the relationship between God and man are from the mythological activities of gods in human affairs, and as different as the polygamous and incestuous pagan society was from the Christian teaching on morals and marriage."[11] At the same time, Boslooper understands the virgin birth as a myth and tends to deny or underplay the historicity of the birth narratives, whereas Barth treats the virgin birth as a mystery with a firm historical basis. Boslooper can be criticized for relating the virgin birth primarily to the humanity of Jesus and not also to his divine origin. Moreover, Boslooper's contention that the virgin birth supports the sanctity of marriage is debatable. His equivocation concerning the historical fact of the virgin birth makes his contribution suspect from my perspective.

Writing as a biblical-historical scholar, Raymond Brown shows that belief in the virgin birth of Christ has some evidential support, though it is by no means conclusive.[12] For Brown the infancy narratives are "folkloric," but they nevertheless contain a historical core that cannot be lightly dismissed. He takes issue with the practice of using these stories to support the traditional belief of the church "that virginal conception is a more noble way of conceiving a child than is marital intercourse."[13] "Mary is depicted as having chosen the married state, and the virginal conception is presented as God's intervention, not as Mary's personal choice."[14]

Wolfhart Pannenberg displays a decidedly more reserved attitude toward the virgin birth, calling it an "aetiological legend." This legend "is Christologically justified only as the expression of a passing stage in the primitive Christian development of tradition."[15] Pannenberg sees the virgin birth narratives as contradicting the high christology of Paul and John, who affirmed the preexistence of Christ as opposed to the position that his sonship began at his conception. Brown poses this question to Pannenberg: "Why is not the Church's reconciliation of pre-existence and virginal conception a genuine step in a developing

christology? Because they are not reconciled in the NT does not mean
. . . that they are irreconcilable."[16]

Eduard Schweizer makes a place for the virgin birth in his theology
but insists that it is not to be ranked with the resurrection of Christ in
importance. The significance of Jesus' birth was not the virginal conception but the naming of Jesus, which reveals that God himself now
dwells among mortals and will thus be the salvation of all peoples.[17]
"Whether a virgin birth is possible is a question only a modern would
ask; virgin birth was an accepted notion to men of the New Testament
period. By no means, therefore, should a man's faith be judged by
whether or not he thinks a miracle like this is possible, the less so
because the virgin birth plays such an infinitesimal role in the New
Testament."[18]

Much more supportive of the virgin birth is Wesleyan Holiness theologian Kenneth Grider, who contends that these biblical stories of the
birth of Christ give historical facticity to the central biblical claim that
God became incarnate in human flesh. The virgin birth is also consonant with God's way of accomplishing his purposes, not by arbitrary
divine fiat but by human participation. "From outside and above the
human experience, He entered into human form and life and experience. From outside and above the historical, He entered into the historical."[19]

A plethora of literature is now available on the reconception of the
virgin birth of Christ and the role of the Virgin Mother by feminist and
liberationist theologians.[20] One of the more significant is Jane
Schaberg, who presents a fairly well-reasoned but ultimately uncon-
vincing case that the infancy narratives are based on the illegitimacy
of Jesus.[21] She claims that some texts are better understood against the
background of the charge of illegitimacy (cf. Mk 6:3; Jn 8:41), and the
infancy narratives were to some degree designed to counteract this
charge. With many other feminists and liberationists she subscribes to
a hermeneutics of suspicion, which claims to uncover an ideological
bias in what is being reported in Scripture. She contends that on this

issue as on others we must explore biblical sexual politics and "the literary strategies that are used by the biblical narrative to promote patriarchal ideology."[22] "We are required to accept the ambiguous nature of the whole Bible with its internal contradictions, to critically assess and evaluate, to discriminate between oppressive and liberating biblical traditions and aspects of traditions, to make decisions about what constitutes the true word of God."[23] She resists the inclination of many feminists to use these stories to promote goddess spirituality. In her view "the data from Hindu and Buddhist countries as well as from many Roman Catholic countries indicates that mother goddess worship stands in inverse relationship with high secular female status."[24] Schaberg agrees with Bultmann that belief in the virginal conception of Jesus developed when the infancy narratives "were heard or read against the background of predominantly Gentile religious heritages and sensibilities and without enough of an ear for the subtle Old Testament allusions and Jewish sensibilities."[25] Schaberg can be criticized for virtually allowing a contemporary ideology (feminism) to dictate her exegesis, but her book is important because it shows that the only biblically viable alternative to the claims of the apostolic church that Jesus was conceived by a virgin is the admission that Jesus was probably illegitimate.[26]

The Traditional Understanding

In church tradition the doctrine of the virgin birth refers primarily to the virginal conception of Jesus. It means that Jesus was conceived apart from a human father. The virginal conception was nonsexual, for "there is no male deity or element to impregnate Mary."[27] Mary was not seduced by God but mysteriously overshadowed by the Holy Spirit. God was not the physical father of Jesus but the preexistent Father. Paul Jewett observed wisely:

> The church uses the language of conception when speaking of the Spirit's mysterious energizing of the Virgin, to avoid the suggestion that in the Incarnation the Spirit assumed the role of the Father of

Jesus by impregnating his mother. Jesus' Father is the first Person, not the third Person, of the Godhead. He is *begotten* of the Father, *conceived* by the Spirit, and *born* of the Virgin Mary. The virgin birth tells us not only that Jesus had no earthly father, but also that he had no heavenly mother.[28]

What we have in the virgin birth of Christ is not a type of *hieros gamos* (holy marriage) in which mortals impregnated by gods produce super-human beings but an incarnation of the living God in humanity—in its poverty and weakness. The virgin birth signified the conception not of an independent human existence but of a human nature. The Son of God united human flesh with his divine person.

The virgin birth also symbolizes the purity of Mary's commitment. She was the mother of Jesus by faith before she was his mother by blood. Luther said the greater miracle beyond her conception of Jesus was the fact that she believed. She conceived by her ear before she conceived in her womb. This must not be taken to mean, however, that Mary cooperated in the work of salvation. She believed and obeyed through divine grace operating upon her and within her. Her only contributions were her receptivity and powerlessness. She was then empowered to celebrate the gift of grace and eventually to be a messenger of grace.

The stories of the virgin birth testify that in the work of human redemption God does not use the will of man or the will of the flesh (cf. Jn 1:13). "God managed without male desire and that proud and complaisant power which subdues and possesses."[29] The virgin birth "may be a sign of God's independence of ordinary human processes, and of our proud masculinity."[30]

In the emerging Catholic tradition Mary was hailed as the Virgin Mother, and this encompassed far more than the virginal conception. It was said that Mary was a virgin not only before Jesus' birth *(ante partu)* but also during his birth *(in partu)* and after his birth *(post partum)*. Many in the church succumbed to a docetic mentality when they envisaged Jesus as simply passing through the wall of Mary's uterus so that her hymen was not ruptured. Their reluctance to affirm that Jesus shared in the ordinary human processes of human birth connoted a gnostic depreciation of earthly existence.

While Protestantism on the whole avoided the pitfalls of gnosticism and docetism in its treatment of the birth of Jesus, it remained remarkably open to the idea of Mary's perpetual virginity. Among others, Luther, Calvin, Zwingli, Wollebius, Bullinger and Wesley claimed that Mary was ever-Virgin *(semper virgo)*.[31] The Second Helvetic Confession and the Geneva Bible of the Reformed faith and the Schmalkald Articles of the Lutheran churches affirm it. The doctrine indubitably has its roots in the exaltation of virginity in the early church rather than in the Bible. The pivotal question is whether Scripture contradicts or supports this belief. Catholic scholars often interpret Mary's reply to the angel, "How shall this be, since I have no husband?" as indicating her resolve to remain a virgin throughout her life.[32] The difficulty with this interpretation is that it stands in conflict with the important role assigned to physical motherhood in the ethos of Judaism, with its attendant joys of children. Celibacy was generally regarded by the Jews as a misfortune rather than a higher state of life, and celibacy within marriage would probably have been an anomaly.[33] When it is said that Joseph "knew her not until she had borne a son" (Mt 1:25), this probably means that Joseph became her husband in fact following the birth of Jesus. Catholic scholars mount a not very compelling case that the text implies only that Joseph did not know Mary up to the time of the virgin birth but says nothing conclusively about the situation after Jesus' birth.

Much more difficult for the Catholic and Orthodox understanding are the many references in the New Testament to the brothers and sisters of Jesus (Mt 12:46-50; 13:55-57; Mk 3:20-21, 31-35; 6:3-4; Lk 8:19-21; Jn 2:12; 7:3, 5, 10; Acts 1:14; 1 Cor 9:5; Gal 1:19). If Mary had other children, this would totally overthrow the doctrine of her perpetual virginity. There is admittedly some internal evidence in Scripture that the brothers of Jesus were not his blood brothers. It is implied that the brothers of Jesus were older than he, since they tried to exercise control over him (Mt 12:46-50; Mk 3:31-35; Lk 8:19-20; Jn 7:3-4).[34] Two of the brothers are mentioned as belonging to another Mary (Mt 27:56; cf. Mk 15:40).[35] There is also the problem of Jesus at the cross asking John to receive Mary as his mother (Jn 19:25-27). This request would be somewhat unusual if Mary had had children of her own. Eastern Orthodox scholars are inclined to interpret the brothers and sisters of Jesus as children of Joseph by another marriage. Catholic scholars generally view them as cousins, for in the extended family network of the ancient world cousins were practically viewed as brothers and sisters.[36]

On the other side of the ledger Luke mentions Jesus as the "firstborn" of Mary (Lk 2:7), thereby implying additional children. Moreover, if the brothers of Jesus were really cousins it would be more natural for the Greek word for "cousin" to be used in this connection rather than "brother." It is well to note that the Lutheran-Catholic task force on Mary in the New Testament concluded that "in using the term 'firstborn'" Luke was not "at all concerned with the question of whether or not Mary had other children after Jesus, and no logically deduced answer to that question is possible from his terminology."[37]

Can evangelical Protestants today uphold Mary as the Virgin Mother? Certainly we must continue to affirm the virginal conception of Jesus, for Scripture testifies to this and the tradition of the whole church supports it. Can we also contend for Mary's virginity at the time of Jesus' birth and after his birth? Mary surely had the status of a virgin when Jesus was born, although this does not imply that this birth was qualitatively different from an ordinary human birth, that Jesus simply passed through Mary and that Mary had no birth pains. But did Mary remain virginal throughout her life? Since Scripture is silent on this matter and the witness of the early church is equivocal, we cannot proclaim Mary as *semper virgo* as an article of faith. That Mary as the Virgin Mother has a long history in the Catholic tradition and was stoutly affirmed by the mainstream Reformation and by many Protestants throughout the succeeding centuries means that we have a basis for holding to this thesis as a pious opinion, but never as a dogma, which would make belief in it necessary for salvation.[38] The Bible seems to indicate that during the active ministry of Jesus Mary was single, since Joseph had passed from the scene.[39] In this singleness she was committed to the mission of her son. She was at the foot of the cross and in the upper room with the disciples when the Holy Spirit was given for the creation of the church. She was virginal in her devotion to Jesus, but we cannot therefore conclude that she did not give birth to Jesus in a natural, human way or that her marriage to Joseph was purely spiritual rather than physical, since such beliefs presuppose a cultural ethos that stands at variance with the Jewish heritage of Old Testament religion. In the early church Origen, reflecting the Platonic cast of his thought, upheld Mary's perpetual virginity, while Tertullian and Irenaeus, who were more resistant to a synthesis with classical philosophy, argued that Mary had normal conjugal relations with Joseph after the birth of Jesus.[40]

While it may be appropriate to view Mary the mother of God as being wholly consecrated to the mission and work of her son in perpetual virginity, the picture of Mary as a mother who lives out her commitment in the midst of family duties also has an appeal to the religious imagination and surely has more direct biblical support. Evangelical theologian Keith Weston echoes the sentiments of probably most (but not all) conservative Protestants today: "For me the natural meaning of the Scripture references takes nothing *from* the beauty of the character of Mary, but rather adds much *to* her attractiveness as a mother who in the grace of God bore all the burdens of motherhood, from real sexuality to real responsibility of a family fraught with problems."[41]

Valid and Compelling Reasons for Believing

In a time when the virgin birth of Christ is increasingly dismissed as a relic of a mythological past, it is important for those who defend this doctrine to give valid and compelling reasons for their belief. First it is unassailable that the virgin birth (and I am here speaking primarily of the virginal conception) safeguards and communicates the event and significance of the incarnation of God in Jesus Christ. The virgin birth is a powerful witness to the paradoxical reality of God in human flesh, a paradox that is not merely useful but indispensable in the affirmation of the historic faith. The virgin birth does not prove the incarnation of Christ but serves to communicate this event. In the first centuries of the church it was used to protect the true humanity of Christ in the face of docetism and Gnosticism. Douglas Edwards, who stood in the "Machen school," astutely perceived that had it not been for the virgin birth it is highly improbable that the doctrine of the incarnation would have ever gained acceptance in the church.[42]

Second, the virgin birth forms part of the authentic New Testament witness. The stories of Jesus' birth in Matthew and Luke are both strikingly Jewish-Christian and Palestinian in form and content (Machen). They have always formed part of the textual tradition. Moreover, they are so different that it leads one to assume that they did not originate from the same source and therefore "must have belonged to the common tradition of the early Church."[43] While the two narratives are radically dissimilar and even conflict at certain points (such as the genealogies),[44] they do have a number of features in common, succinctly summarized by Richard Longenecker: "(1) the principal characters are Jesus, Mary and Joseph; (2) Jesus' birth occurred during the reign of Herod the Great; (3) Mary was betrothed to Joseph; (4) Joseph was of Davidic descent; (5) Jesus was born in Bethlehem; (6) Jesus was given his name by heavenly direction; (7) Jesus as (reputedly) Joseph's son was also of Davidic descent; and (8) the family finally settled in Nazareth."[45]

Biblical scholars now agree that the infancy narratives are composite, representing various traditions. They reveal an editor (or editors) at work, not merely an author. They give the impression of being midrashic in that one can detect in them the retelling of older stories for homiletical or theological purposes.[46] Raymond Brown calls them "imaginative" and "folkloric."[47] Fitzmyer uses the term "imitative historiography" to describe their literary genre.[48] They are not exact history, but neither are they nonhistorical myth (as David Strauss maintained). It would be a profound error to view Matthew and Luke as mythmakers in the sense that they fabricated the virgin birth and the various miraculous phenomena associated with it in order to speak to the sensibilities of the peoples of that time. To the contrary, they built upon traditions that were firmly rooted in history, giving a creative interpretation in the form of narrative and poetry. They "were not rigid editors of their sources, but creative shapers of their material who used their sources to highlight their own theological emphases and successfully integrated this material into the larger schemas of their respective Gospels."[49]

We are not to infer, however, that everything in these narratives is historical, and it is presumptuous for any scholar to designate what is truly historical and what is theological interpretation in the form of symbolic narrative. The historical record in the Bible cannot easily be separated from the mythopoetic imagery in which it is relayed to us, but we can at least assume that the historical does not exhaust the meaning of any particular biblical text. We also have grounds for maintaining that symbolic narrative, which covers a large portion of the Bible, has its source not in human creative imagination but in the events of sacred history that shape the biblical ethos, events that are rightly interpreted only from the perspective of faith. Luke's pastoral narrative may have drawn upon David's shepherd origin or the tradition that Bethlehem had a "flock tower" (Gen 35:21; 1 Sam 16:11), but one cannot prove this.[50] The attempts to find pagan antecedents in the Roman tale of Romulus and Remus, who were nurtured by shepherds, or in the Persian accounts of shepherds who watched over the birth of Mithra are much more dubious. Matthew's notion of a guiding star for the wise men may have derived from Numbers 24:17: "A star shall come forth out of Jacob, and a scepter shall rise out of Israel." Isaiah 60 tells of the nations coming to the light and kings bringing gold and frankincense. Song of Songs 3:6 refers to "myrrh and frankincense" coming from the wilderness. None of this precludes real shepherds who celebrated Jesus' birth and real magi from the East who visited Jesus, but it is unwise "to impose the prose of history on the poetry of faith."[51] We should also keep in mind that Old Testament allusions to either shepherds or wise men reinforce rather than dissolve the historical basis of the infancy narratives, since a realistic interpretation of the events in the New Testament includes the fulfillment of Old Testament prophecy.

The infancy narratives in Matthew and Luke have a wholesome reserve that sets them apart from the so-called apocryphal gospels, which portray Jesus as exercising omniscience and omnipotence even in the cradle, confounding his teachers with the mysteries of the Hebrew letters and so on.[52] They carry the ring of truth rather than the presumption of human speculation and fantasy. These stories are self-authenticating. The Christ they attest is indubitably the Christ of biblical revelation, not of mythology. While allowing for legendary materials in these narratives, the New Testament scholar John Knox nevertheless concluded: "It is inconceivable that these stories will ever be surrendered; and this can be said, not because they are familiar stories or beautiful stories, but because they are in the profoundest sense true stories."[53]

One should acknowledge that the infancy narratives in Matthew and Luke furnish the only solid basis for the virgin birth of Christ in the New Testament. Paul describes Jesus as "born of a woman" (Gal 4:4), which testifies to his radical historicity, but there is no hint of Jesus' being born of a virgin. Paul was probably not acquainted with the virgin birth stories. Mark referred to Jesus as "the son of Mary" (Mk 6:3), which would be somewhat puzzling if Joseph were still living at the time. This text makes no allusion to the virgin birth, but it may reflect a widespread opinion that there was something irregular about Jesus' birth.[54]

John 1:12-13 may allude to the virgin birth of Christ. Two of the oldest Latin fathers, Irenaeus and Tertullian, quote the text with a verb in the singular: "To those who believe on the Name of Him who *was* begotten not of bloods, nor of the will of the flesh, nor of the will of a husband—but of God" (italics mine). Given the absence of any known Greek manuscripts as old as these early church fathers, some scholars (Theodor Zahn, C. C. Torrey and Oscar Cullmann) have concluded that the singular is the original reading.[55] According to Jaroslav Pelikan most of the quotations of Christian writers in the second and third centuries contained the reading "who was."[56] Whatever the case, it is probably safe to assume that in the mind of the early church the virgin birth was a type of the new birth. William Childs Robinson perhaps goes too far in his contention that "the use of the singular shows that the plural of the Greek manuscripts is built upon the analogy of Jesus' virgin birth. And the analogy implies the fact."[57] John was probably not familiar with the infancy narratives in Matthew and Luke, but his deepest intuitions regarding the new birth are in striking harmony with the then emerging doctrine of the virgin birth of Christ.

Still another reason for affirming the virgin birth of Christ is that it constitutes an essential truth of the catholic tradition. The popular appeal of these stories in the apostolic church and in the church through the ages further attests to their intrinsic power and reliability. Christians widely acknowledged the virgin birth already in the early second century and possibly by the end of the first century. Aristides in 140 described the virgin birth as a fact of Christianity. When writing of the virgin birth, Ignatius felt no need to defend it, taking its acceptance for granted. The date of his martyrdom is 117, and his firm belief in the miraculous character of Jesus' birth suggests that this belief arose already toward the end of the first century. The Palestinian noncanonical *Odes of Solomon,* composed in the first century by a Jewish Christian, unequivocally affirms the virginal conception of Jesus. In the middle of the second century Justin Martyr vigorously upheld the virgin birth, but perhaps somewhat surprisingly like Ignatius and Aristides he did not appeal to the birth narratives in Matthew and Luke and may have been unfamiliar with them. Justin based his case on

Isaiah 7:14, though, as we shall see, this text has been a matter of dispute in current scholarship.[58] The consensus of the universal church is not in and of itself an infallible criterion in evangelical theology, but when it is shown to have firm scriptural support it becomes virtually binding on the believer.

Another legitimate reason for including the virgin birth among the essentials of the faith is that it is a powerful testimony to the breadth and wonder of God's grace. It graphically shows that salvation comes "from above" and that the source of our hope and confidence lies in the living God who entered into human history in the historical figure of Jesus Christ. The virgin birth marks off the origin of Christ from the human race just as his end is marked off by the resurrection (Karl Barth). It is a witness to both *sola gratia* and *sola fide,* for Mary believed before she conceived. It should be recognized that these points corroborate the truth of these stories but by no means establish their truth.

Finally we need to consider the fact that the virgin birth is the fulfillment of the prophecy in Isaiah 7:14: "Therefore the Lord himself shall give you a sign; Behold, a virgin shall conceive, and bear a son, and shall call his name Immanuel" (KJV). While in its original context the verse alludes to an immediate birth by a prophetess in that time, Matthew perceived its being fulfilled in the virgin birth of the messianic Christ (Mt 1:22-23). Matthew quoted from the Greek version, the Septuagint, which contains the word *parthenos,* meaning "virgin," though the original Hebrew word *'almâh* is best translated as "maiden" or "young woman," who would be generally taken for a virgin. J. Gresham Machen observed:

> In our passage, the prophet, when he placed before the rebellious Ahaz that strange picture of the mother and the child, was not merely promising deliverance to Judah in the period before a child then born should know how to refuse the evil and choose the good, but also, moved by the Spirit of God, was looking forward, as in a dim and mysterious vision, to the day when the true Immanuel, the mighty God and Prince of Peace, should lie as a little babe in a virgin's arms.[59]

According to Jan Ridderbos the prophecy clearly refers to events in that time, not directly to Christ. Even so, the momentous birth in Isaiah 7 prefigures the coming of Christ in a special way. The salvation of the Lord is "only for the mother with her child and for the remnant of which that child is representative. But judgment will fall on Ahaz and his house."[60] Yet there is a further meaning:

> The child of faith is a type of the Messiah (cf. 8:8-9). Over against the world power on which Ahaz puts his hopes, this boy with his wondrous name is a sign of the work of God for the redemption of His people and is a type of Him in whom the message "God with us" is fully realized. The manner in which the prophet here, without mentioning a father, refers to the young woman who becomes a mother, suggests the divine wisdom by which the birth of Christ from the virgin Mary, without the involvement of a man, was prefigured—just as the Redeemer was already called "the seed of the woman" in Paradise (Gen 3:15; cf. also Micah 5:2).[61]

John Oswalt likewise finds a messianic thrust in Isaiah 7:10-17, especially when seen in relation to its larger context (Is 8, 9). He detects a parallelism between Isaiah 7:10-17 and 8:1-4 and contends that both passages are linked to Isaiah 9:6-7.

> Maher-shalal-hash-baz, or someone else who may have constituted the initial fulfillment of the sign, was not the ultimate fulfillment. Ultimately, Immanuel is the owner of the land, the one against whom Assyria's threats are ultimately lodged, the one upon whom deliverance finally depends. That cannot be Isaiah's son, nor even some unknown son of Ahaz. It can only be the Messiah, in whom all hope resides. It is as if Isaiah, plunging deeper and deeper into the dark implications of his sign, is suddenly brought up short by the deepest implication: God *is* with us and, best of all, will be with us, not merely in the impersonal developments of history, but somehow as a person.[62]

Some scholars have speculated that this prophecy must be understood "in the light of the expectation, widespread in the ancient world, that a divine mother would give birth to a redeemer babe who would supplant the reigning king (cf. Matt. 2:1-12). Mic. 5:2-3 is cited as evidence that such a belief was held in some Judean prophetic circles."[63] Along similar lines W. F. Albright and C. S. Mann surmise that it is possible "that Isaiah was using mythological terms current in his own time to demonstrate an expected deliverer's birth. The LXX translators would appear to have so understood the passage, and only later did Greek translations of the Hebrew appear with the word one would expect, *neanis,* 'young maiden' instead of *parthenos.*"[64]

According to a number of scholars the virgin birth of Christ is best understood against the background of the wonder births in the Old Testament. There was indeed a tradition in Israel of divine intervention in the birth of God's chosen agents (Gen 18:11-14; 25:21; Judg 13:3; 1 Sam 1:4-20).[65] It is sometimes assumed that Philo's (c. 20 B.C.-A.D. 50) interpretation of miraculous conceptions in the Old Testament had a bearing on the Fourth Gospel and perhaps on other circles in the early church. For example, Philo depicts Sarah as pregnant when she was alone and being visited by God.[66] Philo's influence has been discounted by Machen and Charles Gore among others, but Thomas Boslooper sees it as significant for understanding the assimilation of the virgin birth into the thought of the apostolic church.[67]

In scholarly circles support is growing for the view that Matthew depended on a pre-Matthean tradition for his knowledge of the virginal conception of Jesus. Some suggest that Matthew probably received his knowledge of the virgin birth not from the Septuagint but from another tradition in which virginal conception is made more explicit. He then used this knowledge to reinterpret the prophecy in Isaiah along the lines of a virgin birth.[68] Another possibility is that the Septuagint translation rests upon "an early Jewish interpretation, later adopted by the evangelist."[69]

Was Mary herself, and perhaps also Joseph, the source of the knowledge of the virgin birth of Jesus? Luke gives some credence to this theory when he describes Mary as pondering the mystery of the virginal conception (Lk 2:19, 51). He may be advancing the idea "that Mary has preserved in her heart the mysterious words and events that surrounded Jesus' birth (or his finding in the Temple) *trying to interpret them*. This would mean that Mary did not grasp immediately all that she had heard but listened willingly, letting the events sink into her memory and seeking to work out their meaning."[70]

Whatever source or sources finally persuaded Matthew to affirm the virginal birth of our Lord, one cannot deny that Isaiah himself did not explicitly teach a virginal conception in chapters 7 and 8 of his book. Yet he may well have been pointing to a miraculous birth that Matthew rightly saw as having its fulfillment in Jesus Christ. I agree with Avery Dulles: "A classic text, even one that is not divinely inspired, contains depths of meaning that escape the original author and appear only in the light of later reflection."[71] The revelational meaning of a text—what the Holy Spirit teaches—may well go beyond its literal or natural connotation, and if the New Testament itself claims that a particular passage witnesses to the Messiah whom we know as Jesus Christ, we as believers are bound to accept it. In the last analysis it is divine revelation that is the source of the New Testament affirmations of the virgin birth of our Lord, though this can be acknowledged only in the community of faith. The Isaiah prophecy is not a proof or rational evidence of Christ's virgin birth, nor does it furnish empirical support for a supernatural Bible. The Holy Spirit, not the author of the Isaiah text, had in mind a virgin birth, but only faith can discern this truth.

Valid Reasons for Emphasizing

Should the doctrine of the virgin birth be given special emphasis in our day in view of the fact that scientific empiricism holds sway over so much of our culture? Will not the proclamation of the virgin birth lead many people, especially in academic circles, to dismiss Christianity as resting on an outmoded worldview? Such has been the position of Bishop Spong, J. A. T. Robinson, Rudolf Bultmann, John Hick and many others.

Yet it is perhaps precisely in a time when the mystery and paradox of faith are being eroded that we need a forthright reaffirmation of the virgin birth of Christ. This doctrine safeguards the central paradox of the faith—God becoming human flesh in Jesus Christ. Even in the conservative religious world the tendency is to dissolve myth and mystery into logic, and an emphasis on the virgin birth of Christ would counter the overemphasis on the cerebral by recognizing the mystical element in religion.[72]

Similarly the virgin birth makes a powerful witness to the supernatural character of divine revelation in a time when revelation is being reduced to religious experience or even human experience. We need to reappropriate the insights of the church fathers and the Reformers that the content of divine revelation exceeds the compass of human understanding and that the mystery of the virgin birth, like the mystery of the incarnation itself, can be discerned only by faith.

Again, the virgin birth testifies that the measure of fruitfulness in the kingdom of God is not natural but spiritual generation. In a climate of mounting nationalism and ethnocentrism we need to be reminded that the kingdom of God is founded not on sex, blood or race but on grace. This affirmation is given graphic expression in the Fourth Gospel: "To all who received him, who believed in his name, he gave power to become children of God; who were born, not of blood nor of the will of the flesh nor of the will of man, but of God" (Jn 1:12-13). We enter the kingdom from above. We are not born into the kingdom but adopted into the kingdom (cf. Ps 2:7). The virgin birth is indeed a type of the new birth. Christ was the son of Mary by faith as well as by blood. But first of all he was her son by divine grace.

As already indicated, one may properly regard the birth of Isaac as a type of the virgin birth. Sarah had been visited by the Lord in her old age. Both the birth of Isaac and the virgin birth of Christ testify to the freedom of God to bring forth life in the midst of a marriage that would otherwise have been barren or in a situation that would argue against it. Sarah could not conceive because she was old; Mary could not conceive because her marriage was not yet consummated.[73]

Finally it is important to bear in mind that adherence to the virgin birth of Christ promotes unity with the Catholic and Orthodox churches. There can be no hope of fraternal relations among the churches, let alone unity, if the virgin birth of our Lord is regarded as an *adiaphora* rather than an essential tenet of the faith. This does not mean, however, that as evangelical Protestants we must dutifully accept the Marian doctrines of the Catholic and Orthodox churches simply for the sake of unity, since the truth of the gospel takes precedence over the unity of the churches. Indeed, unity can be founded only on the basis of truth. Doctrines such as the perpetual virginity of Mary or the intact virginity of Mary in the act of birth tend to create a docetic Mariology, and this is equally if not more true of the immaculate conception of Mary. With our Catholic and Orthodox brothers and sisters we need to affirm Mary as the Virgin Mother but always make certain that our understanding is in harmony with the witness of the New Testament and the apostolic church.

Invalid Reasons for Believing

It is incumbent on earnest, searching Christians to question not the doctrines of the faith but the often tendentious reasons for holding many of these doctrines. One invalid reason for affirming the virgin birth is that it *proves* the deity of Christ or that it is inseparable from his deity. This stance does not take into consideration that the Arians also believed in the virgin birth, though they denied that Jesus Christ was God in human flesh. Likewise the Jehovah's Witnesses (a modern form of Arianism), the Way and even many Muslims assent to the virgin birth but openly oppose the doctrine of the incarnation and Christ's deity. Moreover, it is possible to affirm the incarnation and deny the virgin birth of Christ, though this is much less likely.

Again it is sometimes said that being born of a virgin is the only way God could have become man. But the God who can raise children of Abraham out of stones (Mt 3:9; Lk 3:8) might easily have chosen some other way to enter the stream of humanity. It is fitting that the Son of God was born of a virgin, since he chooses the powerless to confound the powerful. He comes to us in our poverty so that we might rely wholly on his grace (cf. Lk 1:52-53).

Then there are those who argue that the virgin birth is proved by biblical prophecy. We can believe in the virgin birth because it is an amazing confirmation of biblical predictions in the Old Testament. We have already seen that in the case of the prophecy in Isaiah 7, we cannot speak of proofs or even of exact fulfillments but only of a witness discernible to the eyes of faith.[74]

Some allege that scientific evidence among lower forms of life for parthenogenesis (the development of eggs from virgin females without fertilization by spermatozoa) shows that the virgin birth is not wholly implausible. Origen used this argument, as did the evangelical scholar Wilbur Smith. According to Smith, "No critic of the Virgin Birth today would dare speak of the 'biological impossibility' of such an event."[75] The irony is that when we try to amass natural explanations for biblical miracles we end by denying what we are trying to prove.[76] Interestingly parthenogenesis is affirmed by the feminist theologian Edward Luther Kessel, who contends that this is "the only satisfactory natural biological explanation for the Virgin Conception."[77] It is well to note that Kessel disputes the maleness of Jesus, arguing that he is androgynous.

Surely the most beguiling reason in the history of theology for holding to the virgin birth of Christ is that the Son of God could not have been born in sin. According to Gregory the Great (c. 540-604), a sinless man must be offered to satisfy God's justice, but only one born of a virgin can be sinless. Ambrose drew the conclusion that to be free of sin Christ had to be free of the normal mode of conception. Augustine used the virgin birth to argue for the sinlessness of Jesus. Thomas Aquinas held that it was befitting to the dignity of Christ's humanity in which there could be no sin. Luther reflected this same mentality: "If it could still happen that a woman could conceive without the male seed, then such a birth would also be pure. This is why Christ was born of a virgin."[78] In the nineteenth century conservative Protestants like Hermann Olshausen and Johann Peter Lange believed that Jesus' sinlessness was dependent on his virgin birth.

Part of the problem lies in viewing original sin as wholly a product of sexual procreation. Equally specious is the now antiquated view that the stain of sin is carried preeminently by the male seed. Both Schleiermacher and Strauss raised the question that Mary's participation in Jesus' birth renders it impossible for Jesus to be free of the inheritance of sinfulness.[79] The idea of Mary's immaculate conception is integrally related to this entire discussion, since it reinforces the belief in Jesus' sinlessness. Anselm had already contended that Mary was in a state of purity when Jesus was born. Jaroslav Pelikan confesses his misgivings with "the chain of reasoning begun by the surmise that the sinlessness of Jesus . . . depends upon his being free of the taint that comes from having two human parents. Now Mary may conceive immaculately because she herself has been conceived immaculately."[80] He adds an ominous note: "The dogma of the catholic church has always run the danger of glorifying Christ so much that it cut him off from the humanity he was to save. Now the dogma of the Roman Catholic Church is running a similar danger in its Mariology."[81]

Invalid Reasons for Not Believing

It is fashionable in liberal academic circles to dismiss the virgin birth on the grounds that Isaiah 7 was speaking only of a young woman ('almâh) and not of a virgin (bᵉṯûlâh). I have already suggested that given the openness in that time to the idea of supernatural intervention, especially in the birth of a child ruler, the theme of a virgin birth is not alien to the context of this prophecy, though it is not explicitly affirmed.

As has been indicated, some have also entertained the possibility of an unknown Hebrew source for the LXX (Septuagint) translation of Isaiah 7:14 or even for Matthew's espousal of Jesus' virgin birth.

Whether Isaiah is really alluding to a supernatural birth in the prophecy under question and whether the cultural context allows for a virginal conception cannot finally be decided. But one cannot dismiss the doctrine of the virgin birth on the basis of unclarity in the Isaiah passage, since both Matthew and Luke explicitly affirm it, and the New Testament is, above all, our infallible standard for faith and practice. The church especially must accept Matthew's verdict that the deepest implications of Isaiah's prophecy point to a virginal conception without a human father.

Then others say that the doctrine of the virgin birth is questionable because Paul does not mention it. Paul, whose letters constitute the earliest testimony to the gospel in the New Testament, probably did not know of the virgin birth of Christ. Mary very likely kept this a secret in the early days of the church. It should also be remembered that Paul does not include any mention of the Beatitudes or of Christ's miracles.

Another common objection to the doctrine of the virgin birth is that myths of a divine birth were quite common in the ancient world, and therefore Jesus' virgin birth belongs to the category of myth. Yet a close examination of these stories shows that they are speaking of the impregnation of mortal women by gods, not of a nonsexual visitation of the Holy Spirit. As Alan Richardson points out, "Pagan mythology is full of legends of a superhuman hero born of intercourse between a god and a human woman. But this is scarcely *virgin* birth."[82] Kierkegaard has these trenchant comments:

> The thesis that it cannot be true that Christ was born of a virgin because something similar is said of Hercules, etc., and in Indian mythology, etc., which is not true, is rather curious, since in a certain respect the opposite conclusion seems more correct: precisely because they say this about so many other great men for whom it was not true—for this very reason it must be true of Christ, for the fact that it has been said so often points to man's need for it.[83]

The virgin birth is also disavowed because it is allegedly based on the spurious notion that human sexuality is sinful and "therefore unacceptable as the means of the incarnation of the holy God."[84] As was discussed earlier, this negative assessment of human sexuality is alien to Jewish life and thought and is simply not found in the birth narratives.[85]

Some modern theologians, including Emil Brunner and Nels Ferré, have rejected the virgin birth on the grounds that it takes away from the full humanity of Christ.[86] Others complain that it makes Jesus into a hybrid—a cross between the human and the divine. If this doctrine concerned the impregnation of a mortal by a divine consort, such criticisms would be on the mark. But we are speaking of a divine miracle, not a purely biological generation. The virgin birth is the sign of the mystery that Jesus' birth was wholly spiritual and wholly physical at the same time. It is not a biological explanation for the emergence of a godlike being in human history but a humble recognition that something of eternal significance happened in the birth of Jesus that utterly transcends human imagination. It signifies not simply an extraordinary human birth but the incarnation of the living God in human flesh. God unites human nature to himself and does not simply appear in human form. It should be noted that Brunner verges toward docetism in his christology. He speaks of the "human disguise" or "mask" of Christ and thereby is unable to do justice to the fact that Jesus Christ was both fully God and truly human at the same time.

Some theologians (Bultmann, Reinhold Niebuhr, Brunner) have dismissed the virgin birth stories because they allegedly arose from a desire to prove the faith.[87] Bultmann claimed that when the gospel was introduced to the Hellenistic world these stories were added in order to make contact with the spiritual searchings of a new cultural ethos.[88] First, it is well to keep in mind that these stories belong to the earliest manuscripts of the two Gospels in question. Second, the evidence seems overwhelming that they were addressed not to the Hellenistic ethos but to the Jewish-Christian community. When these stories are taken together they contain too many discrepancies to be of much apologetic value—either to Greeks or to Jews. Rather than offering a proof of Jesus' divinity they were more likely designed to counter the contention that Jesus was illegitimate and to highlight his unique mission in view of the Old Testament prophecy.[89] David Scaer gives this effective rebuttal to Bultmann:

> If the Virgin Birth is taken over from Hellenized communities, then one might expect to find explicit references to it in Mark, John, and Paul's epistles. The argument that the origins of the Virgin Birth can be traced back to Hellenistic and not Jewish communities is fraught with too many difficulties to justify its use in denying its historicity.[90]

The fact that the virgin birth contradicts the canons of naturalistic science is still another invalid reason for rejecting this doctrine. According to Bultmann, science tells us that a virgin birth cannot happen. In Frances Young's opinion, "it is virtually inconceivable in the light of modern knowledge of genetics and reproduction."[91] Yet it is well to bear in mind that science in the strict sense describes; it does not make metaphysical judgments. The biblical miracles stand in tension with scientism, but not with science.

Epilogue

In our treatment of this controversial doctrine we must not claim too much—that it is the basis and evidence of the incarnation of Christ; but we dare not claim too little—that it is only a mythical expression of an eternal truth. The virgin birth does not have its roots in the sequence of events that make up human history. Its basis is in the unique and incomparable visitation of the Spirit to Mary. It is an ineradicable sign that God's great gift to humanity is entirely by grace. Belief in the virgin birth is not necessary for salvation, since it did not form a part of the New Testament kerygma. Belief in this miracle is necessary to maintain the integrity and consistency of the witness of the church through the centuries. The virgin birth serves to safeguard the faith against any heresy that separates or obscures the two natures of Christ, especially docetism, adoptionism and ebionitism.

It is injudicious to deny the virgin birth on the basis of the insufficiency of biblical evidence. What about the ascension of Christ, which is mentioned less than the virgin birth? Or the resurrection, which is mentioned more but is still historically improbable? Does what is historically possible or probable determine the content of our faith? To be sure, Christian faith has an incontestable historical matrix, and historical research can tell us something—about the virgin birth, the bodily resurrection of Christ and many other biblical miracles. It can show that the reports of these phenomena rest upon credible witnesses, but it cannot prove that the events themselves actually happened. Still less can it furnish a rational basis for the mystery of the incarnation or the mystery of Christ's resurrection from the dead for our justification.

The graphic and poetic framework of these stories tempts many sophisticated people to question their historical authenticity. We live in a culture where truth is identified with clarity and precision. We cannot dismiss the veracity of these stories simply because they come to us in the form of dramatic and symbolic language. Nor can we summarily disregard the reports of the witnesses simply on the grounds that they testify to the reality of the supernatural in human history.

The stories of both the virgin birth and the empty tomb can be likened to the husk in the Bible; the gospel is the kernel. We must not confound the husk and the kernel. Yet it is fallacious to deny that the husk is of any importance and to treat the virgin birth only as a symbol (as do Paul Tillich and John Hick). The virgin birth itself is not the mystery, but like the empty tomb, it is a sign that serves to communicate the mystery. It is not itself the stumbling block, but it serves to convey and reveal the real stumbling block of faith—the gospel of God coming into the world in order to suffer and thereby secure our redemption. The virgin birth and the empty tomb refer to the *how* of faith as well as to the *why*. Can we have the *why* without the *how*? Yet much is left unanswered even in the *how*. It is my conviction that we cannot have the internal meaning of the biblical witness apart from the external signs. Although in good conscience we may make the attempt to affirm the truth of the incarnation and the atonement while dismissing the stories of the virgin birth and the empty tomb as poetic lore, the probability is that we will finally be driven to underplay either the human or the divine nature of Christ and thereby lose sight of the paradox that Jesus Christ was truly God and truly human in one person.

I heartily agree with Karl Barth that the virgin birth cannot be the foundation for an independent Mariology. Mary assented to what was already decreed and made possible and inevitable by God. She did not give her consent to something that would otherwise not have taken place. She simply acknowledged that God would work a miracle in her life and in the life of humanity: "Behold, I am the handmaid of the Lord; let it be to me according to your word" (Lk 1:38). The hypostatic union took place when the Holy Spirit descended on Mary. She duly recognized this fact but did not cause it. This does not mean that she was totally passive; rather she was active in her receptivity. Faith is both an inner awakening and an existential decision, but the latter flows out of the former.

This position is quite different from that of Rosemary Ruether, who maintains that the virgin birth illustrates God's radical dependence on humanity.

> Only through that free human responsiveness to God is God enabled to become the transformer of history. Without such faith, no miracles can happen. When such faith is absent, Christ can do nothing. This is the radical dependence of God on humanity, the other side of our dependence on God, which patriarchal theology has generally denied. Mary's faith makes possible God's entrance into history.[92]

Although a liberal Catholic, Ruether is here expressing the traditional Roman Catholic position on the need for human cooperation in the realization of divine salvation. Those who stand in the Reformation tradition limit cooperation to making known the salvation that has already taken place in Jesus Christ.

In our affirmation of the virgin birth we need to battle against gnosticism as well as skepticism. In gnosticism the important thing is the idea that the event supposedly carries rather than the event itself. For Geddes MacGregor, it seems, the historicity of the virgin birth is not crucial, only what the virgin birth conveys.[93] Similarly Carl Jung is willing to affirm that the virgin birth of Christ is psychologically true. We should not be concerned whether the virgin birth actually occurred, only that such an idea contributes to the fullness of the psychic vision that sustains our life.[94] By contrast, the faith of the church holds firmly to the reality of the events of sacred history, though these events need to be interpreted in the light of the revelatory vision given by Jesus Christ himself in the encounter of faith.

The scientific mind has a problem with the stories of the virgin birth, since they palpably conflict with what we know to be true in ordinary experience. Nels Ferré, who did not dismiss the reality of the supernatural, is typical of the reaction of modernity: "The birth stories are, to be sure, most improbable . . . and perhaps, for this reason, the simplest thing to believe may be that Joseph was the natural father of Jesus."[95] As I have already intimated, scientific and historical study can show that the virgin birth was affirmed by credible witnesses—the two biblical evangelists—as well as by the early church. When the Holy Spirit unites this historical witness with his own interior witness to Jesus Christ, we can then be convinced of the truth of these stories and join the community of faith, which celebrates these stories as God's own witness to the miracle of the incarnation. Historical research can give us confirmatory evidence, but this evidence is finally persuasive only to those whose inward eyes have been opened, who have experienced the transforming reality of the Spirit of God at work in the narratives of the Gospel. The virgin birth is an integral truth of the holy catholic faith, but it is not the pivotal truth that saves us from sin and death. This is Jesus Christ himself, who is attested by the witness of the whole Scripture and who brings this witness alive by his Spirit to those who seek the truth that can make them free.

Appendix B: The Role of Mary

Mary, the mother of Jesus, may well be the new frontier in ecumenicity, since the devotion accorded her by Roman Catholics and Eastern

Orthodox constitutes a formidable barrier in relations with evangelical Protestants. Part of the problem is that there seems to be an ineradicable gulf between the Mary of the Gospels and the Mary of dogma. Whereas the former portray Mary as the lowly "handmaid of the Lord" (Lk 1:38), traditionalist Catholics acclaim her as "the Queen of Heaven" and "the Mediatrix of All Graces." Whereas in the New Testament she is definitely subordinate to Christ, in popular Catholic devotion she is often seen as a coworker with Christ in gaining our redemption. Sometimes her prayers are alleged to be even more effective than those of her Son.[96]

The Second Vatican Council sought to contain Marian devotion by treating Mary within the "Constitution of the Church."[97] The message was that Mariology should be subordinated to christology and to an ecclesiology of the people of God. At the same time Mary was pictured as sharing in the atoning suffering of her Son, which gives impetus to the cult of Mary as coredemptrix.[98] Pope John Paul II has abetted Marian devotion by visiting Marian shrines and admonishing his church to honor Mary as well as Jesus.[99]

The pivotal question is whether Mariology is a legitimate product of the church's self-understanding or the recrudescence of the ancient religion of the Great Mother that dominated the Mediterranean world in the early centuries of the church. Jesuit scholar Karl Prümm presents a credible case that Mary could never have become a goddess in the pagan sense because the New Testament presents her as a human mother giving birth to a son in human history.[100] Yet other scholars such as Stephen Benko and Geoffrey Ashe have contended with some acuity that Mariology has its roots more in ancient mythology than in the gospel.[101] According to Benko, "Mary is the direct continuation of the pagan goddesses and unites in herself the basic principles that in Mediterranean piety underlay and determined the worship of mother goddesses."[102] "Mariology does not simply resemble pagan customs and ideas, but . . . it is paganism baptized, pure and simple."[103] Lutheran theologian Jaroslav Pelikan gives a more cautious assessment, arguing that while the church's reflection on Mary has not always been controlled by Scripture, Scripture has nevertheless played a prominent role in this reflection.[104]

Themes in a Developing Mariology. In the first two centuries of the church Mariology was virtually dormant. Irenaeus and Justin Martyr referred to Mary as the second Eve, but the focus was on christology, not on Mariology as such. Just as Eve prepared the way for humanity's fall, so Mary prepared the way for humanity's redemption, but the Redeemer was Jesus Christ alone. For the most part, the extravagant speculations of the apocryphal gospels, in which Mary was treated as a worker of wonders and miracles, were resisted by church theologians and authorities. The rise of a world-denying asceticism drawing upon Gnosticism and Manichaeism was to exert a significant change in the way the church understood Mary—her person and her mission.

The idea of Mary as the Eternal Virgin did not gain real lodging in the mind of the church until the fourth century, though the apocryphal gospel *The Protoevangelium of James* argued for Mary's perpetual virginity already in the late second century. It appears that the author was deeply influenced by the worship of the Mediterranean goddess Cybele.[105] At the end of the fifth century *The Book of the Birth of the Blessed Mary and the Infancy of the Savior* circulated and did much to foster Mary's status as Eternal Virgin. Jerome disputed the view still widely held that Jesus had blood brothers and instead described them as cousins of Jesus. At the Second Council of Constantinople (553) Mary was referred to as "ever virgin," reflecting the growing Christian consensus.

In the fifth century Mary was given the title "Mother of God" at the Council of Ephesus (431). Yet the purpose was not to glorify Mary but to affirm the deity of Jesus Christ. The position of Nestorius—that Mary was only the mother of Christ or of Jesus—was roundly repudiated. It was made clear, however, that Mary was not a goddess and that she was mother of our Lord only "according to the flesh." At the same time, the acclamation of Mary as *theotokos* (God-bearer or mother of God) had far-reaching effects on the spirituality of the church, since it fostered the yearnings of the time for a goddess figure, which the church had hitherto suppressed. Benko comments: "The fact that Mary was officially declared to be *theotokos* in Ephesus, where 'the temple of the great goddess Artemis' stood, must not be set aside as insignificant. The people of Ephesus reacted to the Council in much the same way their ancestors had almost 400 years before when they thought that the honor of Artemis was at stake."[106] In the sixteenth century Luther and Zwingli reaffirmed the decision of the Council of Ephesus, whereas Calvin had reservations about calling Mary "mother of God."

The immaculate conception of Mary was a much later doctrine, though the idea of Mary's purity goes back to the early church period and perhaps even to the New Testament, since the angel addressed Mary as one who was "full of grace" (Lk 1:28 DRV) or "endowed with grace" *(kecharitōmenē).*[107] The dogma of the immaculate conception, defined in 1854 by Pius IX, asserts that Mary was preserved from original sin by the singular grace of God. This idea is nowhere present in the New Testament, nor is it found in the early church. Augustine maintained that Mary lived without sin but denied that she was conceived without sin. For Anselm "Mary was not only conceived but born in sin like all the sons of Adam."[108] Bernard of Clairvaux, who did much to foster Marian devotion, held that Mary "was certainly sanctified before her birth," but he objected to the theological novelty of the immaculate conception.[109] Thomas Aquinas acknowledged that there was no scriptural basis for the sanctification of Mary *in utero,* though he believed that it could be supported rationally. Duns Scotus (d. 1308) argued for Mary's immaculate conception, and his view finally came to dominate in the church. This doctrine signifies a decisive break with Catholic tradition, since it in effect rejects the Augustinian view that all of humanity is under the curse of original sin and that we are helpless to help ourselves apart from the death and resurrection of Jesus Christ.

Protestants have held to the purification of Mary but not to her exemption from original sin.[110] The holiness of Mary means that she was set apart for a special vocation. Her holiness lies not in her sinless perfection but in the perfection of faith that triumphs over sin. The Catholic view seems to make Mary exempt from human failings and thereby calls into question the viability of Mary as a model of holiness. It is well to note that various church fathers, such as John Chrysostom, Cyril of Alexandria, Origen and Basil, held that Mary was guilty of such things as vanity, doubt and ambition.

The assumption of Mary, defined in the papal bull *Munificentissimus Deus* in 1950, asserts that Mary was translated both in body and in soul into heaven, though it leaves open the question of whether she actually experienced death. This doctrine has its origins in the apocryphal legends concerning the transition of Mary into glory. These legends were condemned by Pope Gelasius (492-496), but they received a new lease on life in the ninth century with the circulation of the *Epistle of Pseudo-Jerome to Paula and Eustochium* and *Pseudo-Augustine*. For Roman Catholics this dogma attests the solidarity of the Son and Mother and the Son and humanity. It is aimed at the individualism that holds sway in the modern world. It is a revelation of what will happen to all Christians. This doctrine has no firm biblical basis and hardly any support in the early church. Both Andrew of Crete (d. 740) and John of Damascus (d. 749) held to the incorruption of Mary but not to her assumption. The Waldensian theologian Giovanni Miegge is not far off the mark when he argues that the real foundation for this dogma is the contemporary consensus of the church.[111] It is interesting to note that Mary's assumption into heaven has also garnered support among Protestants, including Luther and Bullinger at the time of the Reformation and Max Thurian, Max Lackmann and John Macquarrie in the contemporary period.[112]

Even more suspect in Protestant eyes is the exaltation of Mary as Queen of Heaven. The queen of heaven is mentioned in the Bible only in Jeremiah, and there she was an object of rebuke rather than praise (Jer 44:17-30). The struggle of Old Testament faith was precisely aimed against the threat of the ancient religion of the Earth Mother with its celebration of nature and fecundity. By the early Middle Ages

"Mary had five holy days of her own, covering the whole course of her earthly life—the Conception, the Nativity, the Annunciation, the Purification and the Assumption."[113] To these was added the feast of Our Lady Queen of Heaven. Over the centuries many minor feasts followed. The last of the fifteen themes of the rosary is devoted to the coronation of Mary as Queen of Heaven. Catholic theologians often appeal to the vision of the apocalyptic woman in Revelation 12 as a basis for holding to both the assumption of Mary and Mary as Queen of Heaven. Yet as Hans von Campenhausen points out, "In the early Church we look in vain for a 'Mariological' exposition of the apocalyptic woman clothed in the sun, and in the same way the prophecy about the woman's seed, who is to bruise the serpent's head, the so-called *protoevangelium* of Genesis, is always related to Christ alone, and never to Mary."[114] It is sometimes argued that if Jesus Christ is king, then his mother is queen or at least queen mother.

Protestant sensibilities are likewise aroused at the current emphasis on Mary as coredemptrix, though it has yet to be declared a dogma of the church. This idea can be traced to Mary as the second Eve, a notion already existent in the second century. Just as Eve helped to bring about the fall of humanity, so Mary plays a causal role in the redemption of humanity.[115] Through the ages Mary has been given such titles as Mediatrix of All Graces, Dispenser of Graces, Mother of Divine Grace, our Heavenly Advocate, and Coredeemer with her Son. Those who use this language commonly appeal to Mary's reply to the angelic visitation: "Behold, I am the handmaid of the Lord; let it be to me according to your word" (Lk 1:38). Catholics and Orthodox interpret this text as implying that the incarnation itself is dependent on Mary's active cooperation. Protestants tend to see this reply as a simple acknowledgment of what is foreordained to take place through the grace of God. Once we view Mary as a collaborator with the Spirit of God, then the incarnation becomes partly her work and partly God's work, as the Orthodox theologian Nicholas Cabasilas made clear:

The Incarnation was not only the work of the Father, of his goodness and his Spirit, but also the work of the will and faith of the Virgin. Without the consent of "the most pure," without the cooperation of her faith, the plan was as impossible as without the intervention of the three divine Persons themselves.[116]

Mary's role as mother of the church (a title given to Mary by Pope Paul VI in 1964) reinforces the idea of coredemptrix. In this view Mary gives birth to the faith of the disciples through her example of fidelity and holiness and her redemptive work of intercession. It is said that she shares in the spiritual motherhood of the church and thereby has a mediating role in our salvation. In the evangelical view she does not give birth to the church, but she plays a modest role in the expansion of the church. She is not over the church, but she is a figure and pro-totype of the church. Some Mary minimalists in the Catholic Church contend that the Holy Spirit is the true mother of the church, but this spiritual motherhood is reflected in the life and work of Mary.[117]

The pivotal question in theology is whether Mary collaborates in the work of objective redemption or only in the distribution of graces. The mainstream of the Marian movement definitely affirms the first, though some Catholic theologians take exception to this view.[118] Among the Marian maximalists Mary is both a mediator of grace and a source of grace. Her mediation is not alongside that of her Son but in and through Christ. Yet even with this qualification Mary becomes a coredeemer of the world rather than simply a servant of the Word. It is said that we go to Jesus through Mary and we go to the Father through Jesus. Mary becomes a midwife who assists Jesus in bringing about the new birth. But does she not then usurp the role of the Holy Spirit in this regard?

Imbalances in Marian Devotion. The Roman Church has not only acknowledged a redemptive role for Mary but has encouraged devo-tion to Mary as well as to her Son. Theologians have frequently made the distinction between *latria* (worship) and *dulia* (veneration). Worship is to be given only to God, but veneration should be given to the saints of God. Since Mary is the preeminent saint she is to be accorded the highest veneration *(hyperdulia),* but the boundaries between this kind of veneration and adoration are not always clear. Once we adore Mary and place our trust in her for our salvation, we are involved in the sin of idolatry. This is recognized by many biblically oriented Catholic and Orthodox theologians as well and presents considerable difficulty for them.

In popular devotion the acclamation of Mary has often exceeded the bounds of what Catholic tradition has deemed proper respect. When Mary is hailed as the spouse of the Holy Spirit, it seems that this would make the Spirit the father of Jesus. Leonardo Boff posits a hypostatic union between Mary and the Spirit analogous to the union between Jesus and the Word.[119] Mary is sometimes identified with Wisdom *(Sophia)* and thereby is acclaimed as a cocreator with God. Occasionally she is praised as "the fourth person of the Trinity" and "the complement of the Trinity."[120] Since the seventeenth century the idea circulated that Mary merits our redemption *de congruo* (according to what is fitting), whereas Jesus merits *de condigno* (according to strict justice). But some have gone further and claim that Mary's merits were sufficient of themselves to gain our redemption, though they must always be subordinated to the superabundant merits of Christ.[121]

Mary is often portrayed as the compassionate mother who will hear our prayers when Jesus seems too distant or intimidating to approach in prayer. Bernard of Clairvaux declared, "Let him who fears the Son seek refuge in Mary."[122] Similarly Richard of St. Victor: "If I approach the judgment and have the Mother of mercy on my side, who will say that the Judge will not be favorable to me?"[123] In this mentality judgment is associated with the Son and mercy with his mother. Mary then becomes our source of hope, the Son and Father being relegated to the background. Bernard claimed, "The Blessed Mother . . . is the ladder of sinners, by which they reascend to the height of divine grace; she is my greatest confidence, she is the whole basis for my hope."[124] She is even hailed as "the peace-maker between sinners and God."[125] Mary tends to displace the Holy Spirit, since she is the one who forms Christ within us and consoles the faithful. Mary, not Christ, is now the focus of piety and faith. Francis Fernandez believes that in Mary "we shall find every grace we need to win through in the fight against temptation. . . . She is our safety, the Love that never fails, the refuge ever open to us, the hand ever ready to caress and console."[126] In the *Salve Regina* prayer, composed around 1100 and sponsored by religious orders, the emphasis is not on the initiative of Christ but on the active role of Mary in securing our redemption. "Mary is indeed to unite us with Christ, but Mary is active and Christ is passive. It is almost as if she were Isis summoning us to approach the child Horus whom she cradles in her arms."[127]

A Marian enthusiasm appears to have compromised the strict monotheism of biblical faith so that trust and hope are directed no longer exclusively to the Creator God but now also to the deified and elevated human creature—Mary. A binitarianism threatens to displace the trinitarianism of the apostolic church. Our salvation is said to be the product of Jesus and Mary rather than of Jesus Christ alone. Goddess spirituality, where the emphasis is on the nurturing qualities of deity, poses a direct challenge to prophetic spirituality, which announces a word of God from the beyond. Prayers are offered not simply to the Father or the Son but now to the heavenly Mother or to Jesus and Mary.

Catholic theologians have often raised protests against this creeping idolatry of Mary and tried to steer popular devotion toward the holy Eucharist and the life, death and resurrection of Christ. René Laurentin is highly critical of the "new view" that "Mary merited quite sufficiently Redemption itself; her merit equals in justice the price of our sins and of our salvation, and now it is the merit of Christ which appears as a surplus addition."[128] It is dangerous, he contends, to say that Mary "also is divine, and strictly so, not in her womanhood but in her motherhood."[129] Edward Schillebeeckx, who at one time regarded Mary as Associate of the Redeemer, came to view her as our "companion in redemption," which places Mary "on our side" in God's saving work.[130]

She is now the "pre-eminent member . . . of the church's community of faith."[131] Elizabeth Johnson warns against confounding the roles of Mary and the Holy Spirit: "It is said that she is spiritually present to guide and inspire; that she forms Christ in believers and is the link between themselves and Christ; and that one goes to Jesus through her. In the Scriptures these are the actions of the Spirit. Furthermore, Mary is called intercessor, mediatrix, helper, advocate, defender, consoler, and counselor, functions that biblically belong to the Paraclete."[132] According to Richard Rohr: "Mary cannot be *the* object of faith. Our trust is in God," but we can "believe *with* Mary." Instead of viewing her as a coredeemer we should acclaim her as our companion in faith and devotion.[133]

Mary in Evangelical Perspective. While Catholicism has frequently veered toward a Marian spirituality that calls into question the gospel affirmation that Jesus Christ is the one and only mediator and savior (1 Tim 2:5), Protestantism has been inclined to reduce Mary to little more than a bystander in the plan of salvation—used by the Spirit at one particular time in history but then largely disappearing from the scene of action. She evinces a historical interest but is assigned no redemptive significance. Hans Asmussen, a noted German Lutheran theologian, posed this question: "Why are the saints of God and Mary, the Mother of God, given no place when we kneel to pray in our homes or when we attend the liturgy in our churches?"[134] According to American Lutheran theologian Joseph Sittler, "It is not strange but right and proper that her meaning should be declared and her praise sung from a Protestant pulpit. If we can find it in our competence to honor the witness to the faith of Augustine, of Luther, of Calvin, of Wesley—how grudging before the gifts of God never to utter an 'Ave Maria—Hail Mary.'"[135] Presbyterian theologian Arthur Cochrane contends that Mary still has significance in the life of the church: "God adopted us in Mary's one son to be His children, and in this sense to be Mary's children."[136]

It is well to note that the notions of Mary's immaculate conception, her assumption, her perpetual virginity and her spiritual motherhood were all present in varying degrees among the Protestant Reformers. Zwingli could refer to Mary as "the Mother of God, the perpetually pure and immaculate Virgin Mary."[137] The Reformed theologian Henry Bullinger seemed to support the assumption of Mary when he declared that "the most pure chamber of the Mother of God and the temple of the Holy Spirit, her most holy body, was taken up by the angels to heaven."[138] Besides his willingness at times to affirm Mary's complete purity, Luther also endorsed Mary's spiritual motherhood: "Mary is the mother of Jesus and the mother of us all. If Christ is ours, we must be where he is, and where he is, we must be also, and all that he has must be ours, and his mother therefore also is ours."[139] At the same time, the Reformers were adamant that Christ is the only mediator and that salvation is entirely by grace. Notions about Mary's purity and special powers were never made a condition for salvation but were allowed so long as they gave glory to Christ.

What divides evangelical Protestants from their Catholic and Orthodox brothers and sisters is the emphasis of the former on the primacy of Scripture—over both church tradition and religious experience. Scripture alone is the infallible standard for faith and practice. If a doctrine cannot be shown to be authentically rooted in the biblical testimony, it cannot be elevated into a dogma of faith and thereby made determinative for salvation. Mary's spiritual motherhood and assumption might be implied in the wider scriptural witness, but there is no solid biblical basis for elevating them into cardinal tenets of the faith. The doctrines of Mary's immaculate conception and of Mary as coredemptrix stand in considerable tension if not actual contradiction with the scriptural witness.[140] When people begin praying to Mary more than they pray to the Father, to Jesus or to the Holy Spirit, something is radically amiss in our spiritual priorities.[141]

Evangelical Protestants caution against the invocation of Mary and the saints because it tends to draw attention away from Christ as sole mediator to the subordinate mediators. This does not mean, however, that Mary and the saints play no role whatever in the work of media-tion and intercession; yet their task is not to procure redemption but to communicate the fruits of Christ's redemption to the world. They can properly be spoken of as intercessors, and we may perhaps in our prayers ask for their intercession, but we do not go to them first in order to get to Christ or to God.[142] The right order is not "through Mary to Jesus" but through Jesus to Mary and the whole company of the saints. It is in Christ that we are related to one another in the commu-nal fellowship of love that is the church. We have access to each other in and through Christ but never directly, as the practice of the invoca-tion of saints implies.

We pray not through the intercession of Mary but through the inter-cession of Jesus Christ and in the power of the Holy Spirit. Mary is an intercessor as are all the saints, but their prayers are effectual only when united with those of Jesus Christ. Mary and the saints are not sources of grace but channels of grace. At the time of the Reformation Protestants relegated the doctrine of the communion of saints to the background and consequently lost sight of the mystery that all people of faith are bound together in holy love, and through their prayers and supplications both build up one another in the faith and reach the world of unbelief for the gospel.

An evangelical catholicity will seek to reclaim Mary for the wider church—not as a goddess figure but as the handmaid of the Lord and therefore as a model of holiness. Mary is both a servant of the Word and the mother of God. She is both handmaid of the Lord and inter-cessor for the world. She is both a prototype of the church and a moth-er to the church. She is both the daughter of Zion and the herald of the new Jerusalem.[143] She is both a sinner saved by grace and a preemi-nent saint who radiates the glory of God. She is not the object of faith but an exemplar of faith. She is not a coredeemer but a witness and sign of Christ's all-sufficient redemption. She does not assist Christ in procuring our salvation, nor is her cooperation a condition for this sal-vation. But she is a special covenant partner with Christ in making this salvation known and in communicating its fruits to both church and world. She is not so much a ladder to heaven as an earthen vessel who humbly receives the grace given from heaven.

With the Reformers we should try to understand Mary christologically. Her importance lies not in her special merits or in her significant role in the spreading of the gospel but in her election by God to be the mother of his Son and therefore the earthen channel of his grace. God reached out to our world of sin and darkness through this particular human instrumentality, but he did not need Mary. He could have raised up other Marys just as he can raise up children of Abraham from stones (cf. Lk 3:8). It is not the person of Mary but the message of the cross that is the divinely ordained means of grace by which people are saved and sin is overcome. Insofar as Mary has a role in the evangelical proclamation she too becomes a means of grace. But she is never a necessary means of grace, for God is not bound to any of the instruments he might use to redeem and deliver a lost humanity. He is not even bound to the gospel proclamation, since he could speak to people directly apart from the external preaching and rites of the church. As Calvin noted, we as Christians are bound to these means of grace, but God is not so bound. We Protestants need to reclaim Mary as the mother of God and as our mother through faith. We may also regard her as our sister and companion in redemption.[144] But we must beware of making her into a goddess, of seeing her as a mediator of redemption alongside Christ rather than a sign of his redemption. We should take care not to elevate her above sin and temptation but rather view her as a model of holiness who battles against sin and temptation and overcomes them through the grace that is not inherent in her but is a free gift of God to undeserving sinners.

The church today is confronted with five options: a sectarian Catholicism (and Orthodoxy), which praises Mary uncritically and does not take into serious account her subordinate role in the plan of salvation;[145] a reductionist evangelicalism, which confines church proclamation to the facts of the gospel and evinces little interest in how these facts are related to the church's self-understanding through the ages; a latitudinarian liberalism, which celebrates the open quest for truth over a definitive revelation of truth in the Bible and is willing to hold on to the doctrines of faith, but only as private opinions; a sectarian liberationism, which reconceives Mary through the lens of a social ideology;[146] and finally an evangelical catholicity, which views Mary always in the light of Christ and his redemption and stays sedulously close to Scripture in its assessing of Mary's significance for Christians in every age.

As evangelicals we should remain steadfast in our affirmation of the primacy of Holy Scripture, but this should not be taken to imply scriptural exclusivity. We need to reason beyond the parameters of Scripture as we relate the doctrines and themes of Scripture to the new challenges to the faith posed in every succeeding generation. Just as the church came to the right conclusion regarding the two natures of Christ and the Trinity through deliberate and prolonged reflection on Scripture but also drawing upon the intellectual tools provided by the culture of that time, so the church throughout history and in our time must wrestle with the implications of the message of faith in dialogue with all other Christian communions. Yet we must never forget that church tradition can be deceptive, that again and again it is tempted to transgress the limitations imposed by Scripture, that it needs itself to be continually purified and reformed in the light of a fresh appropriation of the truth of faith through the power and illumination of the Holy Spirit.[147] Church tradition can be a salutary guide to faith but only when it functions under the ruling authority of Holy Scripture. May this be our method and motto as we seek to reclaim Mary for our churches today.

Appendix C: Myth and Reality in the Bible

The debate over the mythical element in the Bible continues to rage in both systematic theology and biblical studies.[148] Depending on how *myth* is defined, almost all parties to the dispute acknowledge some mythical dimension in the biblical stories, but how this is related to history is the pressing issue. Theologians or philosophers who have entertained a basically negative view of myth include David Strauss,[149] Rudolf Bultmann, Uta Ranke-Heinemann, Karl Barth, Gerhard von Rad, Kenneth Hamilton, Emil Brunner, Elizabeth Achtemeier, Bruno Bauer, James Frazer, Lucien Lévy-Bruhl and Brevard Childs. Among those who treat myth more positively are Wolfhart Pannenberg, Paul Ricoeur, Hans Küng, Jacques Ellul, John Hick, Helmut Thielicke, Mircea Eliade, Paul Tillich, Reinhold Niebuhr, Amos Wilder, Bernard F. Batto, Joseph Campbell, James P. Mackey, Karl Jaspers, C. S. Lewis, C. Stephen Evans, John Polkinghorne, John Shelby Spong, Avery Dulles and Geiko Müller-Fahrenholz.

Those who harbor misgivings about the role of myth in biblical interpretation typically contend that myth must not be confounded with reality. Even many who allow a more positive function for myth warn against literalizing myth (Hick, Spong, Tillich, Niebuhr). For David Strauss the whole gospel tradition was only the "historical garb fashioned for primitive Christian ideas by naive poetic mythmakers and consolidated in an historical personality."[150] Rudolf Bultmann understood myth as a prescientific way of viewing reality, and the task of the exegete is to penetrate through myth to the existential meaning of the biblical passage.[151] Uta Ranke-Heinemann, who studied under Bultmann, believes that the stories of the virgin birth and the empty tomb as well as of other alleged miracles are creations of a fertile imagination and must not be allowed to stand in the way of a critical assessment of the claims of the gospel.[152] Karl Barth was firmly convinced of the ahistorical nature of myth and therefore maintained that *myth* is not the most felicitous word to describe the stories and events of biblical history. His preference was for *saga*, an intuitive, imaginative narration of happenings in prophetic history that are not susceptible to scientific corroboration.[153]

A significant number of scholars in our time take a surprisingly positive approach to the problem of myth in the Bible, but they are by no means agreed in their appraisal of myth. Joseph Campbell, who has exerted a wide influence on contemporary secular and religious culture, regards mythology as a pictorial language that puts us in touch with the basic rhythms of human existence.[154] Bernard Batto sees the mythical mode of consciousness as "a proven path by which to approach the divine *mysterium tremendum.*"[155] In his view the stories in the Bible are the product of "mythopoeic speculation."[156] By contrast, C. S. Lewis views the Bible as a basically historical narrative but one that comes to us in the form of mythology.[157] Evangelical philosopher C. Stephen Evans follows Lewis in finding promise in myth, for such language has the "capacity to engage the imagination as well as the intellect."[158] Also standing in the tradition of Christian orthodoxy is John Polkinghorne, who contends that "the power of myth and the power of actuality fuse in the incarnation."[159]

Myth in Recent Theology. Instead of exploring the wide diversity of views on myth, I think it more helpful to examine three contemporary theologians who have made an in-depth study of the role of myth in biblical history. The first is Rudolf Bultmann, who defined myth as a mode of conceiving reality by projecting on the plane of history images that elucidate human experience.[160] He reflects the position of the history of religions school, which viewed myth as sacred stories set outside of profane or secular time whose function was "to reveal the exemplary models for all human rites and significant human activities."[161] Myth seeks to describe this world in terms of the other world and thereby confounds the empirical and the transcendental. The story of gods and goddesses interacting with mortals reveals something about human longings and hopes but should not be treated as a historically accurate depiction of reality. Because we live in a scientific era the stories spawned by mythology are stumbling blocks to the acceptance of the Christian message. Our task is to demythologize the pictorial language in which the truth of the Bible comes to us so that the gospel can be presented as a credible option in today's world. Myth should not be discarded but interpreted so that people can be challenged to live lives of authenticity and courage. Not surprisingly, Bultmann has been criticized for imposing a naturalistic worldview on the Bible and ruling out a priori the very possibility of supernatural intervention in history.[162]

A quite different assessment of myth is given by Emil Brunner, who forthrightly acknowledged the reality of a supernatural realm beyond human existence. Brunner recognized that the mythical element is omnipresent in the Bible, since the events of sacred history are invariably described in symbolic or figurative language. This language is drawn for the most part from the contemporary pagan culture of that time, but it is put into another framework of meaning. Brunner regarded the doctrine of the incarnation of God in Jesus Christ as a direct challenge to the mythical worldview. "Through the incarnation of God in Jesus Christ the myth has been done away—the myth of gods who become men and yet are not real human beings, the myth of the dying and rising Saviour-God who yet never really died, and never really rose again, because he never really lived at all."[163] Pagan myth allows for "an infinitely varied divine series of events," but it has no conception of "one serious decisive event." "All its conceptions are based on the idea of recurrence."[164] Brunner sometimes referred to "the Christian myth," but he did so with much caution, since it belongs to an entirely different category than pagan mythology.[165] It belongs to superhistory rather than to history as such. It signifies "the crossing of that frontier which separates all history from God," "that event which takes place between time and eternity."[166] Brunner had no compunction in acknowledging that all our statements of faith have a mythical cast, since they express the heights of religious imagination as well as witness to the reality of divine revelation. Indeed, this is the only form in which the drama of sacred history could be expressed and preserved.[167]

Like Brunner, Wolfhart Pannenberg sees the Bible as bearing the imprint of myth while at the same time challenging and overcoming myth.[168] In tension with Bultmann, Pannenberg maintains that we should not hastily reject myth as a suitable vehicle for conveying divine revelation. It has positive value in illumining and clarifying the biblical witness. Pannenberg views original myth as descriptive of the primal age and containing archetypes that reappear throughout history. Myth is rooted in religious sensibility even more than in poetic imagination. It seeks to explain the human condition in terms of stories of the visitation of the gods, stories that have a universal significance. Pannenberg speaks of the Christian "new myth" that focuses on "the conception of the redeemer who came down from heaven."[169] What we have in the incarnation is "the association of historical fact and myth."[170] The incarnation challenges the mythical worldview because it focuses on an unrepeatable event in human history, whereas mythical events are continuously repeated in the cults and ceremonies of a people. Moreover, the Christian message opens us to a new future rather than reduplicates the past. Yet the presence of God in history cannot be expressed otherwise than in the language of myth. But "the function of the mythical language remains only that of an interpretive vehicle for the significance of a historical event."[171] Pannenberg detects a movement away from myth already in the Old Testament. Both Jewish and Christian eschatology do not signal a return to a primal age but instead await a future that surpasses and supersedes the mythical primal age. He sees typology, not mythology, in the Old Testament denouement of history. The biblical prophets do not anticipate a return to the first things but "in the image of the important things that have already happened they look for something hitherto unexampled which is still to come."[172]

Pannenberg insists that "myth is not eliminated in Christianity but integrated and transcended."[173] This is true not only for the biblical witness but for the early church as well. Myth did not shape the witness of the church fathers but was "reduced to a device for interpreting history, and this explains the dazzling combination, foreshadowed by Hellenistic syncretism, of fragmentary mythical elements in patristic literature."[174] The early church gave new content to the day of

Helios (the mythical sun god) by relating it to the mystery of the resurrection. "The myth of the sun was not merely reinterpreted, but was superseded for Christians; this was because the resurrection of Jesus was understood as the epiphany of a divine reality greater than that of the sun."[175]

Part of the problem with Pannenberg is that while holding on to the historical facts of the incarnation and the resurrection, he is quite willing to dismiss the historicity of the Adamic fall, the virgin birth, the empty tomb and the nature miracles of Jesus. In his theology the supernatural claims of the faith are muted because history in many cases seems to be dissolved into myth. A clearer statement needs to be made on the reconception of myth as a literary tool for interpreting God's redeeming acts in a particular history as opposed to a mode of apprehending cosmic reality that simply throws light on universal human experience and existence.

Reassessing Myth. Drawing upon the tradition of the history of religions school, I would define myth as a poetic narration concerning supernatural phenomena that take place in primal time and consequently have an ahistorical orientation.[176] The experiences that the story embodies are relived in the rites and ceremonies that shape the ethos of a culture. Sometimes the impression is given that the mythical events transpire in eschatological time, but this proves to be simply a duplication of primal time. Myth employs dramatic, vivid language to describe occurrences of a preternatural character that have their ultimate source in the poetic imagination. The focus of myth is on dramatic encounters between gods and mortals that transcend the parameters of ordinary discourse.

The pivotal question is whether we have this kind of myth in the Bible. My position is that there is no myth of this sort in Scripture because mythical stories, unlike the biblical ones, have no solid basis in human history but refer only to the rhythms of nature and universal human experience. At the same time, it can be shown that there are remnants or trappings of myth in the Bible in the sense that the language and imagery of myth is brought into the service of a divine revelation. We can speak with Helmut Thielicke of disarmed myth in the Bible, myth that has been extricated from its original setting and given a historical focus.[177] The Bible does not contain original myth—stories of gods and goddesses—but it does contain mythopoetic language that pertains to real interventions of the living God in human history.

Genuine myth is concerned with theophanies, direct manifestations of gods to mortals. Scripture by contrast speaks of a revelation of God to humanity in which God remains veiled even in the revelation. The biblical God is the hidden God *(Deus absconditus)* who cannot be possessed in direct perception and who can be grasped only by faith. The Bible does record encounters between godlike beings and mortals, but these beings are angelic intermediaries between God and mortals. The true God cannot be seen (cf. Ex 33:20; Jn 1:18), and can be known only when he chooses to make himself known through the mouths of his seers and prophets.[178] God remained hidden even in his revelation in Jesus Christ, for Christ's messianic identity was veiled even from his disciples.

At the same time, it is incontestable that mythological themes and imagery pervade Holy Scripture, though these themes are invariably given new content and direction. The narrative in Genesis 1 bears a remarkable resemblance to mythological accounts of creation that depict creation as the outcome of a conflict between the gods and chaos. Yet as Pannenberg astutely shows,

By being incorporated into the chronology of the priestly document, the character of the creation narrative as the account of a primal age lost the possibility of being repeated in the cult; it became an event which was definitively in the past, and in precisely this way provided the basis of the later history of the world. It thus lost the essential feature of myth, the ability, as the events of the primal age, at the same time to be present in any age through the events of the cult.[179] This historicizing thrust of the biblical authors is also apparent in many other stories that refer to interaction between God and humanity. The story of the Fall in Genesis 3 does not simply concern a primeval event outside historical time but points to a future resolution within history. We do not merely repeat the Fall in our lives but look forward to its overcoming in the dawning of a new creation. The lost paradise is made to serve an eschatological hope: the coming of the Messiah (cf. Gen 3:15). The biblical stories of the great flood are superficially similar to the Babylonian Gilgamesh Epic. Yet in the biblical perspective the flood is the expression not of polytheistic caprice but of God's judgment on a sinful humanity. Second, Isaiah transforms the Babylonian myth of creation into the history of the exodus and the crossing of the Red Sea (Is 51:9-10). The millennium in Revelation 20 is not a return to a primal state of innocence but an entirely new stage in history when the promises of God to the earth will be fulfilled.

The language of Scripture is for the most part dramatic and symbolic, which presents problems for modern people who identify truth with precision and technical accuracy.[180] The term *mythopoetic* can also be guardedly applied to much of the language of Scripture, first because it is akin to the figurative language of ancient mythology, and second because many expressions actually have a mythological source. The crucial difference is that the scriptural language is oriented around the unfolding of sacred history, not the repetitions of nature.[181]

While real history is recorded in the Bible, it is often interspersed with mythical themes so that what is recounted is not simply external events in space and time but the hand of God in these events. It is history not in the sense of *Historie* (objective history) but of *Geschichte* (theologically interpreted history). There is somewhat of a consensus in biblical scholarship that 1 and 2 Maccabees are among the most historical of the sacred books, though they form part of the Apocrypha, not of canonical Scripture, at least for Protestants.[182] In the context of a historical report the author relates this incident: "While they were still in the neighborhood of Jerusalem, there appeared at their head a horseman arrayed in white and brandishing golden weapons. With one voice they praised their merciful God and felt so strong in spirit that they could have attacked not only men but also the most savage animals, or even walls of iron" (2 Macc 11:8-9 REB). Was this a straightforward account of what actually transpired or a poetic description of a divine intervention that only faith can recognize and appreciate? In accord with a great many of the fathers and doctors of the church I contend that the language of Scripture when referring to God and his actions is not identical with the reality described but congruent. We know God not univocally but analogically and symbolically.[183]

In contradistinction to Bultmann I hold that many of the events in the Bible that suppose the direct intervention of God in human affairs really happened; yet they cannot be described in the language of historical precision but only in dramatic, parabolic language. The resurrection of Jesus Christ from the dead really happened, but the opening of the graves of the saints who joined Jesus in his resurrection (Mt 27:52-53) was surely a symbolic way of affirming the solidarity of Christ with Old Testament believers.[184] The outpouring of the Holy Spirit really happened, but the tongues of fire that appeared in the upper room were probably a symbolic rendition of the flaming presence of the Spirit of God (Acts 2:3). Jesus really did cast out demonic spirits from the bodies of broken and hurting people, but this is a poetic way of describing how Jesus liberated the human will from bondage to Satan, the superhistorical adversary of God and humanity.[185] Bultmann was right that the ancients, including the biblical writers, believed in a three-story universe: the heavens above, the earth beneath and the waters under the earth (cf. Ex 20:4). But whereas Bultmann wished to substitute the modern view of a single closed universe, I continue to use the biblical picture but interpret it as an affirmation of a supernatural or transcendent reality beyond and above the world of human perception and experience. The mythical framework remains but is not literalized; it is now understood as symbolic of a real transcendent realm outside the compass of ordinary human experience. There are real angels, real devils, real miracles, but they are best grasped only by a sanctified imagination. The view of life and the world that comes with biblical revelation is postscientific rather than prescientific and ipso facto poses a formidable challenge to both the mythological worldview of the ancients and the modern worldview of empirical science.

I see myth in both positive and negative terms. Positively it supplies the language for describing the hidden and enigmatic actions of God in human history. It engages the intuitive side of our being, not just the intellectual side. It preserves the depth dimension of human existence and experience that is otherwise dissolved by the rigors of logic. It also resonates with the deepest yearnings and longings of humanity for the transcendent (as C. S. Lewis so astutely observed). Negatively myth is tied to the human search for meaning in life rather than God's search for humanity. Its focus is on the opening of humanity to a new horizon rather than the descent of God into human experience. Its concern is with the unraveling of the riddle of human existence rather than obedience to the will of God as revealed in a particular human history.

The biblical authors were not mythmakers in the sense that they deliberately concocted stories of divine-human encounters in order to speak meaningfully about the human condition in terms that their contemporaries could understand. Instead they were transformers of myth, historicizers of myth. They brought mythical images into a new framework of meaning that signaled the overturning of the mythical vision but at the same time the fulfillment of mythical aspirations. I agree with W. M. Schmidt that Israel did not create mythical narratives but only "took over foreign . . . myths in fragmentary form and changed them."[186]

What we have in the Bible is the imprint of myth rather than its delineation. We find mythical allusions rather than a bona fide mythical religion. We are confronted with the transcendence and transformation of myth rather than its unfolding. The primary category in Scripture is not myth, story, saga or narrative but *witness*.[187] The scriptural writers sought to give a stirring and reliable witness to the events of sacred history that focus not on the human ascent to God but on God's descent to humanity. In making their witness they now and again felt free to employ the mythological language of their time. The truth of their witness cannot be separated from the mythopoetic form in which it comes to us. We must avoid two errors: to literalize what is intended to be understood symbolically, and to symbolize—to see the historical matrix in which the truth of God is enunciated as expendable. In one sense the Bible is both history and myth, since historical narrative is relayed through symbolic, dramatic language.[188] In another sense the Bible is neither history nor myth, since its focus is neither on history as such nor on the rhythms of nature but on God's amazing entrance into history. Its language, moreover, is not so much that of myth as that of faith, for its source is not the creative depths of the human psyche (as in myth) but the experience of being confronted by the living God who issues a call to action and obedience.

The mythic mode of the biblical language does not determine the historicity of the events described in the Bible. Reflection on these events may well involve the use of semiconceptual language as well as poetic or symbolic language (as in the apostle Paul), but language is not the key to either truth or historicity. A truly free historical-critical scholarship—liberated from naturalistic presuppositions—can tell us much about the historical basis of the biblical claims, though it cannot guarantee that any of these events really happened just as described. Neither can it lead us to the revelational meaning of these events, the truth of the Word of God, that is given finally only by the Spirit in conjunction with the wrestling of the believer with the biblical text and hearing the biblical word proclaimed.

Basically the Bible is not a poem or artistic narration (as in narrative theology). Nor is the Bible precise history or an amazingly accurate record of historical happenings (as in fundamentalist theology).[189] Instead the Bible is a prism through which light from the beyond shines—via both historical narrative and poetry (as in the evangelical theology I espouse).

The purpose of God's revelation attested in Holy Scripture was not to bring enlightenment to humanity but to create a new humanity and a new world. It was not to raise human consciousness to a vision that transcends history but to herald the descent of the transcendent God into history. Its focus was not on the fulfillment of human aspirations to divinity but on the incarnation of God in human flesh.[190]

The biblical narrative is the true life story of a people of faith as they are encountered by the living God in history. This story is not a projection of the longings and hopes of humanity upon the screen of history (as Bultmann and Spong maintain). Nor is it a means of demonstrating "the inner meaning of the universe and of human life" (as Norman Perrin alleges).[191] Instead it is a proclamation of a new heaven and a new earth that will come in God's own time and way. A future kingdom is breaking into present experience, and human language is strained to the limit to depict this new reality. The poetry of faith is more felicitous in this task than is the prose of history, but one should keep in mind that what is generally being described are real objective happenings, not merely subjective states of human consciousness (as in Joseph Campbell, Carl Jung and the New Age movement).

Because the term *myth* is ambiguous in today's climate of discourse and often carries a pejorative meaning, I have a slight preference for such terms as *symbolic, dramatic* and *narrational* to describe the tenor of biblical language.[192] Yet *myth* and *mythopoetic* have the merit of reminding us that the biblical revelation broke into a world dominated by a mythological worldview. This worldview was overturned by divine revelation, but its mode of language was preserved as a vehicle for mysteries that cannot be fully contained in ordinary, straightforward language.

·FIVE·

THE PREEXISTENCE OF JESUS CHRIST

No one has gone up into heaven except the one who came
down from heaven, the Son of Man who is in heaven.
JOHN 3:13 REB

The first man was from the earth, a man of dust;
the second man is from heaven.
1 CORINTHIANS 15:47

We believe . . . in one Lord Jesus Christ, God's only-begotten Son,
born of the Father before all time.
NICENO-CONSTANTINOPOLITAN CREED

The birth of our Saviour in Bethlehem of Judea was not His *origin*.
HARRY RIMMER

I do not understand how one can hold the doctrine of
pre-existence. . . . This doctrine comes from pagan philosophy.
ADOLF VON HARNACK

The issue of the preexistence of Jesus Christ has been with the church since apostolic times. It is inseparably related to the doctrine of Christ's deity. If Jesus Christ is indeed divine, then he must have preexisted in heaven with God or in God. In addition to this question, however, is that of the preexistence of Christ's humanity. If there is no Logos apart from the flesh *(Logos asarkos)*, as Karl

Barth maintains, then Jesus too and not just the Word preexisted with God in eternity. But if this is so, can we then speak of a real incarnation?

Adolf von Harnack has been helpful in his analysis of the two theories of preexistence that have emerged in the course of church history.[1] The first, which he labels the Hebraic, contends that everything of real value that from time to time appears on earth has its existence in heaven. It exists with God and therefore has real being. Its manifestation on earth is merely a transition from concealment to publicity. Hebrews 9:23 speaks of "copies of the heavenly things" on earth. This understanding may also be reflected in Wisdom of Solomon 9:8: "Thou hast given command to build a temple on thy holy mountain, and an altar in the city of thy habitation, a copy of the holy tent which thou didst prepare from the beginning."[2] Insofar as the earthly copy is deemed inferior to the original, however, this passage seems to betray a Hellenistic influence.[3] The preexistence of the man Jesus is not inconsistent with the Hebraic view.

In the Hellenic conception the idea of preexistence is based on "the contrast between spirit and matter, between the infinite and finite, found in the cosmos itself."[4] What preexists is not the flesh but the spiritual side of the human creature. Spirit is eternal and with God. In this view the preexistence of Jesus can refer only to his Spirit or to the Word. According to Harnack, Paul leans more toward the Hellenic view, since he believed that the flesh is "something inadequate" and indeed "hostile" to the divine.[5] Preexistence can here refer only to the spiritual part of Jesus Christ. But Paul gave life to this spiritual nature by viewing the preexistent Christ as "a being who, even during his preexistence, stands independently side by side with God."[6] Harnack does not fully consider that when Paul condemns the "flesh" he means body and soul under the sway of sin; indeed, Paul has a remarkably positive view of the body and of materiality as a creation of God.

H. R. Mackintosh also wrestled with the doctrine of Christ's preexistence. Among the Jews, "not only were great men credited with preexistence, such as Adam, Enoch, or Moses, but even the tabernacle, the temple, and the tables of the Divine law. The idea, in short, was one which primitive Christianity found ready-made, and which naturally it utilized to set forth the enduring value and felt mystery of Jesus' person."[7] Mackintosh held that the Jewish and Christian ideas are nevertheless very different. "In Rabbinism the celestial archetype is only a double of the earthly object; in the New Testament, the very signature of Christology is the faith that the Divine Son passed from glory to humiliation; and it is mere inaccuracy to say that these ideas are equivalent, or analogous, or that one of them suffices to explain the other."[8] Faith must see "the pre-incarnate One *in* God, not alongside of God, not as an entity to be known and appreciated in abstraction from God. Thus in a purely religious interest it is equally misleading to regard the eternal 'Son' as a mere impersonal law or force or principle on the one hand, and on the other as an independent Divine individuality."[9]

Mackintosh was firm that the Christian idea of preexistence does not include Jesus' humanity: "The Church has never affirmed that the humanity of Christ was real prior to the birth in Bethlehem; and if, as must be admitted, certain apostolic statements, interpreted *au pied de la lettre*, have the appearance of saying quite the opposite, it must be considered that this was inevitable in the case of men using the intensely concrete language of religion, not the coldly correct phraseology of the schools."[10]

A Historical Overview

The preexistent Word is a salient theme in the Fourth Gospel, but does this idea also include the preexistent humanity of Jesus? A credible case could be made that it does. John the Baptist acknowledged the preexistent person—Jesus: "This was he of whom I said, 'He who comes after me ranks before me, for he was before me'" (Jn 1:15). Jesus' words in 17:5 also point to a preexistent humanity: "So now, Father, glorify me in your own presence with the glory that I had in your presence before the world existed" (NRSV). In 17:24 Jesus confesses, "Thou didst love me before the foundation of the world"

(NASB). Preexistent humanity is certainly implied in 6:62: "Then what if you were to see the Son of man ascending where he was before?" (cf. 3:13; 7:29; 8:38). John 13:3 portrays Jesus as knowing that he had come from God and was now going to God. In 8:58 Jesus utters the enigmatic words "Before Abraham was, I am."

The concept of preexistent humanity is also found in the Pauline writings. Colossians 1:15 describes Jesus as "the first-born of all creation." In 1 Corinthians 8:6 Paul declares that there is "one Lord, Jesus Christ, through whom are all things and through whom we exist." In 15:47 of the same epistle Paul links Jesus with the supernatural Son of Man: "The first man was from the earth, a man of dust; the second man is from heaven." The apostle also affirms the self-emptying of Jesus Christ: "You know the grace of our Lord Jesus Christ, that though he was rich, yet for your sake he became poor, so that by his poverty you might become rich" (2 Cor 8:9; cf. Phil 2:5-11). The Pauline author of 2 Timothy 1:9 says that God "hath saved us, and called us with a holy calling, not according to our works, but according to his own purpose and grace, which was given us in Christ Jesus before the world began" (KJV).[11]

Other New Testament books also suggest the preexistent humanity of Jesus Christ. The author of Hebrews avows, "Jesus Christ is the same yesterday, today, and for ever" (13:8 REB; cf. Heb 5:5-6). In the book of Revelation the glorified Redeemer declares himself as "the Alpha and the Omega," coequal with the Father "who is and who was and who is to come" (Rev 1:8). Revelation 13:8 describes Jesus as "the Lamb slain from the foundation of the world" (KJV). First Peter 1:20 affirms that Jesus "was chosen before the creation of the world" (NIV).

The Hellenistic idea of preexistence is apparent in Origen (d. 254), who conceived of the incarnation of the Logos in two stages: the assumption of the soul and the assumption of the body. Before the creation of the world the Logos took to himself the untainted human soul of Jesus, who did not participate in the fall of the preexistent souls from their eternal origin but instead cleaved to the Logos in fidelity and submission. This soul assumed a human body conceived by the Spirit in the Virgin Mary. The human soul of Jesus was inseparably united with the eternal Word just as iron can be penetrated by fire.[12]

The preexistence of the humanity of Jesus reappeared in the radical or left-wing Reformation among those whom scholars call "Spiritualists."[13] Caspar Schwenckfeld (d. 1561) rejected the doctrine of the dual nature of Christ as both human and divine, contending that Christ was altogether divine and uncreated. He was from all eternity the God-man having a body of "spiritual flesh."[14] He lived in this body on earth and continues to possess it in his exalted state in heaven. This meant that Christ's humanity was in no sense creaturely but that he brought it with him from heaven. Similarly Sebastian Franck and Valentin Weigel maintained that the Son "from all eternity put on human nature."[15] He was from all eternity "the complete and perfect image of God." This divine humanity is incarnate wherever mortals rise into union with God. Such a position denies that Christ assumed our sinful flesh.

In the eighteenth century Isaac Watts, nonconformist preacher and hymn writer, stoutly affirmed the preexistence of the humanity of Christ. Manifesting an affinity to Origen, he conceived of a preexistent human soul created in personal union with the Logos. This soul had such exalted power that he was the greatest of all created spirits.[16] Watts entertained reservations about the doctrine of the Trinity and argued that it should not be mandatory for ministers in independent churches.

Another proponent of Christ's preexistent humanity, Emanuel Swedenborg, taught that Jesus Christ was God and man from eternity. The incarnation of Christ was simply his manifestation in the flesh, the revelation on the earthly plane of the eternal God-Man. True to the Hellenistic tradition, he viewed reality as an organized hierarchy ascending toward God, who is pure Spirit. Swedenborg rejected the doctrine of the Trinity, claiming that it masks a commitment to tritheism. Instead of affirming God as triune he saw the Father and the Son as one person and the Holy Spirit as "their efficiency, or sanctifying influence."[17]

With the rise of modernity in the eighteenth and nineteenth centuries the emphasis shifted from the preexistence of the Word to the reinterpretation of the Word as a principle for the moral life. According to Harnack the idea of preexistence simply means the consciousness that Jesus had of being united with his Father in will and action.[18] This general position is reaffirmed in our own day by Catholic theologian Karl-Josef Kuschel, who reinterprets the preexistence of Christ "historically."[19] For Kuschel the allusions to the preexistence of Christ in the New Testament are attempts to deify him, "to turn him into a mythical or semi-mythical being."[20] Like his mentor Rudolf Bultmann, Kuschel holds that we must penetrate through the mythical imagery in order to comprehend "the historical depth and universal significance of the 'event of Jesus.'"[21] We may confess Jesus of Nazareth as the "eternal Son" because in him "the 'eternal God and Father' has revealed himself."[22]

The traditional view that the Word preexisted but not the humanity of Jesus indubitably remains the dominant position in conservative Christianity. Donald Baillie was firmly convinced that Jesus is not consubstantial with God but consubstantial with humanity.[23] According to the New Testament scholar John Knox, "We can have the humanity without the pre-existence and we can have the pre-existence without the humanity. There is absolutely no way of having both."[24]

At the same time, a significant number of scholars have come to accept the preexistent humanity of Jesus. Klaas Runia of the Reformed Church in the Netherlands contends that there is solid biblical evidence for affirming "the pre-existence of the man Jesus of Nazareth as the Eternal Son of God."[25] Harry Rimmer argues that Jehovah of the Old Testament and Jesus of the New Testament are the same person.[26] Other scholars who affirm Jesus' preexistent humanity are Robert Jenson, Ray Anderson, Arthur Pink, Wilhelm Vischer and Karl Barth. It is the last who has advanced this view with systematic precision and whose influence is conspicuous among many of its defenders, including Jenson and Anderson.

Karl Barth's Position

In Karl Barth's theology we see a reaffirmation of Hebraic themes, including the preexistent humanity of Christ as opposed to the Hellenic understanding, which posits a preexistent spirit of the man Jesus. Barth speaks of Jesus as "the electing God" and also as the "elected man."[27] Before the creation of the world the Son of God took upon himself the identity of Jesus of Nazareth, and therefore we may speak of Jesus Christ as "the uncreated prototype of the humanity which is to be linked with God."[28] Indeed, "the man Jesus already was even before He was."[29] Barth does not believe that Jesus existed in the flesh from all eternity (as some Radical Reformers alleged) but that the man Jesus was prefigured in the eternal Word of God. The Word of God already identified himself with Jesus before the incarnation, but he did not assume human flesh until his conception. Yet the flesh was not foreign to his nature, since it was foreknown and selected from all eternity. He had the form of flesh, and this is why he could enter into a body of flesh. The flesh was latent or implicit in the Word.

Barth argues that the incarnation happened in eternity before all time, and its occurrence in time is a transition from concealment to publicity. He does not mean that the male Jesus preexisted as a pretemporal spirit but that the Son of God chose to become Jesus before the actual incarnation in history. In Barth's theology "between the eternal being of the Second Person of the Trinity and the temporal existence of the man Jesus there is a 'third' reality—the reality of the choice in which the Son chooses to be *and is* one with man."[30] To understand this choice we must look upward "to the place where the eternal God not only foresees and foreordains this person, but where He Himself . . . actually is this person."[31]

Barth's position becomes more intelligible when we see it against the background of his conception of the humanity of God.[32] Because humanity is already latent within God, because God is already characterized by vulnerability and dependency in the fellowship of the holy Trinity, he can assume the humanity of Jesus Christ without contradicting his own nature. By going out of himself into the world of human history he does not abdicate his divinity but realizes it in a new way. In Barthian terms he is exalted in his humiliation. He gives up his divine prerogatives but not his divine nature.

Not surprisingly Barth's position has met with gnawing reservations in the Christian scholarly community. Some have argued that by identifying the Jesus Christ of history with the eternal Logos Barth denies the real incarnation of God in humanity. It seems that Christ only appeared in the flesh rather than incarnated himself in flesh. Could Barth be speaking of a theophany, a visible manifestation of God, rather than a genuine incarnation? Barth is very insistent in affirming a *Logos ensarkos,* the Word inseparable from the flesh, rather than a *Logos asarkos,* which supposes the Word outside the flesh.[33] This means that we can speak not of an eternal Logos apart from Christ that is generally accessible to reason but only of the Logos of divine revelation—God in Jesus Christ.

Helmut Thielicke has raised serious objections to what he regards as Barth's theological innovation. One implication is that "the incarnation is no new event, it is not the inauguration of a new covenant; it cannot be the historical juncture of the aeons, but simply recapitulates, clarifies, and reveals events which, as enacted and completed facts, belong to the perfect tense of Old Testament salvation history, or even to the pluperfect tense of pre-temporality."[34] Thielicke then cites Barth's *Kirchliche Dogmatik* in support of his contention that Barth's view of the incarnation does not involve a new revelation but only a further stage of the one revelation of God to Israel:

The *Word of God,* which has come so near in the act of the divine mercy [performed on Israel] . . . is identical with the *Word of faith* proclaimed by the apostles of the Church. . . . The apostolic message of God's mercy actualized in Jesus Christ does *not* speak of any *new revelation* . . . the *one old* revelation of God in which Israel partici-pates is as such the message which is proclaimed by the apostles.[35] One should keep in mind that Thielicke as a Lutheran sees two dis-pensations—one of law and one of grace, and the first is annulled by the coming of Jesus Christ. By contrast, Barth, who is here close to Calvin, affirms one covenant of grace that pervades both Testaments, and this means that Jesus Christ stands in continuity with what has gone before. For Barth the revelation of God in Christ is the culmina-tion of his revelation in the sacred history of Israel, so it is not entire-ly new or unexpected.

One profound implication of Barth's position is that Jesus Christ is already in the Old Testament. Barth could affirm with Luther regarding the angel who wrestled with Jacob in Genesis 32: "Without the slight-est contradiction this man was not an angel, but our Lord Jesus Christ, who is the eternal God and yet was to become a man whom the Jews would crucify."[36] His position also lends weight to Arthur Pink's exege-sis of Joshua 5:13-14, where Joshua fell on his face and worshiped the one who called himself "commander of the army of the Lord": "It was one of the pre-incarnate appearings of the Son of God in human form, which brings before us a most blessed yet profoundly-mysterious sub-ject."[37] In evangelical tradition Melchizedek of Genesis 14:17-18 is identical with the Son of God, "who continues a priest for ever" (Heb 7:3). Similarly the fourth person in the fiery furnace with Daniel and his friends is said to be like the "Son of God" (Dan 3:25 KJV) and therefore quite possibly the preexistent Jesus Christ.

American evangelical theologian Ray Anderson interprets preexis-tence in such a way as to avoid the common charge leveled at Barthians that they postulate Jesus as a separate human being existing before the incarnation. The right way of expressing this doctrine is "that the relation of Jesus as the obedient Son to God as loving and sending Father has its origin within the very being of God's existence. This is what is meant by the 'pre-existence' of Jesus of Nazareth in the form of the divine Son of God before the historical event of incarnation. There is no pre-existence as such of Jesus the male Jew, born of Mary."[38]

While Barth's position is more Hebraic than Hellenic, it definitely goes beyond the notion found in Jewish writings "that the Messiah is the man who is with God in heaven; and who will make his appearance at his own time."[39] Jesus is not simply with God, but Jesus is God—the Son of God who takes upon himself the human identity of Jesus of Nazareth. The Jesus of history is not a copy of an original prototype in heaven but the enactment in human flesh of the eternal decision of the Son of God to unite himself with the sin, death and travail of a lost humanity so that the redemption of the whole world will be effected through the life, death and resurrection of this one person— Jesus Christ, who is both true God and true man, our Savior, Redeemer and Lord.

Epilogue

With Karl Barth I hold to the preexistent humanity of Jesus Christ, but not in the sense that the man Jesus preexisted in heaven as a separate being (Barth would agree). I contend that God the Son took upon himself the identity of the man Jesus and thereby united himself with humanity. By "humanity" I am thinking not of flesh and bones but instead of individuality, embodiment, vulnerability and dependency. The Son of God could become human because the Godhead already embraces characteristics that we attribute to humanity. Barth insightfully declared that "genuine deity includes in itself genuine humanity."[40] Those who are closer to Greek metaphysics might object that this position makes God an anthropomorphic being. Divinity, however, does not signify timeless essence (as in the Greek view) but dynamic existence (as in the Hebraic view). Because God is a Trinity he interacts dynamically within himself, and this is why he can also go out of himself and interact dynamically with his human subjects.

To affirm the preexistent humanity of Jesus means that the incarnation was not an absolute beginning. It implies that there is a continu-

ity between the historical Jesus and the eternal Christ. The full meaning of the incarnation is not simply that the Word became flesh, but
that Jesus Christ assumed human flesh (1 Jn 4:2).

God is not man (Hos 11:9), but the God of the Bible is a humanlike
being. Both man and woman are created in the image of God and *eo
ipso* in the image of Jesus Christ. The living God infinitely transcends
gender but at the same time includes gender within himself in that he
is its source and ground. God's actions within his triune life as well as
upon the creation can be described in terms of gender. The Father
begets the Son, and the mystical body of Christ, the church, gives birth
to sons and daughters.

When did Jesus become the Son of God? Adoptionists hold that this
occurred at the time of his baptism. Pannenberg, at least in his earlier
phase, suggested at the time of the resurrection of Jesus. Classical theology has always contended that this event is associated with his conception. Barth held that Jesus was already the Son of God before his
incarnation in human history. While this statement can easily be mis-
understood, it nonetheless contains the element of truth that the Son
of God willed to unite himself to the human Jesus before his actual
experience of living an incarnate life on earth. Even before the event
of the incarnation the Son of God adopted the name of Jesus, so it is
appropriate to refer to him not only as the Son or the Word but also as
Jesus Christ, God made man in human flesh.

Those who are involved in process theology have considerable difficulty with this conception, since they tend to interpret the whole universe as the incarnation.[41] The incarnation of God in Jesus Christ is not
an event in a particular history but an eternal process in which God
continually goes out of himself into the world and seeks to realize
himself with the aid of his human creation. One could argue that
process theology makes a place for the preexistent Word or Logos
insofar as it speaks of a primordial nature of God as well as a conse-
quent and superject nature. Yet the primordial nature in Whitehead's
philosophy is purely abstract and is insufficient to explain either the

preexistent Christ or the preexistent Jesus. What is preexistent in process theology and philosophy is the power of creativity, which is envisaged in suprapersonal rather than personal terms.

Speaking in terms of the ancient creeds, the person of the eternal Son of God is also the person of Jesus, God in human flesh. This person adopted the human nature of Jesus in his incarnation in history, but this was a human nature already conceived in the mind of God. The eternal Word of God to be sure did not experience the sin, death and travail of humanity until he actually entered history—in the covenant people of Israel and then in Jesus Christ, the Messiah of Israel. Yet this experience was not alien to his being: it was already anticipated by the humbling of himself and giving of himself in the experience of joy and love that he has in his triune life. The god of Hellenism has joy simply by gazing upon his inimitable beauty and goodness. The God of biblical faith has joy by interacting within himself in joyous acts of celebration and by interacting with the world of humanity in loving acts of humiliation and exaltation.

I do not begin in my theological speculation with an abstract idea of a preexistent man nor with the dogma of the preexistent Word or Son of God (a christology from above). Nor do I begin with a historical investigation of the available evidence concerning the life and death of Jesus (a christology from below). I begin with the incarnation itself— God assuming human flesh in a particular time and place in history (a christology from the center). By seeing the eternal God in the Jesus of history we are then able to understand why this God is already named Jesus Christ and how Jesus' humanity becomes a mode of his divinity. To claim that Jesus is victor (Johann Christoph Blumhardt) is also to claim that Jesus is God—not God in the abstract but God in humanity, God in history. This is the God who enters the world of sin and death in order to overcome sin and death by making atonement for sin on the cross and by breaking the power of death through rising from the dead and ascending into heaven.

·SIX·

CHRIST'S

ATONING

SACRIFICE

He has appeared once for all at the end of the age
to put away sin by the sacrifice of himself.
HEBREWS 9:26

He is the atoning sacrifice for our sins,
and not only for ours but also for the sins of the whole world.
1 JOHN 2:2 NIV

He, then, was sin, as we are righteousness; but this righteousness
is not our own but God's, not in ourselves but in Him,
just as He was sin, not His own but ours.
AUGUSTINE

He does not give grace so freely that He has demanded no
satisfaction, but rather He has given Christ as the one
who makes the satisfaction for us.
MARTIN LUTHER

The feeble gospel preaches, "God is ready to forgive";
the mighty gospel preaches, "God has redeemed."
P. T. FORSYTH

Christ does not simply offer himself to God in the name of man,
so that God is the object of atonement. He also offers himself
to man in the name of God and as God's sacrifice.
HELMUT THIELICKE

The relation of the incarnation to the atonement has always
been a source of contention in the history of theology.[1] A major
strand in Christian tradition associates the incarnation with the

person of Christ and the atonement with his work of redemption. Another strand sees Christ's atoning work as beginning with his birth and culminating with his death on the cross and his resurrection from the grave. Catholic and patristic theology has generally subordinated the atonement to the incarnation, whereas evangelical theology has put the emphasis on the cross.

For Karl Barth the incarnation accomplishes the reconciliation of God and sinful humanity. "Jesus Christ is not what He is—very God, very man, very God-man—in order as such to mean and do and accomplish something else which is atonement. But His being as God and man and God-man consists in the completed act of the reconciliation of man with God."[2] It seems that for Barth the cross and resurrection of Christ have essentially revelatory significance, since they reveal the reconciliation that already occurred through the incarnation. At the same time, Barth indicates that the cross of Christ fulfills God's reconciling will and purpose and therefore has some role in effecting reconciliation.

In my position the incarnation sets the stage for the atonement, though the work of redemption already begins in the decision of Christ to incarnate himself in human flesh. Moreover, we come to appreciate and understand the mystery of the incarnation only in the light of the cross and resurrection of Christ. The incarnation and the atonement are inseparable, but the gospel message focuses on the latter rather than the former.

The Purpose of the Incarnation

Various answers have been given concerning the purpose of the incarnation. They do not necessarily conflict but often admirably complement one another. At the same time, each one indicates a definite theory of the atonement that serves to shape one's understanding of the work and mission of Jesus Christ.

One tradition within the church contends that Christ came to save us from death and corruptibility and to unite us with the divine nature.

These theologians often appeal to 1 Corinthians 15:26 and 2 Peter 1:4. Salvation becomes identified with the gift of immortality (cf. Wisdom of Solomon 8:13, 17; 6:18-19). This was indeed the emphasis in the early church. According to Jaroslav Pelikan the affliction that seemed to command the most attention at that time was the universality of death, not the inevitability of sin.[3] While sin and the devil also played a significant role in the soteriology of patristic theologians, they generally saw the fundamental human dilemma as mortality. In the view of Theodore of Mopsuestia, "Because we shall be made immortal after our resurrection, we shall no longer be able to sin; for it follows from our being mortal that we sin."[4]

Another closely related position held by many of the church fathers and very much present in the mystical tradition of the church is that Christ came to prepare the way for the reunion of the soul with God. Salvation is depicted as a return to undivided unity with God (cf. Jn 16:28). Here as in the first position one can discern the pervasive influence of Platonic and Neoplatonic philosophy.[5] The renowned medieval mystic Meister Eckhart gave voice to this understanding: "Our Lord Jesus Christ besought his Father that we should be made one—not merely united—but joined together in him and with him in the one single One. . . . When I return to God, I shall be without form and thus my reentry will be far more exalted than my setting out."[6]

Still other theologians emphasize that Christ came to save us from sin and the divine judgment. This position is especially prominent in the medieval and Reformation periods, though it is conspicuous among the patristic fathers as well. These theologians appeal to such texts as Romans 3:23-25, 2 Corinthians 5:21, 1 Timothy 1:15 and Hebrews 2:17. Luther declared that Christ "makes us so secure in relationship to God and gives peace to our conscience that God is no longer against us, or we ourselves. This is a far greater act than making [the powers] harmless for us; for guilt and sin are far greater than pain and death."[7] According to G. C. Berkouwer, the purpose of the incarnation was "not the 'deification of man,' but this propitiatory

CHRIST'S ATONING SACRIFICE

restoration into the service of God."[8] As Barth put it, "The incarnation, the taking of the *forma servi,* means not only God's becoming a creature, becoming a man . . . but it means His giving Himself up to the contradiction of man against Him, His placing Himself under the judgment under which man has fallen in this contradiction, under the curse of death which rests upon Him."[9]

Then there are those who argue that Christ's primary motivation to incarnate himself was to reconcile and unite sinful humanity to God. The pivotal text is 2 Corinthians 5:19: "God was in Christ reconciling the world to Himself, not imputing their trespasses to them" (NKJ). This was a special emphasis of Barth, for he subsumed justification and sanctification under reconciliation. Barth rejected the idea of a human sacrifice appeasing the wrath of God, but he affirmed that Jesus Christ bore the punishment made necessary by the wrath of God. For Barth reconciliation signifies the heart of the atonement. It involves bringing about peace with God through the overcoming of sin. As reconciler Jesus Christ heals the breach and restores the broken communion between God and humanity.

One significant place where Barth diverges from the Reformation and from a great part of church tradition is his insistence that God does not need to be reconciled with humanity, though humanity stands in need of being reconciled to God. Barth is not always consistent in this area, for some of his statements presuppose that God too is affected by the change in relationship. I affirm with Arthur Crabtree, William Sanday and Arthur Headlam among many others that reconciliation is mutual.[10] It consists not only in a change of attitude on the part of the human creature but also in a change of attitude on the part of God.[11]

We must also consider the position that Christ saves us from the demonic powers of darkness. This motif, especially prominent in the early church, was revived by Martin Luther and various other Reformers in the sixteenth century. It has a firm basis in such texts as Matthew 20:28, Mark 10:45, 1 Timothy 2:6, Hebrews 2:14-15, 1 John 3:8 and Revelation 5:9. It is also found in Barth, who contended that salvation is primarily from the chaos (the powers of darkness) and only secondarily from sin and death.[12] This understanding portrays Jesus as victor over the powers of darkness that hold the human race in servile subjection.

Finally, there are those who claim that Christ came to demonstrate and reveal God's love for us. Texts in which this note is discernible are 1 John 3:16 and 4:7-12. This view is often embraced by mystics and pietists and has found a lodging in liberal Christianity as well. These theologians hold that Christ came to show us the right way to live. We ought to love as he has loved us. The role of Jesus Christ is to bring us into contact with God's love and transform us in his image.

While all of the above positions contain some truth, they have given rise to conflicting doctrines of the atonement. More than a few of the divisions within the church through the centuries are anchored in the divergences in understanding the work and mission of Christ.

Theories of the Atonement

Among the theories of the atonement is what Gustaf Aulén calls "the classic view" inasmuch as it is deeply embedded in the patristic fathers of the church.[13] In this perspective military metaphors abound. Christ's death is depicted as a victory over the powers of darkness: death, sin and Satan. Christ's sacrifice is sometimes described as a ransom to the demonic powers, which could not hold on to it because of Christ's resurrection. In the classic theory God takes the initiative and carries through. He himself performs the sacrifice in the person of his Son. According to Luther, who revived the classic theory, satisfaction is given not only *to* God but also *by* God. Luther added the law of God and the wrath of God to the powers that Christ overcomes. In the classic view the resurrection is supremely important, for it reveals and fulfills the work of Christ on the cross. Christ's redeeming work is continued by the Holy Spirit. His victory is therefore an eternal victory, present as well as past. Christ *for* us and Christ *in* us are two aspects of the same work. This means that the atonement is both objective and subjective.

The manhood of Christ is significant, for it is in Christ as a man that God carries out his work of deliverance.

The classic view is characterized by a moral dualism in which good triumphs over evil. John Chrysostom claimed that "the devil was overcome by that through which he had power," the weapon of "death" through which "Christ smote him." "What a great blessing death has wrought. . . . It is no longer terrible, but it has been trodden underfoot; it has been despised."[14] Luther portrayed the devil as an unwitting instrument in the hands of God:

> God promotes and completes His work by means of an alien deed, and by His wonderful wisdom He compels the devil to work through death nothing else than life, so that in this way, while he acts most of all against the work of God, he acts for the work of God and against his own work with his own deed. For thus he worked death in Christ, but Christ completely swallowed up death in Himself through the immortality of His divinity and rose again in glory.[15]

The classic view also reappeared in Barth. For him the heart of Christ's atonement is neither the punishment of sin nor the satisfaction or placating of the wrath of God but the overcoming of sin and the chaos, the victory of grace over human sin.[16] While the deepest meaning of the cross is the victory over the nothingness or chaos, Barth still made a place for expiation and satisfaction. Yet he did not see God's forgiveness as conditional upon a prior satisfaction for the hurt done to his glory (as in Anselm) but maintained that this forgiveness itself satisfied the demands of his righteousness.[17]

What Aulén refers to as the Latin view also has deep roots in church tradition. Here legal and cultic metaphors abound. A sacrifice for sin must be offered in order to satisfy the demands of God's righteousness. This sacrifice, as Anselm stressed, must come from the side of humanity, but at the same time it must be acceptable by a holy God.[18] Christ's sacrifice meets these conditions, for it is offered by Jesus as a perfectly righteous man. The union with the divine nature gives the perfect sacrifice infinite value. In the classic view God is the reconciled and the reconciler. In the Latin view God is the reconciled and the human agent the reconciler. In the classic view the idea of the atonement is inseparable from the incarnation. This is not so in the Latin view, which holds that God is not the direct agent in the atoning work. Aulén is probably right in his contention that the God of the Latin view is distant. There is no direct contact between God and humanity except in Jesus Christ. Mortals have nothing to do with the act of satisfaction except that Christ is our representative. While the payment is primarily the work of Christ's human nature, this work gains increased meritorious value by virtue of the union of the human and divine natures. This theory was given systematic explication by Anselm (c. 1033-1109), but it goes back to the Latin fathers, including Tertullian, who held that satisfaction must be made to the justice of God before he could be persuaded to grant us his forgiveness.[19]

The Latin or juridical theory was amplified and developed by Thomas Aquinas. Thomas taught explicitly that the human nature of Christ makes the offering; yet because he is God the merit of his work is not only sufficient but superabundant. Christ's work of satisfaction includes the endurance of punishment on our behalf. This idea of Christ undergoing vicarious punishment is also found in Anselm, though not in his *Cur Deus Homo*. Whereas Anselm tended to conceive of the atonement as basically an objective act, Thomas made a place for the subjective dimension as well: the remission of sins involves not only the pardon of sin but also its expulsion through the infusion of Christ's righteousness. Whereas Anselm taught that satisfaction to God is an absolute necessity for humanity's salvation, Thomas held that God could have saved us in some other way without violating his justice. Moreover, Thomas associated merit with the whole life of Christ, not just with his death.

A synthesis of the Latin and classic views is to be found in the Protestant Reformers. In Luther Christ suffered not for his own sake or for the sake of divine justice but for the sake of a lost humanity. Therefore Christ abrogated the law even while fulfilling it. It seems that for Luther Christ suffered and satisfied the wrath of God as Representative Man, but he conquered the powers as the Son of God.

Calvin subordinated satisfaction to the theme of election. The satisfaction of Christ on the cross is not the meritorious cause of our salvation but only the instrumental cause in carrying out the purpose of redemption. Calvin ascribed the origin of Christ's merits not to Jesus as man but to the decree and ordinance of God, which is their cause. He claimed that "Jesus Christ was unable to merit anything but by God's good pleasure."[20] According to François Wendel, Calvin seemed to deprive the obedience and passion of Christ of any value independent of the divine will.[21] In line with the classic view Calvin held that God takes the initiative in our salvation and carries through. Christ was the mediator even before his manifestation in the flesh. He invaded this world held in captivity by Satan through his conception by the Virgin Mary, and he conquered the powers through his death on the cross and his resurrection. He is now at work in restoring the world to its original purpose through the power of his Word in unity with the Spirit.[22]

In addition to the *Christus Victor* motif, we find the theme of penal redemption in Reformation theology and even more so in Protestant orthodoxy. Franz Burmann typifies the legalistic tenor of orthodoxy: "The effect of the satisfaction offered by Christ to the Father for the elect . . . is on the one hand the expiation of the elect and the reconciliation of God to them, and on the other hand the merit which Christ has acquired for himself, in virtue of which on the basis of his eternal pact with the Father he can demand of Him the pardon of the elect."[23] Francis Turretin conceived of God basically as creditor, judge and ruler. This tradition is continued in A. A. Hodge, who maintained that "it was necessary that Christ should expiate sin by his death, to the end that God might be justified and the justifier of him that believeth in Jesus; . . . that is, to enable God to pardon the sinner without violating his own essential righteousness."[24] In the classic theory, to the contrary, the atonement represents not an example of rational justice that expresses God's calculation but instead the mystery of his unfathomable love. The atonement is accomplished not by strict fulfillment of the demands of justice but in spite of them.

Where Protestant orthodoxy made an advance over the Reformation is its contention that the life of Christ as a whole atones for our sin and not simply his death on the cross. This idea is also to be found among various church fathers (esp. Irenaeus). In a manner unlike Anselm Protestant orthodoxy held that both natures of Christ participate in the atoning sacrifice, but it is still made from humanity's side and it is still seen basically as a human sacrifice, though having divine significance and efficacy.[25]

Whereas the classic and Latin theories focus on the objective character of the atonement,[26] the moral influence theory places the accent on the subjective response of an awakened humanity. The atonement is exemplary rather than propitiatory or expiatory. It is a dramatic testimony to the power of suffering love, that good triumphs through suffering. The cross of Christ is an unsurpassable demonstration of God's love.

In this perspective Christ is our pattern for life. He is the embodiment of divine love. It is through our conversion and obedience to the teachings of Christ that we achieve reconciliation. The difference between Christ and other human beings is one of degree, not kind. The moral influence theory has a venerable tradition in the church. Both Clement of Rome and Justin Martyr emphasized Christ as teacher and example. For Justin the primary purpose of the incarnation was didactic.

In the medieval period Peter Abelard (d. 1142) held that the cross is a supreme demonstration of the love of God, which would kindle a similar love in our hearts. Our reconciliation with God rests upon whether we have the love that we see in Jesus.[27] For Abelard the compassion of God is the motivating force that enables us to live out the imperatives of our faith. Jesus was a compelling moral teacher who "in all that he did in the flesh . . . had the intention of our instruction."[28] Jesus did in a higher degree what Socrates and Plato had done before him.

The doctrine of substitutionary atonement was also countermanded by Laelius Socinus and Faustus Socinus (sixteenth century), who regarded

Christ's death as a shining example of the obedience that every Christian should manifest. Socinianism reflected the spirit of the Renaissance, though it also appealed to Scripture, albeit Scripture interpreted by reason. Socinian views on christology gained ready acceptance in the Enlightenment of the eighteenth century.

Protestant theologians in the modern period who espouse the moral influence theory of the atonement include Albrecht Ritschl, Horace Bushnell, Walter Rauschenbusch, F. D. Maurice, Hastings Rashdall and Kirby Page. Among moderns the atonement signifies a new attitude to the world characterized by inner assurance, peace of mind, harmony and self-fulfillment.

For Ritschl Jesus was the bearer of a religio-ethical ideal. His sacrifice was one of obedience, not a penal sacrifice. Jesus makes justification accessible to the human creation by revealing it. Justification is effective only in reconciliation, which is a human work. In this theology reconciliation is the realized ideal of human life.[29]

Rauschenbusch's theology was similar, though it was more oriented toward the reshaping of society. In his view "Jesus set love into the center of the spiritual universe, and all life is illuminated from that center."[30] From Jesus we derive spiritual freedom and an awakened social consciousness. Jesus initiated the kingdom of God, and we continue in his steps. Rauschenbusch saw the death of Christ as a potent reminder of the depth of human sin and a supreme revelation of the power of love. The function of the atonement is to assimilate us to the mind of Christ. "We can either be saved by non-ethical sacramental methods, or by absorbing the moral character of Jesus into our own character."[31] The social gospel "is based on the belief that love is the only true working principle of human society."[32]

Another subjective approach to the atonement is the mystical theory, which sees the work of Christ as primarily the inward work of personal renewal. Salvation involves both God's identification with humanity in its misery and the elevation of humanity to God. The object of God's condescension is to bring us into mystical contact with

Christ and to show us the way to union with God. Christ entered the world as a transforming leaven, and its resulting transformation constitutes his redemption. By being assimilated to Christ we will gain incorruptibility and salvation. Simeon the New Theologian (d. 1022) declared, "When the Christian receives the grace of the Holy Spirit and thus becomes a partaker of the Divine Nature in our Lord Jesus Christ, he is transformed and changed by His power into a quasi-divine condition."[33] For Dionysius the Pseudo-Areopagite (c. 500) Jesus is the chief symbol of the transcendent reality of the union of humanity with God through mystical ascent. Through Jesus, who reveals the eternal divine-human unity, we ascend to the Godhead. In the mystical theory the role of Jesus is to reveal the presence of God latent within all mortals and to communicate the knowledge of salvation. Jesus is the prototype of divinity that lies within the realm of possibility for all mortals. He is the supreme embodiment of the inner light, which all people can discover and cultivate.

The mystical theory was prominent among the church fathers (Clement of Alexandria, Athanasius, Irenaeus) as well as the great Christian mystics in the late medieval and early modern periods (Meister Eckhart, Bonaventure, John Tauler, Richard Rolle, Bernard of Clairvaux, John of the Cross). In the age of the Reformation it was conspicuous in Andreas Osiander, who saw the motive of the incarnation as the union of God and humanity. It was also a cardinal theme in William Law (d. 1761), who claimed that all mortals possess the seed of divinity within them.[34] By being joined to Christ they allow the seed of divinity to burst forth into life. For Law it is Christ born in us who redeems us, not Christ given for us on the cross as a vicarious, substitutionary sacrifice for sin.[35]

In the nineteenth century the mystical note is strikingly apparent in the theology of Friedrich Schleiermacher, who held that we are justified by the power of the indwelling Christ. Christ is the pattern for the Christian, but a pattern with power. Salvation is the realization of God-consciousness within us when we confront Christ. Jesus is not a sin-bearer but a mediator of God-consciousness.

Closer to our time is the eminent Catholic thinker Karl Rahner (b. 1904), who sought to combine mystical themes with Catholic orthodoxy. He affirmed the Anselmian idea of satisfaction but interpreted salvation as primarily existential healing and fulfillment of life. He spoke of the "divinization" and "transfiguration" of humankind as one of the principal purposes of the incarnation.

Mystical motifs can also be discerned in the Anabaptist theologian Eberhard Arnold (d. 1935), founder of the Bruderhof, a Christian communal society. He believed that the relationship "between the divine and the human" is present in every person, but in Jesus "this relationship attained such a unique and decisive power" that early Christians were compelled to recognize him as "the highest type of man" as well as "the highest revelation of God." Salvation is deliverance from the prison of self-isolation to loving participation in "the all-embracing life power of God's unity," realized preeminently in Jesus Christ.[36]

The governmental theory advanced by Hugo Grotius in the seventeenth century is also mainly subjective, though it contains objective elements. Grotius sought a middle way between Calvinism and Socinianism. In this view God is moral ruler and sin is an offense against God's law. God may pardon if he chooses, but if he pardoned in too facile a manner his law would be brought into contempt. The sacrifice of Christ is a divine tribute to offended law, not a payment to God for human sin. The penalty was not executed on Christ, but Christ powerfully revealed God's antipathy to sin. He suffered as an example of punishment to counteract the evil effects of sin in a moral universe. Grotius attached principal importance to the moral impression that the death of Christ was intended to produce. The aim of Christ's suffering was not to satisfy divine justice but to deter mortals from future offenses against God's law. The ground of our justification is faith *and* evangelical obedience. The death of Christ does not make us righteous but makes it possible for us to become righteous. In the nineteenth century a prominent American Arminian theologian, John Miley, presented a credible case for the governmental theory.[37]

Finally we need to consider the theory of vicarious repentance or vicarious identification, also known as the representative theory. This theory, which contains both objective and subjective elements, is associated with J. McLeod Campbell, Vincent Taylor, Robert Campbell Moberly and Malcolm Furness. It is also found in a modified form in P. T. Forsyth and Barth. Here the cross is viewed as a symbol of God's anguish and sorrow over sin, not as a payment for sin. Vicarious identification is favored over substitutionary expiation and penal redemption. For J. McLeod Campbell and Vincent Taylor, what Christ offers is a sacrifice of penitence, thereby showing his solidarity with the human race. His sufferings were not penal but moral and spiritual. They satisfy the moral claims of the universe rather than the demands of an objective law. They effect a moral satisfaction rather than a legal satisfaction. Interestingly Barth at one place also spoke of Jesus giving the perfect penitence and of Jesus' sacrifice as one of obedience.[38]

This view assumes a different slant in P. T. Forsyth, who argued that the ground of our forgiveness is not our confession of sin or even Christ's confession of our sin but "His agonized confession of God's holiness, and its absorbing effect on us."[39] Showing an affinity to the older view Forsyth declared that "the blood of Christ stands not simply for the sting of sin on God but the scourge of God on sin, not simply for God's sorrow over sin but for God's wrath on sin."[40] Christ did not suffer the pains of hell that the human race deserved, but he suffered vicariously for us and with us so that we might be restored to God's favor by repentance and obedience. He tasted of the depth of our guilt by "the moral sympathy possible only to the holy."[41] In criticism of the traditional view Forsyth contended that satisfaction is offered not to a distributive justice, not to a legal claim, but to a holy person. "It is an offering, primarily, not of pity but of sanctity, and neither by God to man nor by man to God, but by God to God, the self-sacrifice of the perfectly holy Son to the perfect holiness of the Father."[42]

While there is truth in all the above theories of the atonement, I believe that the biblical note is most evident in the classic and Latin views. The vicarious, substitutionary atonement is fully affirmed only in the classic and Latin theories, though some of those associated with the theory of vicarious repentance also try to incorporate a substitutionary theme. The idea of divine pardon for sin is found in all the theories under discussion, but unconditional pardon is especially prominent in the classic view.

The atonement, of course, involves much more than divine forgiveness. It entails liberation, satisfaction, expiation and propitiation. The sacrifice of Christ on the cross effects not only pardon for sin but release from the power of sin. It involves not only the propitiation of God but also the liberation of the sinner. It removes not simply the sense of guilt but the very stain of guilt. The theme of reconciliation is found in the so-called subjective theories of the atonement, but they fail to do justice to expiation, satisfaction and propitiation.

The cross reveals not only the suffering of Jesus but also the suffering of God in the person of his Son. God has taken pity on our sad condition and has decisively acted to save us. But before the cross in history there was a cross in the heart of God (cf. Rev 13:8). God vicariously identifies with our pain and misery, but he does so voluntarily. He suffers not by necessity or compulsion but in his sovereign freedom.

The atonement is made by Jesus Christ as the God-Man who turns away God's wrath because he embodies God's righteousness and love. It should be understood as both a royal victory and a priestly sacrifice. In the cross both God's holiness and mercy are made manifest. Aulén has done the Christian world a signal service by recapturing the vision of the church fathers in describing the atonement as God's act of deliverance in Jesus Christ. Yet he did not do justice to the concepts of penal redemption and satisfaction, which are certainly found in Luther, Calvin and Barth. The classic view as he has delineated it needs to be united with certain aspects of the Latin view particularly as found in Thomas Aquinas and Calvin. Aulén does not sufficiently consider that the agent of our redemption is the God-Man, even though it is begun and carried through by God.

While Aulén and his colleague Anders Nygren[43] tended to minimize the idea of the satisfaction of the law of God and the propitiation of the wrath and holiness of God, they rightly rejected a legalistic view of the atonement that reduces the sacrifice of Christ to a payment that fulfills the requirements of law. A more biblical view would see both God's holiness and God's love as the ground of the atonement. Today we are prone to underplay the demands of God's holiness and depict God as exhaustively love. Forsyth rightly saw that it is not only God's love that sin has injured but also his holy law.[44] I heartily concur with A. E. Garvie: "It is *love* that wills redemption and reconciliation, while it is *holiness* that requires the means towards this end."[45]

The wrath of God is a subordinate reality to both God's holiness and God's love. It can be defined as the immediate and severe reaction of God's holiness to human sin. Although wrath is not in the essence of God, it still must be taken seriously. The far more overwhelming reality is the love of God. Yet this is a love informed by God's holiness, just as his holiness is informed by his love. So we may therefore speak of a holy love that characterizes the inner nature of God.[46] For the liberal theologian Albrecht Ritschl, justification is nothing more than an act of forgiveness bestowed on sinful humanity. It is not tied to a sacrifice for sin that meets the requirements of God's holy law. For Forsyth the atonement is an act of God to satisfy his holiness before it is a forgiveness to sinful humanity.

Christ as Our Substitute
Evangelical theology affirms the vicarious, substitutionary atonement of Jesus Christ. It does not claim that this theory does justice to all aspects of Christ's atoning work, but it does see substitution as the heart of the atonement. The crucial point is that Jesus suffers in our stead, and he also conquers in our stead. Christ is our representative: he represents God to humanity and humanity to God.

Jesus Christ is prophet, priest and king. As prophet he fulfills the law as well as heralds the gospel, the higher righteousness of the kingdom. As priest he makes a once-for-all sacrifice, the offering for sin. He himself is this offering, this sacrifice, this propitiation. He is the one who reconciles the sinful human race to God. He is both priest and victim. At the same time, he was the mediator of our redemption even before the incarnation. And his priestly ministry continues even after his resurrection (cf. Ps 110:4). As king he conquers the powers of darkness and delivers mortals from their bondage to these powers. His sacrifice is not only an offering for sin but a royal victory over the powers that hold humanity in subjection: sin, death, the devil and hell.

The idea of substitution is pervasive in Scripture. Second Isaiah says regarding the suffering servant: "The Lord has laid on him the iniquity of us all" (53:6). Paul declares, "For our sake he made him to be sin who knew no sin, so that in him we might become the righteousness of God" (2 Cor 5:21); "He is the source of your life in Christ Jesus, whom God made our wisdom, our righteousness and sanctification and redemption" (1 Cor 1:30); "Christ redeemed us from the curse of the law, having become a curse for us" (Gal 3:13). And in the words of 1 Peter: "Christ . . . died for sins once for all, the righteous for the unrighteous, that he might bring us to God" (3:18).

Luther referred to the "happy exchange." Christ's righteousness is imputed to us; our sin is imputed to him. His righteousness covers our sin; our sin is hidden in his righteousness. Our justification is grounded in his sacrifice; his sacrifice is the altar on which our sins are laid.

This evangelical truth was also conspicuous in the Anabaptist theologian Menno Simons (d. 1561):

I pray and desire that you will betake yourself wholly both as to what is inward and what is outward unto Christ Jesus and His merits, believing and confessing that His precious blood alone is your cleansing; His righteousness your piety; His death your life; and His resurrection your justification; for He is the forgiveness of all your sins; His bloody wounds are your reconciliation; and His victorious strength is the staff and consolation of your weakness.[47]

The idea of substitution is qualified in Forsyth and subordinated to the idea of representation. "We are not disposed to speak of substitution so much as of representation. But it is representation by One who creates by His act the Humanity He represents, and does not merely sponsor it."[48] When Forsyth spoke of substitution he mainly had in mind Christ's substitution of his holiness for human sinfulness rather than Christ's carrying the penalty for human sin in his person, though he did not dismiss the concept of penal redemption altogether.[49]

Barth vigorously affirmed substitution but deepened its meaning: "We can be rescued from eternal death and translated into life only by total and unceasing substitution, the substitution which God Himself undertakes on our behalf."[50] "There is an exchange of status between Him and us: His righteousness and holiness are ours, our sin is His; He is lost for us, and we for His sake are saved. By this exchange . . . revelation stands or falls."[51] Barth's peculiar twist to substitution was that he saw Christ becoming "the reprobate man" in our place so that we and the whole world might be elected to salvation in him.

Evangelical theology sees Christ as our present substitute as well as our past sin-bearer. The exchanged life is an ongoing reality and not simply a change in our status before God. It is characterized by the substitution of Christ's humility for our vanity, his courage for our fear, his love for our bitterness, his power for our weakness, his holiness for our sin (J. Hudson Taylor).[52]

Yet Christians are not exempt from suffering. We must take up our cross and follow him (Mt 10:38; 16:24-25). Our cross does not atone for sin, but it is a witness and sign of his atoning sacrifice. Like Augustine, Luther saw Christ's passion as both a "sacrament" and an "example." His sacrifice is a sacrament in that it effectively kills the power of sin. But it is also an example in that we should follow after Christ in suffering, even to the point of dying physically if this is what is required of us.[53]

Liberal theology denies the substitutionary sacrifice of Christ for sin. According to Ritschl, Jesus procured justification for all people by his obedience. His was a sacrifice of obedience, not a penal sacrifice. Jesus is the revelation of God's love to humanity. Jesus is seen basically as a moral ideal rather than a sin-bearer. Donald Baillie tried to make a place for traditional ideas of salvation like sacrifice, expiation and atonement.[54] Yet his theology falls short of affirming vicarious substitution and all that this entails. God carries out the atonement, but God does not need to be reconciled. It is sinful humanity that needs to be reconciled to God. The cross is not the propitiation of an angry God but simply the means by which guilt is annulled. In my view Jesus not only revealed and demonstrated God's costly reconciliation but also paid the penalty that God's justice demands. We are saved not only from personal sin but also from God's judgment.

The drama of the atonement began in the incarnation, even before history (cf. 2 Cor 8:9; Gal 4:4; Phil 2:5-8; Heb 2:17; 5:5-6). I concur with Calvin that Christ was our mediator even before his condescension in human form. Yet his saving work was not accomplished until he became human and suffered and died on the cross. The suffering of his life was also atoning but only in an anticipatory sense (cf. Heb 5:8-9). His atonement was not yet fulfilled until his cross and resurrection. It is not the sacrifices in his life but the sacrifice on Calvary that purchased our redemption. "He . . . has offered one single sacrifice for sins, and then taken his place for ever, at the right hand of God" (Heb 10:12 JB). We are redeemed not by Christ's life, not by his teachings, but by his death (Rom 5:10; Col 1:22; Heb 2:14; 9:15; Mt 20:28; Jn 21:19). "For where a will is involved, the death of the one who made it must be established. For a will takes effect only at death, since it is not in force as long as the one who made it is alive" (Heb 9:16-17). "Without the shedding of blood there is no forgiveness of sins" (Heb 9:22; cf. Rom 5:9).

Yet the cross in and of itself is not enough. Apart from the resurrection of Christ the cross is a catastrophe. He "was put to death for our trespasses and raised for our justification" (Rom 4:25; cf. 6:4). The atonement is a royal victory because of the resurrection. It is in the resurrection that we see the conquest of sin, death and the devil. Luther could attribute the victory of Christ to both the cross and the resurrection. He could say that Christ "rose again to make us righteous and in so doing, He hath overcome the Law, sin, death, hell, and all evils."[55] Yet he could also contend that in the cross Christ "performed His mightiest work and vanquished sin, death, world, hell, devil, and all evil."[56]

Because the guilt of sin has been remitted through Christ's atoning work, the Christian no longer suffers penalties for sin but only disciplines. Our suffering effects a change in our character (cf. Rom 5:3-4), but it does not make reparation for sin. The debts of our sin have already been fully paid in Jesus Christ. God allows sin to afflict us in order to remind us of how much we owe to Christ and in order to equip us to carry the good news of Christ to the world.

The Two Poles of the Atonement

The atonement is an objective sacrifice that reverberates throughout history in the lives of those who trust in this sacrifice for their redemption. It includes both God's atoning work for us in the life history of Jesus Christ and the faith of the human subject in this work.

The objectivity of the atonement is clearly affirmed in the New Testament. Christ does not simply offer reconciliation and redemption, but he also accomplishes what he sets out to do (cf. Jn 17:4; Rom 5:6, 8; 1 Cor 1:30; 2 Cor 5:19). Christ not only died for all but in Christ all died (2 Cor 5:14). Emil Brunner trenchantly observed: "His death on the Cross is not only a parabolic suggestion of the divine reconciliation, *it is* this reconciliation, its completion, its reality."[57]

Yet we must appropriate what Christ has done for us in faith. It is not enough to see Christ from afar, but "the morning star" must rise in our hearts (2 Pet 1:19). His reconciliation needs to be fulfilled in the experience of redemption made possible by the Holy Spirit. God put forward the redemption in Christ "as an expiation by his blood, to be received by faith" (Rom 3:25). Paul declares, "In Christ Jesus you are all sons of God, through faith" (Gal 3:26). The gospel "is the power of God for salvation to every one who has faith" (Rom 1:16). According to Brunner, "It is only in this subjective experience, in faith, that the Atonement becomes real. But this subjective experience is completely objective in character."[58] The Heidelberg Catechism is unequivocal on the necessity for personal faith: "The satisfaction, righteousness and holiness of Christ is my sole righteousness before God," provided that I "accept this and appropriate it for myself through faith" (q. 61).[59]

Salvation is not simply an objective reality but an objective-subjective reality. In one sense Jesus Christ himself is the subjective side. Jesus as our representative appropriates the salvation of God on our behalf. Yet salvation remains incomplete until we ourselves participate in Christ's appropriation. The experience of faith constitutes the subjective side of salvation. The Christian life can also be said to comprise the subjective pole of the atonement. Jesus' life and obedience are the ground of our salvation, but our lives and obedience are the fruit and culmination of Christ's work of salvation. We are not adopted into the kingdom of Christ de facto until we respond to the calling of God. There is no accomplished adoption or realized election apart from personal faith. We are not reconciled in fact until we acknowledge Jesus Christ as reconciler. We are not redeemed in fact until we rise to claim our pardon, until we act and live in the knowledge that we are pardoned. His redemption on the cross is our redemption in fact if we are united to it in faith. Yet it is dangerously misguided to contend that the real salvation is only what happens in us. The real salvation happened in Jesus Christ *for* us and happens *in* us through faith. Our salvation is effected not only through the death of Christ on the cross but also through the application of the benefits of his death by the Spirit of the risen Christ. The descent of God to humanity and humanity's ascent to God through faith and the life of obedience must be held together in paradoxical tension.

Anselm erred by conceiving of the atonement as essentially a transaction between Christ as man and God. Thomas Aquinas criticized

Anselm for this supposed objectivism. Thomas was insistent that "when a sufficient satisfaction has been rendered, liability to punishment is removed . . . though the satisfaction of Christ takes effect in us only in so far as we become one body with Him as members with their head."[60]

Bultmann erred on the subjective side. In his theology the atonement or salvation is wholly or primarily subjective. He rejected the vicarious, substitutionary atonement of Christ on the cross. "What a primitive mythology it is, that a divine Being should become incarnate, and atone for the sins of men through his own blood!"[61] Christ has not merited salvation through his death, but he reveals that salvation is a human possibility. The cross reveals our impotence to liberate ourselves through our own efforts. For Bultmann the cross of Christ is not the accomplishment of salvation but the revelation that salvation is available. Salvation is a redemptive experience in which one comes to self-understanding. Bultmann recognized in his *Jesus Christ and Mythology* that "the facts of redemption constitute the grounds of faith, but only as perceived by faith itself."[62] They have no redemptive significance or efficacy apart from faith. How utterly different was Calvin's understanding that in the death of Christ we have "the complete fulfillment of salvation" and that we "have been born anew" through the resurrection of Christ.[63]

Much closer to Calvin and in open conflict with Bultmann was Barth. For Barth, even more than for Calvin, the atonement is essentially and primarily objective. All people are saved and delivered by virtue of the condescension of Christ and his substitutionary sacrifice on the cross. All are justified, sanctified and called into Christ's kingdom. This signifies a divergence from Calvin as well as a contradiction of existentialism. Calvin was adamant that only those who have faith are included in the electing grace of Jesus Christ. According to Barth we are in Christ whether we believe or not because Jesus Christ represents the whole of humanity. In Christ we are all elected to a glorious destiny. We are claimed for inclusion in the family of God even in the state of our spiritual blindness and ignorance. Faith is an awakening to what has already been accomplished for us rather than the realization of salvation in our lives. Barth can aver that redemption "has happened fully and exclusively in Him, excluding any need for completion."[64] The life of Christ "in all the narrowness of its limits is the theatre of the whole action of loss and salvation."[65] Faith "is simply the confirmation of a change which has already taken place, the change in the whole human situation which took place in the death of Jesus Christ."[66] Faith "is not the event of the redemptive act of God. It can only follow this. It is subsequent and at the deepest possible level subordinate to it."[67] Barth acknowledged a subjective side to the atonement, but this refers to the noetic change in the human person rather than an ontic change, which has occurred exclusively in Jesus Christ. Yet Barth time and again sought to balance some of his extreme statements that can only be described as objectivism with the recognition that the human person must participate in Christ's saving action if he or she is to benefit from it. Barth could say that the atonement is "both a divine act and offer and also an active human participation in it: the unique history of Jesus Christ; but enclosed and exemplified in this the history of many other men of many other ages."[68]

In his discussion of the Holy Spirit Barth made a real place for the subjective pole of salvation. Yet the Holy Spirit does not create a further salvation but brings to light what has already happened to us and all humankind in Jesus Christ. The Holy Spirit makes manifest the reconciliation and redemption in Christ. Faith, which is a gift of the Spirit, entails "not our new creation and regeneration as accomplished in the cross and resurrection of Jesus Christ, but its present manifestation."[69]

My principal criticism of Barth is that he depicted the subjective pole of the atonement as wholly subordinate to the objective pole. It therefore has only epistemological and not ontological or soteriological significance. Barth admitted that the logic of his theology leads to the assertion that the very body of Christ includes and unites all peoples.[70] While Barth acknowledged that the world is not yet redeemed in the sense that all have come to a knowledge of their redemption in Christ, in another sense the world is already redeemed since the spiritual situation of the human race has been irrevocably altered through the condescension and incarnation of Jesus Christ in human history. In his later writings Barth gave more prominence to the subjective dimension of salvation and to the pivotal role of the Holy Spirit, who makes the cross and resurrection of Christ effective in the world.[71]

Abraham Kuyper too veered toward objectivism because of his conviction that the plan of salvation has already been ordained in the counsels of God. He confessed that "justification does not occur when we become conscious of it, but that, on the contrary, our justification was decided from eternity in the holy judgment-seat of our God."[72] For Kuyper the role of the Holy Spirit is to bring us the knowledge of our justification. In this view the cross of Christ becomes an instrument of the eternal decree of God. Despite this objectivistic bent Kuyper also insisted that we are justified the instant we believe. Yet what he had in mind is our coming to the awareness that we already have been justified.

Objectivism comes in various shades. The predestinarian type of objectivism places the emphasis on divine predetermination, as in Augustine, Calvin, Zwingli, Turretin, Kuyper, Cornelius Van Til and Barth. Then there is the sacramental type, which presupposes that salvation is accomplished in external rites of the church, particularly in baptism. We see this strand in Roman Catholicism, Eastern Orthodoxy, Anglo-Catholicism and some forms of high Lutheranism. The covenant theology associated with Reformed Christianity holds that children are justified by virtue of being born into the covenant community. The critics of this view contend that it actually teaches regeneration by procreation. Finally there is the christological objectivism of Barth, which is really a variant of the predestinarian view. Salvation is here equated with the eternal decision of God to elect all of humanity to his kingdom in Jesus Christ.

We must also be wary of subjectivism, which comes primarily in two different forms. First we find the mystical-pietist view that reduces salvation to an inner experience of God or Christ. The existentialist position as seen in Bultmann is a variant of this view. Here it is the act of faith or an existential decision for authenticity that saves. In the ethical-humanistic view we are saved by ethical obedience. The decisive factor is our ethical response to God's saving grace.

The biblical-evangelical view takes into consideration both God's gracious initiative and the need for human decision and obedience. Salvation involves both the objective work of Christ on the cross and the response of faith in a Christian life, made possible by the outpouring of the Holy Spirit. Salvation is a past accomplishment, a present experience and a future hope. The objective-subjective character of Christian salvation is strikingly apparent in Revelation 12:11: "They have conquered him by the blood of the Lamb and by the word of their testimony, for they loved not their lives even unto death."

Limited or Universal Atonement

An ongoing controversy in the church is whether the atoning work of Christ is intended for all humankind or only for a select group. In the Calvinist tradition the idea of particular redemption is very important. For Calvin Christ's sacrifice is *sufficient* for the salvation of all peoples but not *efficient* for their salvation. Calvin acknowledged that God, "by exhibiting to all the gospel and Christ the Mediator, shows that He wishes all men to be saved."[73] Yet he also taught that the ungodly have been created for the specific purpose of perishing.[74] In his system the elect alone are saved, and the reprobate are forsaken by God. God's love is for the elect and his wrath and judgment for the reprobate. Calvin distinguished between the revealed will of God, which is for salvation, and his secret will by which he withholds his saving grace. Here we are confronted by the awesome mystery of double predestination, which tends to create a bifurcation within the very heart of God. Calvin conceded that Christ died for all, but Christ intercedes in heaven only for the elect. Our salvation is not completed until his ascension. His death is offered for all, but it becomes efficacious only by virtue of the ascension.[75]

Calvin's legacy is very pronounced in the history of Reformed theology. The Reformed theologian L. Riissen stated, "Christ died sufficiently for all, but effectually only for the elect."[76] In the words of John Brown of the United Secession Church: "In the sense . . . that Christ died so as to secure salvation, I hold that he died only for the elect."[77] A. A. Hodge declared: "God, eternally anterior to their creation and irrespective of their character, loved the elect, and hated the non-elect, predestinating the first to holiness and happiness, and the other to sin and misery for ever."[78]

The Calvinist position, especially as transmitted through Reformed orthodoxy, stands in palpable conflict with the New Testament witness.[79] Titus 2:11 assures us that "the grace of God has appeared for the salvation of all men." The Pauline writer of 1 Timothy contends that Jesus Christ sacrificed himself "to win freedom for all mankind" (2:6 NEB). Second Peter affirms that "it is not his will for any to be lost, but for all to come to repentance" (3:9 NEB). When John avers that "God so loved the world" (Jn 3:16) he manifestly has in mind not simply the elect (as some hyper-Reformed allege) but the whole human creation.

Probably the dominant segment of the church has held to the universal atonement—that Christ dies for all and desires to lead all into his kingdom. Universal atonement does not necessarily mean universal salvation, but it does imply that all people are the beneficiaries of God's grace in some way or to some degree. John Wesley contended against Calvinistic Puritanism that every person is "a blood-bought soul." Charles Wesley was emphatic that Christ paid the ransom even for those who "will not come to him."[80] Nicholas Ludwig von Zinzendorf argued that the whole world was set free by the sacrifice of Christ. "On the wood of the Cross the world was saved all at once, and whoever is lost loses himself, because he will not receive the Saviour, because he falls again and repeats the fall of Adam."[81] Barth maintained that all people stand under the wrath and love of God, but God's wrath is penultimate whereas his love is ultimate. All people are under the sign of God's gracious election, all are recipients of the promise of Christ's salvation, though they have de facto participation in this salvation only by faith.

With Barth I hold that through the sacrifice of Christ on the cross and his glorious resurrection from the grave the human situation has been irrevocably altered. The powers of sin, death and hell have been decisively vanquished, though they continue to resist the advance of the kingdom of God through the power of the lie. All people, irrespective of their moral and spiritual state, are claimed for the kingdom, but only some respond in faith and obedience. Christ has reconciled and justified the whole human race but in principle *(de jure)*, not in fact *(de facto)* except for those who believe. All are heirs to the kingdom, but not all become members of the church of Christ. The treasure in the field is there for all, but only those benefit who give up everything to attain it (Mt 13:44). The gates of the prison in which we find ourselves are now open, but only those who rise up and walk through these gates to freedom are truly free.

I do not wish to deny the truth in predestination, a doctrine that is integral to the whole of Scripture. Yet predestination must be preached as good news if it is to serve the evangelistic mandate of the church.[82] Predestination in its biblical context is a message of hope, for it simply means that before we respond in faith we are already claimed by God's unconditional grace. Predestination is not something finalized in the past but something realized in the present and consummated in the future. We can resist and deny our predestination, but we cannot permanently thwart the stream of God's irresistible grace.[83] We will ultimately be brought into submission, though not necessarily into salvation. Yet predestination means life even though we may choose death. Predestination does not necessarily eventuate in fellowship with Christ, but it does mean that every person is brought into inescapable relatedness to Christ. Even though incorrigible sinners may find themselves in hell, outside the holy city, they are not outside the compass of God's love and protection.[84] The atonement of Christ is universal in its intention and outreach but conditional in the way its efficacy is realized in the lives of God's people. God's election and predestination are realized in a different way for those who spurn the offer of the gospel; yet we can still hope and pray even for these condemned mortals, since we know that they are in the hands of a God whose justice is evenhanded but whose mercy is boundless. I affirm no ultimate dualism (as in Augustinianism and Calvinism) but a duality within an ultimate unity, and this means that the pain of hell itself will be made to serve the glory of heaven.

Appendix D: The Death of God

Since the emergence of Christianity theologians have debated the question of whether God himself really suffered in the person of his Son. Patripassianism contended that since the Father, Son and Spirit are simply modes of the one divine person, the Father himself was therefore crucified on the cross and not just the Son. Against this view the church fathers vigorously affirmed the impassibility of God, which means that God in himself is not subject to pain and discord, since he embodies the perfection of all beatitude. We can speak of the death of Jesus Christ on the cross but not the death of the Father or even of the Logos. By excluding God from the pain of suffering, orthodox theology succumbed to the Greek idea of God as the unmoved mover characterized by imperturbability and insensibility.[85] It was commonly held that Christ suffered in his human nature but not in his divine nature. In the nineteenth century philosophers like Hegel and Nietzsche reintroduced the concept of the death of God, though their understandings were by no means the same. Hegel envisioned the Spirit of God incarnating himself in the whole of history and thereby participating in the pain of death as well as the joy of new life.[86] Nietzsche saw the death of God as the demise of conventional piety in the world come of age and the deepened awareness that human survival depends on the human will alone.[87]

In contemporary theology the idea of divine impassibility has largely been discarded and replaced by the vision of a God who is vulnerable to pain and distress and who is to a high degree dependent on the world. Narrative theologian William Placher argues that in the biblical story God is neither essentially omnipotent nor impassible.[88] A God defined in terms of power is a God who cannot be relied upon because "power provides no guarantee of concern."[89] "Only a God 'weak in power but strong in love' can be strong enough to take on all the world's pain and die on a cross."[90] In process theology (John Cobb, Bernard Meland, Norman Pittenger, Charles Hartshorne, David Griffin, Lewis Ford, Henry Nelson Wieman) God empathizes with our suffering and strives with us for a cosmic perfection in which pain prepares the way for beatitude.[91] God is neither the self-contained Absolute nor the Lord of the universe but "the fellow-sufferer who understands."[92] Jürgen Moltmann, who leans heavily on the panentheism of Hegel, holds that God has not died but God experiences death, and this fact is revealed preeminently in the cross of Christ. What we see in the crucifixion is not the death *of* God but death *in* God.[93]

With Barth I aver that God in himself is impervious to pain and suffering, but God nevertheless wills to enter the world of pain and contingency in order to redeem it.[94] He is not subject to the ravages of sin and the turmoil of finitude, but he makes himself subject to these things so that they may be overcome. He shares in our afflictions and ignominy in the person of Jesus Christ, but he transmutes the pain of death and sin into the joy that exists in the midst of pain. The conflicts on the human plane are resolved in the perfect beatitude and composure of his inner being.

God does not suffer *as* humanity suffers, for his suffering is creative and redemptive, not destructive and corrosive. Yet God suffers *in* humanity, and such suffering reflects the self-abnegation within the inner life of the Trinity, the self-emptying that is the hallmark of trinitarian love. In one sense God's suffering greatly exceeds that of humanity because it is deeper and more extensive. In another sense God's suffering is less intolerable than human suffering because it does not contain the meaninglessness and despair that mar the life of the sinner.

God is affected by human pain and suffering, but he is not thereby diminished because self-sacrificing love is integral to his very nature. In contrast to process theology I hold that God is free to remain above the world of pain and death, but he willingly enters this world out of inexplicable love. Process theology can speak of a primordial nature of God that transcends the world of contingency and relativity, but God in his primordial nature is entirely abstract and therefore deficient. In the biblical view God in his essence is concrete and wholly self-sufficient. God is a personal, luminous being rather than a creative process or life principle within the universe. Moreover, in the process view God does not enter into death but expels all that is death-begetting from his own life.

Those in our era who defend the idea of a finite God are prone to argue that God's knowledge is limited, since the future of history is open, not closed.[95] If human beings are really free, then even God cannot know exactly how they will choose in shaping their own destiny. I continue to affirm the omniscience of God, but this does not mean that God always knows the events of history in the very same way. God has theoretical knowledge of the future but not experiential knowledge. He cannot experience the future before it happens, but he can know theoretically what the future contains. He is omniscient in that he knows the whole future, but he has more than one mode of knowledge. Classical theism reduced the knowledge of God to his intellectual cognition. Process theism confounds the knowledge of God with passing experiences. In the biblical view God comes to experience what he already knows will come to pass through his perfect foresight.

God is not pure actuality *(actus purus)* in the classical sense of excluding all movement and possibility from his inner life. But he is *actus purus* in the sense of a ceaseless overflowing of his goodness and mercy.[96] The summit of perfection is not isolated self-sufficiency and sublime independence from all that is creaturely but outgoing love to the creaturely.

God is the supreme contingency, but at the same time he towers above contingency. He is supremely free—from the fate of history— and supremely bound—to his own nature as love. He is both vulnerable and in control. He alone is the primary cause, but he allows for secondary causes. He realizes his purposes not to the exclusion of human freedom and participation but in conjunction with human efforts. He can enter the world of contingency because he already encompasses contingency in himself.

God foreordains both our creation and our redemption, but he does not redeem us apart from ourselves. He allows us to thwart and resist his greater will for our lives only in order to realize the fullness of his will for us in cooperation with our efforts and strivings. The divine permission serves the divine predetermination. He accomplishes his purposes by entering into our suffering and tasting death in the dying of his Son on the cross. He experiences our travail—not as despairing humanity but as self-giving and triumphant deity.[97] He takes our despair upon himself and thereby allays and conquers it. The nothingness or chaos does not belong to God's kingdom but is radically excluded and dispelled. The death of God signifies not that God ceases to exist but that the forces of darkness and evil cease to present a real threat to God's good creation, by being countermanded and superseded in the sacrifice and resurrection of Jesus Christ.

In the person of Jesus God identifies with our guilt and shame, but vicariously, not univocally. He enters into our history, but he does not empty himself into human history. He remains above history even while he enters into it. He remains God even when he incarnates himself in human flesh. The living God of the Bible is neither finite nor infinite in the sense of being without any limits whatsoever. He is the infinite in the finite—not by necessity but by his free decision to be in solidarity with us.

The God who incarnated himself in Jesus Christ and thereby entered human history is the God who makes himself passible even while he remains in his own inner life impassible. God's knowledge is not curtailed when we say that he is still open to new experiences.[98] God is not an Eternal Now who knows all things simultaneously but a living God who experiences the world ever anew.[99] He knows what will happen and how we will respond. But he does not experience the event until it occurs. His knowledge is not ever expanding (as in the process view) but is continuously operative. He realizes in fact what he already knows in principle. He does not give up his power when he becomes human in Jesus Christ, but he chooses to exercise his power in a new way—a way that confounds the wisdom of the philosophers as well as challenges the presumption of those who would be his followers.

The death of God in the Christian sense means God *with* us and *for* us. God did not cease to be God when he went to the cross in the person of Jesus; on the contrary, he demonstrated his deity in a way that only people under the cross can appreciate and understand. The death of God does not remove God from our lives but confirms his inescapable presence in our lives. The death of God means God triumphant over sin and death, and faith in this God as the key to overcoming the power of sin in our own lives.

·SEVEN·

SALVATION IN EVANGELICAL PROTESTANTISM

For all alike have sinned, and are deprived of the divine glory;
and all are justified by God's free grace alone.
ROMANS 3:23-4 REB

For Christ also died for sins once for all, the righteous for the
unrighteous, that he might bring us to God.
1 PETER 3:18

The blood of Christ stands not simply for the sting of sin on God
but the scourge of God on sin, not simply for God's sorrow
over sin but for God's wrath on sin.
P. T. FORSYTH

Justification . . . is the heart of the gospel and unique to
Christianity. No other system, ideology or religion proclaims a
free forgiveness and new life to those who
have done nothing to deserve it.
JOHN R. W. STOTT

In delineating the doctrine of salvation in evangelical
Protestantism, I am fully aware of the wide diversity of views on
this subject, reflecting the myriad of Protestant denominations
that have divided over this and other issues. It can nevertheless be
shown that those denominations that trace their heritage to the
Protestant Reformation of the sixteenth century generally share a

common understanding of how the salvation of fallen humanity is accomplished, stressing the cruciality of the cross, the priority of grace and the indispensability of personal faith. Differences begin to emerge when a greater role is assigned human freedom and responsibility than either the Bible or the Reformation allows. Many Protestants, especially those influenced by the Enlightenment, take issue with the Reformation doctrine of total depravity, which regards fallen humanity as totally unable to help itself morally or spiritually.

Evangelical theology has a marked predilection for biblical words in articulating the dogmas of faith. It generally tries to stay clear of extrabiblical words like *deification* (popular among the church fathers) and *satisfaction* (anchored in early Christian tradition and becoming determinative in medieval thought),[1] even though these words may resonate with certain themes in Scripture. It has even more difficulty with unbiblical words like *amorization* and *christification* (both from Teilhard de Chardin). At the same time, it recognizes that in some contexts nonbiblical or extrabiblical words may be appropriate, especially if they have an enduring basis in sacred tradition. Its reservations with regard to *deification* and *divinization* are based on its determination to maintain the infinite qualitative difference between God and the human creation.[2]

Biblical Christianity defines salvation first of all as redemption— being bought back or delivered from the slavery of sin. Closely related are expiation, in which our sins are blotted out, and propitiation, in which the holy wrath of God against sin is turned away. Atonement is making reparation for sin, which occurred sufficiently and once for all times in the sacrificial life and death of Jesus Christ. Reconciliation is the act by which God overcomes the alienation that sin creates between the Creator and the creature. Regeneration is the inward cleansing that is done by the Holy Spirit as he applies the fruits of Christ's redemption to the sinner. Justification is the act by which God imputes the perfect righteousness of Christ to the one who believes. Sanctification is the act by which God separates his people from the pollution of the world and remolds them in the image of Christ. Vocation or calling is the grace that equips the Christian for service in the world. Adoption is the privilege of being made a son or daughter in the family of God. Election and predestination refer to God's prior act of love that shapes human decision and commitment. Glorification is the final transformation of the sinner by the glory of God so that he or she becomes transparent to this glory. It is roughly equivalent to the vision of God in which we enter into direct fellowship with our Creator and Redeemer.

In most theologies one or other of these facets of salvation takes on special significance. Luther made justification central, virtually equating salvation with justification. While acknowledging the priority of justification, Calvin gave more attention to regeneration and sanctification. The later Calvin and Calvinism assigned priority to divine predestination and election. John Wesley focused on sanctification, which he described as "a still higher salvation."[3] Karl Barth made reconciliation the comprehensive principle and saw justification, sanctification and calling as aspects of reconciliation.[4] The mystical heritage of the church (which has had considerable impact on both Roman Catholicism and Eastern Orthodoxy) stresses the importance of inward purification, leading finally to the transforming vision of God. In the Anabaptist tradition discipleship rather than justification or sanctification is the key element in Christian identity.[5]

Justification

There is little doubt that in the magisterial Reformation justification is not the preliminary thing but the ultimate thing. It is the act by which God declares the sinner righteous by virtue of faith in the perfect holiness of Jesus Christ, thereby restoring the sinner to the positive favor of God. Justification includes both the remission of sins and the liberation of the human will from bondage to sin. While its primary meaning is forensic or legal (and this is especially evident in the Pauline epistles),[6] it also contains a mystical meaning in which righteousness is implanted in us as a life-giving principle.[7] We are not only declared righteous but made righteous; whereas the former is complete the latter is incomplete. Inwardly we still remain sinners, for our regeneration is only begun; but outwardly in the sight of God we are fully righteous because our sins are covered by the perfect righteousness of Christ. The entire Christian life must be one of repentance, since we are summoned to fight against the sin within and around us, but we are assured of victory because of the presence and power of the Holy Spirit. Faith is the sole means by which we apprehend and receive the righteousness of Christ; love is the means by which we demonstrate and manifest this righteousness. Faith is not a virtue that merits God's favor but an empty vessel that receives what is produced wholly by God. Faith does not have to be formed by love in order to be effective, but faith is always accompanied by love if it is genuine faith.

The point the Reformers were trying to make was that our salvation is due solely to the free, unmerited grace of God made concrete and effective in history in the person and work of Jesus Christ. We are justified by faith alone *(sola fide)* and grace alone *(sola gratia),* since Christ alone accomplishes our salvation *(solus Christus),* which is acknowledged by faith through the power that comes from the Spirit of God. Not only faith but the very condition to receive faith is a work of the Spirit of God within us.

Our redemption is wrought wholly by Christ—without our cooperation and aid. But we need to make experiential contact with this redemption if it is to be effective in our lives. It is not enough to believe in Christ: we also need to be engrafted into his righteousness. Justification is inseparable from regeneration, which might be called the subjective pole of justification. Those whom God forgives he also makes alive in the power of his Spirit. Justification is both a forensic judgment and a dynamic action. It embraces not only the decree of God in Christ but also the work of the Spirit, who communicates this decree to the people of God. Calvin rightly maintained that the saving work of Christ constitutes a twofold blessing: grace *for* us and grace *in* us.[8] Yet with Luther he insisted that our inward renewal by the Spirit is not the precondition for justification but its effect and consequence. We are justified not on the ground of our faith or works but on the ground of God's free, unmerited mercy revealed in Jesus Christ. We do not play a positive role in procuring our salvation, but we are made covenant partners by the Spirit of God in manifesting and celebrating this salvation.

The gulf between Reformation theology and Roman Catholic theology revolves around this issue: Is our salvation a cooperative endeavor in which we are assisted by grace in preparing the way for justification, or is our salvation an act accomplished by Christ alone *(solus Christus)* whose benefits are then applied to us by the Spirit?[9] In Catholic theology defined at the Council of Trent (1545-63) justification becomes a lifelong process of inward purification by which we make progress toward Christian perfection with the assistance of the church, Mary and the whole company of the saints. In the Roman view we are justified only in proportion as and insofar as we are morally renewed. The Catholic position as well as that of the Eastern church confounds justification and sanctification whereas the Reformed view sharply distinguishes them but regards them as inseparable.[10] In Reformed theology grace is not primarily an infused energy that enables us to climb the mystical ladder to heaven but the free, unmerited favor of Christ by which he accepts us even though we are basically unacceptable in the light of the standard of his law. Grace is power as well as personal favor, but it is the latter before it is the former. It is the power, moreover, that wholly converts us, changes us into new creatures rather than simply assists us in the struggle for righteousness. In the Catholic view grace builds upon nature; in the Reformed view grace brings us a new nature.

Justification in evangelical and Reformed theology is basically an event, not a process. It is an event in which God declares us righteous because of the perfect sacrifice of Jesus Christ on the cross and his glorious resurrection from the grave. Yet it is not simply the event that initiates the process of salvation: it is the event on which our salvation is forever based. Justification is not merely a past event that inaugurates the process of sanctification; it is the enduring event that we must constantly draw upon as we live out the Christian life. Because we remain sinners, even as Christians, we need to repent again and again and throw ourselves continually on God's mercy. When the Westminster divine Samuel Rutherford was reminded of his achievements at his death, he replied, "I disclaim all. The port I would be in at is redemption and salvation through his Blood."[11]

In his groundbreaking work *Justification* Hans Küng tries to overcome the cleavage between Reformation Protestantism and Roman Catholicism, a cleavage that he attributes in large measure to a misunderstanding in terminology.[12] Both Catholic and Protestant parties in this dispute were using the same terms but with different meanings, thus creating an insuperable obstacle to agreement and reconciliation. Küng accepts the Protestant argument that justification in the New Testament basically has a declarative or forensic thrust, but he holds that it has a creative dimension as well. The Catholic side would be willing to accept that justifying righteousness is imputed to us by God's grace, but they insist that justification is not wholly extrinsic to the sinner: it must enter into us and transform us. Evangelical Protestantism avers that the ground of justification is extrinsic, but its effects are intrinsic. Küng is willing to assert *sola fide,* but he insists that justifying faith has the seed of love within it and therefore has something positive to offer.[13] Both Reformation and Barthian theology are adamant that faith makes no positive contribution to the gaining of salvation: it is simply the instrument that the Spirit uses to bring Christ and all of his saving benefits into our lives.

Sanctification

Sanctification is the act by which God separates his people from the world of sin and implants within them a yearning for holiness. It involves being born from above and continuous conversion as the

Spirit works within us, purifying us and making us fit for heaven. Spiritual growth follows spiritual rebirth, though this growth does not take us beyond justification but roots us more deeply in it.

Sanctification is inseparable from justification; yet these are not parallel or identical but complementary terms.[14] Those whom God justifies he also sanctifies. But his justification is based not on our personal holiness, which is always imperfect and rudimentary, but on Christ's alien righteousness, which is perfect and complete. In justification we are delivered from the guilt of sin, in sanctification from the power and pollution of sin. Justification indicates primarily a change in status, sanctification a change in being. Justification is complete whereas sanctification is incomplete. Justification is imputed righteousness; sanctification is imparted righteousness.

Like justification, sanctification is both objective and subjective, a historical reality as well as an inward experience. It is objective because Christ has been made our sanctification as well as our justification (1 Cor 1:30). It is subjective because the Holy Spirit works within us what has already been imputed to us. We are justified by faith and sanctified by love. But even as faith is a gift of God, so love is also a gift, since this kind of love (agape) is not an element within our created human nature. But just as faith is also a task calling for repentance and obedience, so love, too, is a task. Through the power of the Holy Spirit we can practice a love that is beyond natural human capacity—the self-sacrificing love of the cross.

While we are active in our sanctification, we do not deserve any credit because it is God who works sanctity within us (2 Cor 3:5; Phil 2:12-13). Luther rightly perceived the necessary correlation between passive sanctity and active holiness.[15] The Holy Spirit works sanctity within us and thereby enables us to practice holy living in the world. We cannot sanctify ourselves, but we can demonstrate and manifest our sanctification in lives of self-giving service. We can also prepare ourselves to receive the gift of the Holy Spirit that enables us to walk the way of the cross. We cannot procure our salvation, but we can set up signs and parables of a salvation already accomplished—for us and for the whole world (Barth).

Justification and sanctification have a relationship of interdependence rather than subordination. Justification is not a preliminary work of grace (as in some strands of Arminianism) but a continuing work of grace that keeps us in faith until the end. Sanctification is not simply a consequence or effect of justification but the crown and goal of justification. It is not a second work of grace that follows justification but the obverse side of the one grace that pardons us and revivifies us. Justification is the enduring foundation; sanctification is the goal. Sin is remitted in justification; it is being overcome in sanctification; it is eliminated in glorification.

The life of sanctification is one of unceasing struggle against sin, death and the devil. Because we remain sinners though we are declared to be saints, we need to die daily to the demands of self and take up the cross daily and follow Christ. Paul enjoins those who are already Christians: "Put off your old nature which belongs to your former manner of life and is corrupt through deceitful lusts, and be renewed in the spirit of your minds, and put on the new nature, created after the likeness of God in true righteousness and holiness" (Eph 4:22-24).

Luther described the Christian as paradoxically "always righteous and sinful at the same time" *(simul iustus et peccator)*. We are sinful because an inclination to sin remains within us even after conversion, though it is counteracted by grace. We are righteous because we are covered by the perfect righteousness of Jesus Christ through faith. Luther's portrayal of the Christian's spiritual state is helpful, but it needs to be united with Calvin's perception that we can make real progress in the Christian life, that grace is victorious over sin as well as being an ever present remedy for sin. Grace not only forgives us our sin but drives sin out of our lives. We are not delivered from the very presence of sin (that will come in glorification), but we are delivered from bondage to sin. We are freed from sin and for righteousness. As

Christians we now have sin behind us and righteousness before us (Barth).

Luther and Lutheranism sometimes create the impression that living the Christian life means continually beginning all over again in repentance and faith, resolving ever again to die to self and live for Christ.[16] Calvin, Wesley and the Pietists rightly perceived that we can grow in sanctification, even though we can never arrive at an absolute perfection in which we are no longer vulnerable to sin. We should never speak of a sinless perfection attainable in this life (as do some in the wider Wesleyan movment), but we can hold up the possibility of perfect love, love that comes from God and takes us into itself, though this is something momentary, something that has to be received again and again. We are given a foretaste of the glory that lies ahead (2 Cor 1:22; Eph 1:13-14), but this glory always remains a goal, never a possession. The great saints of the church almost unanimously testify that the deeper we grow in the faith the more conscious we are of our imperfections and the more dependent we become on God's grace and mercy.

In sanctification we go forward and upward, but we also fall backward, not once but many times. Growth in grace makes us more vulnerable to the sin of pride, and this is why the great saints underscored the constant need for humility in the Christian life. Christian perfection does not mean achieving moral rectitude but persevering in faith, remaining true to the gospel even in the midst of affliction and temptation. We are able to endure and overcome only on the basis of the forgiveness of sins, which keeps us humble even while it sets us free to be holy as we strive to follow Christ as our Lord and Master.

Only the righteousness of faith justifies us, but the righteousness of life proves the genuineness of our faith (cf. 1 Thess 2:10-12; Phil 1:27; Eph 4:24; 1 Pet 1:15; 1 Tim 6:11; Jas 3:18). The righteousness of life or holy living does not merit the remission of sins because it is always accompanied by unholy thoughts and actions (Is 64:6). Only the righteousness of faith redeems us from sin, but the righteousness of life benefits us by strengthening our resolve to do God's will, by deepening our commitment to kingdom service. It also benefits our neighbor who is oppressed by sin, for it brings that person into contact with agape—the love that binds up wounds and heals afflictions (1 Pet 2:12). The righteousness of faith is invisible, hidden from all sight and natural understanding; the righteousness of life is visible to those around us, though it remains partially hidden from ourselves (cf. Mt 7:16; 12:33; 2 Cor 3:2-3; 1 Tim 5:25).

Continuing Issues

One of the hotly debated issues in the history of theology has been the role of free will in our salvation. Pelagius (fifth century) taught that on our own we can live a virtuous life, though grace is necessary for a true understanding of God's will.[17] The semi-Pelagians acknowledged that we need to be assisted by grace if we are ever to reach our goal, but we can do something for ourselves even before grace reaches us. Augustine contended to the contrary that our natural freedom has been so severely impaired by sin that our will is in bondage until grace breaks into our lives and turns us around. The Augustinian position was basically reaffirmed and deepened by the magisterial Reformation.[18] By contrast, Wesleyanism asserted that we contribute to our salvation on the basis of grace, that grace assists the human will to do the good.

If we wish to remain faithful to both Scripture and the witness of the Reformation, we need to affirm that God alone works salvation for us and in us, though we can receive and respond to this salvation through the power of his Spirit. This is neither monergism (in which God is the sole actor) nor synergism (in which God and the human person are partial causes). We are speaking of a mystery in which God does all but through human effort and decision. Sinful humanity still has a free will, but this free will does not cooperate with grace in achieving salvation. Instead, God's grace liberates our will from its bondage to sin so that we can believe and obey in the power of the Spirit. As sinners we are still free in the things below, but we are not free in the things above. We are not free to dispose ourselves to the good or to come to God. We need to be set free by grace to live a life of holiness, a life pleasing to God. In evangelical Protestantism the natural person is not merely weakened by sin but is dead in sin and therefore must be raised by grace to new life in Christ (cf. Rom 6:13; Eph 2:1-6).[19]

In the Catholic position as developed by Thomas Aquinas we are able to do the good that lies within us but only on the basis of a prior or prevenient grace.[20] Once we do the good we can merit a further increase of grace. For Thomas our free will plays an important role in the transition from nature to grace, but it is always a free will healed and renewed by grace. In Reformation theology there is a discontinuity between nature and grace. Grace is not primarily the infusion of supernatural power (as in the Catholic and Orthodox view) nor the stimulation of our natural powers (the liberal view). Instead it is the invasion of the Holy Spirit, which makes us altogether new creatures. Grace is the Spirit of the living Christ dwelling within us and taking possession of our lives. We are given a new will, new motivations, new goals. Our will is not so much assisted by grace as turned around by grace. Because they are always accompanied by sinful motivations, our works are not meritorious, but Christ's perfect work on the cross is supremely meritorious, and it is this work alone that saves and redeems.

The temptation in evangelical Protestantism is to overlook or downplay the many biblical passages that promise rewards for faithful diligence (cf. Mt 5:12; 6:6, 20; 10:41-42; 16:27; Mk 9:41; Col 3:24). God does reward us if we persevere in the right, but this is out of the bounty of his goodness, not on the basis of any legal claim on our part. God is under no necessity to reward us because our good works fall far short of the perfection his law demands. But if we rest our efforts and hopes in the perfect work of Christ on the cross, God is pleased to give us beyond what we deserve so that others might see the light of the Lord Jesus Christ shining in and through our actions.

We are justified by faith alone, but faith does not remain alone. It takes the form of obedience under the cross and perseverance in the truth. This obedience is a necessary fruit and consequence of our faith, but it is not the ground of our justification. The ground of God's justifying work is the sacrifice of Jesus Christ on Calvary. The means by which he transmits the fruits of this justifying work to our lives is faith. The effect of his justifying work is faith working through love (Gal 5:6).

We can never say that we are coredeemers with Christ in procuring salvation. Nor are Mary and the great saints of the church coredeemers. Christ alone achieves redemption for lost sinners, but he makes us covenant partners in proclaiming the good news of this redemption. He makes us active and busy—not in acquiring salvation through our industry and merits but in celebrating and demonstrating the salvation that is already completed and perfected. We are not agents in bringing about salvation but signs and witnesses of the salvation that he alone accomplished for our sake *(solus Christus)*. Our decision and our obedience are not preconditions for salvation but the outworking of a salvation already extended to us by the gracious hand of God.

Salvation, to be sure, has a subjective as well as an objective pole.[21] It is enacted in history in the life, death and resurrection of Jesus Christ, but its fruits must be applied to our personal histories by the Holy Spirit. This does not mean, however, that Christ simply brings us the possibility of a salvation that is yet to be realized. Christ has truly and really saved us by his atoning work on the cross, but we need to make contact with this work. The human situation is drastically and irrevocably changed by virtue of Christ's atoning death and glorious resurrection. We are saved by Christ de facto as well as de jure, but this is Christ in his inseparable unity with the Holy Spirit, who awakens us to the truth and significance of the cross and resurrection. Christ's saving work reaches its goal in our faith and obedience, but our faith is already presupposed and made practically inevitable by his determination to include us in his family as his sons and daughters. The prison doors have already been opened, but those who lack faith have still to pass through these doors to freedom. We need to claim the salvation that is already assured to us and extended to us. To be sure, in our folly we might choose to remain in the security and darkness of the prison house of sin, but we have the assurance that even if we make our bed in hell Christ is still with us and for us (Ps 139:8; 2 Tim 2:13).

As we have seen, evangelical Protestantism has been divided on whether Christ's atonement is universal or particular.[22] The Calvinist tradition has emphasized particular atonement—that Christ died only for the elect.[23] Luther and Wesley were adamant that Christ died for all, but only those who respond to his atoning work will be saved. Barth argued that not only did Christ die for all but all have already been reconciled to Christ by virtue of his atoning and electing work, which is all-inclusive and unalterable. In the view that I am propounding, Christ died for all, but not all die to self for Christ, and a universal atonement therefore does not mean a final universal salvation. It is interesting to note that Barth refused to follow through the logic of his position and insisted that entrance into the kingdom of God is contingent on personal faith and repentance. We are all elected to salvation, but we are not all adopted into the family of God as his sons and daughters except through faith.

Another divisive issue in the church is the question of certainty of salvation. The Catholic position has been that because faith is incomplete apart from love we cannot be certain that we are truly saved on the basis of faith alone. Our certainty is grounded in the hope that Christ will reward those who diligently seek him and follow his will.[24] By contrast, the Reformers contended that faith already gives certainty because it unites us with Christ, who remains true to his own (Jn 10:28). If we have faith, we know that we are saved because Christ's promises never deceive and his Spirit is all-victorious. Wesley maintained that the assurance of faith follows the gift of faith but is not a necessary element in this faith. Jonathan Edwards found the source of certainty in the practice of faith: we become ever more certain as we press on to do the will of God in daily life.

Finally we should consider the role of the sacraments in our salvation. In the Catholic view baptism saves us from original sin and its penalty *ex opere operato* (by the work performed). But sins committed after baptism need to be confessed and remitted by the church in the sacrament of penance.[25] Because penance involves not only the absolution of the priest but also acts of contrition and reparation prescribed by the church, it creates the impression that good works have a determinative role in our salvation after all. In Reformation theology baptism saves only in conjunction with the Word of God and personal faith. The privilege of baptism is extended to the children of Christian parents, but baptism with water must be united with baptism by the Spirit if we are to be truly engrafted in the body of Christ. If we sin after our baptism we do not need a new sacrament that absolves us from sin; instead, we are obliged simply to return to the promises we made at our baptism (or that were made on our behalf at that time). We are to look back to our baptism as the sign of the invisible grace of God revealed in Jesus Christ—in his sacrificial life, death and resurrection.

According to Barth, if we fall into sin after our baptism or conversion, we need only remind ourselves of the cross of Christ that alone gives assurance of God's grace and forgiveness. We do not have to suffer additional penalties for sin but only disciplines that equip us in the battle against sin. We do not need to make reparation for sin, only claim the reparation already made on our behalf by Jesus Christ. Barth interprets baptism as a sign and witness to Christ's victory over sin and death rather than a means of grace by which we gain access to the fruits of his victory. Baptism also provides the occasion to make a public profession of our faith and to resolve to live out our vocation of being ambassadors and witnesses of the Lord Jesus Christ.

My own view, reflective of an abiding strand in the Reformed tradition, is that baptism is both a sign and a means: a sign of God's redeeming action on our behalf and a means by which this action reaches us—moving us to faith and repentance. In the case of believers who are baptized, baptism is the confirmation and completion of the redeeming action of God in Christ. I affirm baptismal grace but not baptismal regeneration. If we are baptized into the body of Christ as infants or small children, we are in contact with God's prevenient grace, but we are not yet regenerated from sin. The Holy Spirit is *with* us but not yet *in* us. He comes to dwell in us in the moment of decision, which ratifies our baptism and initiates us in the Christian walk with Christ.

Models of Salvation

The following diagrams might prove helpful in comparing the different Christian understandings of the relationship between justification and sanctification. Some of these stand in partial conflict, but most of them reveal a true grasp of the mystery of salvific revelation. All of them are limited and need to be complemented by the others. Some are palpably more biblical than others. I find Calvin's position as set forth in his *Institutes* very close to the biblical vision, but I also find much I can agree with in Luther's and Barth's positions. Wesley and the mystics also have something positive to offer. What makes Calvin's insights particularly helpful is that he makes a real place for progress in the Christian life while nevertheless continuing to see justification as its enduring basis.

Christian Mysticism. The mystical model of salvation is representative of the spirituality in Roman Catholicism and Eastern Orthodoxy (see figure 1), though it is also reflected in some pietistic and gnostic strands within Protestantism.[26] Mysticism draws on the conceptuality provided by Neoplatonism (esp. Plotinus and Proclus), which envisaged an outgoing of the One (ultimate reality), thereby accounting for the material creation, and a return to the One, reunion with the Eternal. In Neoplatonism the creation and the fall are practically identical; sin means separation from the divine ground and source of our being. Christian theologians who have drawn upon this tradition have tried to unite it with biblical themes. It is by the incarnation of God in Christ that we are enabled to ascend to the beatitude from which we have fallen. The descent is not an inevitable overflow of divine goodness (as in Neoplatonism) but the free decision of a beneficent Creator to create and redeem humanity made in his image. Justification and sanctification are aspects of deification in which we are continuously purified and transformed by God's glory. This perspective is found in Origen, Hilary of Poitiers, Evagrius Ponticus, Gregory of Nyssa, Dionysius the Pseudo-Areopagite, Augustine, Maximus the Confessor, Bonaventure, Thomas Aquinas,[27] Gregory Palamas, Meister Eckhart, Jan van Ruysbroeck, John Tauler, John of the Cross and Teresa of Ávila. In the twentieth century it is reflected in Paul Tillich, Thomas Merton, Evelyn Underhill, Vladimir Lossky, Christoforos Stavropoulos, Carlo Carretto, George Maloney and Gerald Heard.[28] The weakness in this view is that sin is interpreted not so much as transgression of God's law as separation from a preexistent union with God. Salvation is seen not primarily as justification, a declaring righteous, but as the return of the soul to its original, undivided unity with God. Those theologians in this tradition seeking a more biblical stance speak of salvation as reunion with God in the fullness of love and joy.

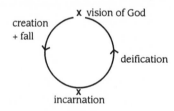

Figure 1. Christian Mystical Model of Salvation

The strength in the mystical understanding is that it keeps alive the call to holiness, relating it to the entire salvific process. This spiritual legacy bids us remember that grace is not only justifying but also elevating; we are not only forgiven our sins but required to live a life above sinful contamination. Mystical theology can appeal to such passages as 2 Corinthians 3:18, which speaks of the Christian being transformed "from one degree of glory to another," and 2 Peter 1:4, which holds out the promise that the faithful will "become partakers of the divine nature." We in the Reformed tradition regard the Christian not as divinized by grace but as liberated for intimate fellowship with the Giver of grace so that we come to share in the very sufferings of Christ (Phil 3:10; 1 Pet 4:13) and thus to experience the glory that is yet to be revealed (1 Pet 5:1).

Luther. For Luther salvation is not faithful humanity climbing the mystical ladder to heaven but Christ descending to fallen humanity and meeting us on our own level (see figure 2). Salvation is solely by grace, not by human effort, though effort is necessary to show our gratitude and joy for a salvation won for us by Christ. Justification is the redemptive act of God in Christ by which he imputes to the sinner the perfect righteousness of Christ and takes the judgment on human sin upon himself in the person and work of Christ.[29] Justification in this conception might be likened to an umbrella that covers our unrighteousness and makes us acceptable to a righteous and holy God.[30] Sanctification or regeneration is the demonstration of a Christian life motivated by outgoing love to our neighbor, not by a desire to ensure the permanence of our salvation. In sanctification we go forward but always under the forgiveness of sins. The Christian life consists of ever new beginnings as we seek to conform ourselves to God's holy will.

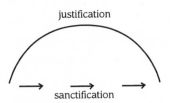

justification

sanctification

Figure 2. Model of Salvation in Luther

Luther rediscovered the heart of the gospel—salvation by free grace alone and sacrificial service through the power of agape love. The question remains whether he did justice to the call to holiness apart from which no one will see the Lord (cf. Heb 12:14; 1 Pet 1:15). For Luther (as with Paul) God justifies us while we are still in our sins, but God does not leave us in our sins: he sends us the Holy Spirit to expel sin from our lives. The justification of the ungodly must be held in tension with the sanctification of the righteous, those who seek to be righteous even though sin persists in their every thought and action. This second note—the sanctification of those seeking holiness—is prominent in Paul but is found only minimally in Luther. The polemics of the sixteenth century prevented him from developing a theology of personal holiness, for he was compelled to give special emphasis to the alien righteousness of Jesus Christ in order to counter a theology of works-righteousness that had penetrated the life and thought of the church at that time.

Calvin. Calvin focused his *Institutes* on the process of regeneration rather than on justification, partly to speak to the concerns of Roman Catholics who accused Protestants of abandoning the call to a devout and holy life. Yet Calvin was adamant that our progress in regeneration or sanctification is contingent on justification, which he interpreted much like Luther as a divine imputation of the righteousness of Christ received only by faith. The basis of our salvation is a simple trust in the efficacy and all-sufficiency of the atoning work of Christ, but the evidence of our salvation is a life of obedience under the cross. At the moment of our salvation we are both justified and sanctified, but this twofold blessing does not mean that God's decision to justify us is dependent in any way on our progress toward holiness. On the contrary, as we proceed upward in sanctification we need to rely wholly on God's justification and forgiveness. If we ever begin to depend even for an instant on our own endeavors to ensure our salvation, we abandon the gospel that we are justified solely by God's grace received in faith. The ultimate goal of both sanctification and justification is glorification, which is also a free, undeserved gift from God (see figure 3). Final salvation is paradoxically both a crown to be won and a gift to be received. We are moved to lay hold of the treasure of eternal life only because it is already assured to us through faith in Jesus Christ. Sanctification is an upward albeit broken ascent to the portals of heaven, for we slip back again and again. The saints, however, those who are truly elect, will persevere to the end because Christ will never abandon his own and will therefore constantly make available to them his grace and beneficence. Justification is the enduring foundation that makes the upward ascent possible.

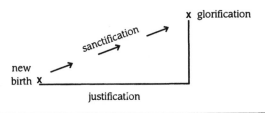

Figure 3. Model of Salvation in Calvin

While Calvin fully affirmed justification by faith alone *(sola fide)*, he was convinced that faith is genuine only when it generates repentance and obedience to the risen Lord. His position must not be confounded with later Reformed orthodoxy, which tended to elevate faith over works.[31] Eastern Orthodox and Roman Catholics might appreciate Calvin's admonition: "We cannot be justified freely by faith alone, if we do not at the same time live in holiness."[32]

Wesley. John Wesley was an avowed opponent of what he called solifidianism and held that faith must be complemented by love if we are ever to gain the salvation promised us in Christ. We are both justified and sanctified by God's undeserved grace, but the gift of his grace is partly contingent on the sincerity of our commitment (see figure 4). Wesley believed in humanity's total depravity, but he also posited a universal prevenient grace that enables all people at least to begin the ascent to salvation. Before we are justified we can seek for salvation on the basis of God's prevenient grace. We can cooperate with the Spirit of God as he calls us to an ever higher spiritual station in life. We cannot compel God either to justify or to sanctify us, but we can prepare ourselves to be open to the movement of his Spirit. Sanctification begins already at the moment of our justification, but Wesley also held out the promise of a second work of grace, a second crisis experience, in which the Spirit of God would sanctify us wholly, filling us with perfect love (cf. 1 Thess 5:23). Even as perfected Christians we need to continue striving for the glory of the eschatological kingdom, since we are still maimed by weaknesses of the flesh, still subject to temptations. It is possible and indeed highly probable that we will fall away from the perfection that is worked within us by his Spirit. It is even possible to fall wholly from the grace of God and become reprobate. This is why salvation and God's grace can never be taken for granted. We must constantly be vigilant as we strive to practice a Christian life that gives glory to God. Wesley's position tends to undercut the eternal security of the Christian, but it does hold out hope for all people, since he affirmed Christ's universal atonement and the universal working of the Spirit of God—even in non-Christian cultures. In Wesley's theology, justification is a preliminary work leading us to the blessing of entire sanctification, which, he insisted, is available to all who truly believe in Christ.

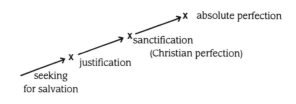

Figure 4.   Model of Salvation in Wesley

Karl Barth. Karl Barth placed the emphasis on the objective ground of salvation, and thus provided a valuable corrective to many other theologians, both past and present. Salvation is something worked for us before it is worked within us. It is an act by which Christ justifies and sanctifies us before he imparts his Spirit to us (see figure 5). In Jesus Christ, in his sacrificial life, death and resurrection, all humankind is elected, justified and sanctified. But the knowledge of this divine favor extended to us is withheld until the Holy Spirit confronts us with the message of the cross and the concrete reality of

Christ's goodness. Salvation is basically an awakening to our changed status in the eyes of a beneficent and holy God, an awakening brought about by the outpouring of the Holy Spirit. In Christ there occurs both objective and subjective salvation, since in his work we see both God's undeserved grace and Jesus' filial obedience. Yet it remains true that we as Christians are also summoned to faith and obedience, and when we respond to this summons we enter the dispensation of Christian freedom. We and all people have already been reconciled to God through Christ, but we need to experience the grace of his reconciling work, and we do so through the work of the Holy Spirit. We are also called to look forward to the goal and crown of his saving work: the coming of the kingdom of righteousness that is already present in our midst but is yet to be revealed to the whole creation. Barth was insistent that though God's grace is free it is not cheap. It demands from us lives of self-sacrificial and abundant service. We are justified by faith, but we are sanctified by love. While the works that proceed from justifying and sanctifying grace do not merit God's favor, they certainly display his favor and mercy to the world. The gospel does not exempt us from the imperatives of the law but sets us free to obey these imperatives in the spirit of love.

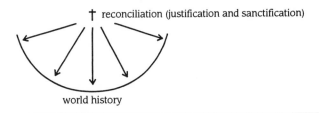

Figure 5. Model of Salvation in Barth

Barth has performed a real service to Christian theology by reminding us that salvation is originally and essentially objective—God's reconciling work in Jesus Christ on our behalf and on behalf of all humanity. Admittedly in some of his earlier writings in particular he unduly minimized the subjective side of salvation, but in his fuller vision he definitely strove to make an important place for this too. The question is whether by the feebleness of our response we can forfeit our salvation and find ourselves once again in an inner darkness. Barth left open the possibility of a final hell in addition to heaven, but its impact is blunted by his firm insistence that God's Yes is more powerful than our No, that God's grace is triumphant even in the disobedience and faithlessness of his people.

Ecumenical Implications

In the growing dialogue involving evangelical Protestants with Eastern Orthodox and Roman Catholics we need to ponder anew the relation between philosophical conceptuality and the imaginative vision of faith. Have Orthodox and Catholics poured new meaning into ancient Greek expressions, such as *deification* and *divinization*, or have they simply expanded and developed meanings already associated with these words in Platonism and Neoplatonism? Does the order of salvation as we find it in the tradition of Christian mysticism (purgation, illumination, union) comport with the biblical schema—election, justification and sanctification? Is the eschatological vision of God an eternal gazing upon the transcendent beauty of God or direct fellowship with God that includes fellowship with the whole company of the saints? Is our final court of appeal Holy Scripture or Scripture *and* sacred tradition? Does a theology of Word and Spirit allow for deeper meanings of the scriptural text that transcend its surface meaning (as with Origen, Cyril of Alexandria, Hilary of Poitiers, Augustine and many other Greek and Latin fathers)?

In this whole discussion it behooves us to draw upon the insights of the fathers of the early church as well as the doctors of the medieval church. But it is also important that all parties give serious attention to the enduring witness of the Protestant Reformation, for it was the Reformers who rediscovered the meaning of the gospel—salvation through the free grace of Jesus Christ received by faith alone. Yet this faith is not content to stand alone but gives rise to works of love that confirm and attest our election and justification.[33] As evangelicals we should be alert to the intrusion into the speculation of faith of a legalistic mentality that interprets the atonement exclusively or primarily in terms of satisfaction of the law of God.

It is imperative that we regain the treasures of the past in all the major Christian traditions, but we are also obliged to restate the ancient faith in the language of the present day and relate that faith to the pivotal issues in modern philosophy and culture. The temptation that beguiles conservatives—Catholic, Orthodox and Protestant—is simply to return to older positions without allowing for deficiencies in these positions and therefore the need for a fresh restatement of truths that have been won in the past but must be rewon in the present. We would do well to remember that when Christians are separated from one another, their perception of the truth of the gospel is thereby dimmed. The way to a fuller understanding of truth is through a deeper cultivation of fellowship with one another. At the same time, no enduring fellowship can exist without a wholehearted commitment to the truth as we find it in Jesus Christ. Truth *(alētheia)* and fellowship *(koinōnia)* belong together, and conservatives have to learn this as much as anyone else.

·EIGHT·

LAW AND GOSPEL: A REFORMED PERSPECTIVE

Does God give you the Spirit and work miracles among you
because you do what the Law requires or
because you hear the gospel and believe it?
GALATIANS 3:5 GNB

The law was given that grace might be sought;
and grace was given, that the law might be fulfilled.
AUGUSTINE

Let us therefore learn to maintain inviolable this sacred tie between
the law and the gospel, which many improperly intend to break.
JOHN CALVIN

Man does the good when he acts according to the imperative
inherent in the gift of freedom. He does evil when he
obeys a law that is contrary to his freedom.
KARL BARTH

The relation of the law and the gospel has been a persistent cause
of dissension among theologians through the ages. The two
main branches of the Reformation—Lutheran and Reformed—
have taken divergent positions on this and related issues. In this chap-

ter I wish to speak out of the Reformed tradition but without dismissing the valid insights proffered by Catholics, Lutherans, Wesleyans and others who together constitute the one holy catholic and apostolic church.

The term *Reformed* has become almost as ambiguous as *evangelical*, but I am using it in a very specific sense. First it means anchored in the Protestant Reformation of the sixteenth century. To be Reformed means to claim the legacy of Calvin, Zwingli, Knox, Bucer and Bullinger. But Reformed people also acknowledge their indebtedness to Luther and Melanchthon, both of whom spearheaded the Lutheran Reformation, and to Augustine, who gave a forthright affirmation of *sola gratia* in the face of the errors of Pelagius. One should keep in mind that Calvin signed one of the early editions of the Augsburg Confession. In the former Evangelical Synod of North America, the church of my childhood, the guiding standards of faith were the Augsburg Confession, Luther's Small Catechism and the Heidelberg Catechism. These remained the confessional standards in the Evangelical and Reformed Church, which came into existence in 1934 (now part of the United Church of Christ).

A second meaning of *Reformed* is the willingness always to be reformed in light of the Word of God *(ecclesia semper reformanda)*. Our creeds and theologies remain under the witness of Holy Scripture and therefore may be corrected and amended on the basis of new insight gleaned from the Word of God. New creeds can be written as new heresies arise to challenge the faith once delivered to the saints. Both Calvin and Luther placed the Word of God above the testimonies of sacred tradition.

Other theologians who have shaped the Reformed tradition and have influenced me personally in various ways are P. T. Forsyth, Charles Hodge, Karl Barth, Jacques Ellul, G. C. Berkouwer, Hendrikus Berkhof, Emil Brunner and Reinhold Niebuhr. My principal mentors in this study are Barth, Calvin and to a lesser extent Niebuhr.

Contrasting Positions

Roman Catholicism often pictures the gospel as a new law, one that fulfills the Mosaic law of Hebraic tradition. Christ is envisaged as the eternal or final law of God. The teachings of Christ as well as the ministry and acts of Christ constitute the gospel as the fulfilled law of God. Thomas Aquinas could describe the "New Law" as "the grace of the Holy Spirit, which is given through faith in Christ." The New Law not only indicates to us what we should do but also helps us to accomplish it.[1] In this same vein Pope John Paul II declares that "the New Law is not content to say what must be done, but also gives the power to 'do what is true.'"[2]

Luther by contrast frequently drew an antithesis between law and gospel. The law is the hammer of God's judgment, which brings about conviction of sin. The gospel is the balm of God's mercy that assures us of divine forgiveness. Like Calvin, Luther also affirmed a political use of the law: to restrain our rapacity and thereby preserve us from injury in the order of creation. While Luther's emphasis was on the spiritual use—to drive us to an awareness of our helplessness and need for God—it is debatable whether he held that the law always accuses. For the person with a stricken conscience, he said, "sin assuredly rules by the law, for no one loves the law by nature; and that is a great sin. Grace, however, makes the law dear to us, and then sin is no more there, and the law is no longer against us, but with us."[3]

For Calvin the principal use of the law is the ethical one: the law as a guide in the Christian life. He acknowledged that the law is also a tutor that leads one to Christ, but he was equally emphatic that the law is a divinely given standard that keeps us in conformity with the will of God as revealed in Christ. Calvin affirmed the basic continuity between law and gospel, though he did perceive the continuing tension between the letter of the law and the evangelical proclamation. According to him the law is always *with* the gospel rather than simply *before* the gospel. The right order is law-gospel-law. The law prepares us for faith in Christ, and the gospel then sends us back to the law, enabling us to obey it in the spirit of love. Reinhold Niebuhr perceptively observed that, unlike Luther, Calvin does not "believe that grace abrogates the law, for he does not think of sanctification as an ecstatic experience of love which transcends all law. He thinks of it rather as a rigorous obedience to law."[4] With regard to justification, however, Calvin contended that our only hope lies in the grace of Christ, not in adherence to the law. We "have to put away all thinking about the Law and our works" and "embrace the mercy of God alone," turning "our eyes away from ourselves and upon Jesus Christ alone."[5]

In contradistinction to the mainstream of Reformation tradition, Karl Barth gave priority to the gospel in the determination of the content of the law. If we are to understand the demand of the law rightly, we must first have been confronted by the promise of the gospel. Barth basically saw one use for the law—a spiritual-ethical use: the law directs us to the gospel and to service in the world in light of the gospel. Or to put it another way, the law leads us to faith in Christ and to obedience to Christ. The law thereby becomes a sign and witness of the gospel. The law is not the gospel, and the gospel is not the law, but the two are inseparable in constituting the one Word of God.[6]

Not surprisingly, natural law has been suspect in Barthian circles, where natural awareness of moral law is deemed insufficient to provide us with valid knowledge of God's will and purpose for human life. Human sin distorts our perceptions of moral order in the universe and subverts the moral sense that is a gift of creation. Jacques Ellul, however, who more or less followed Barthian theology, made a place for the fact of natural law as opposed to a theology of natural law.[7] Despite human limitation and sin, all societies construct moral norms simply to preserve a semblance of justice and order. These moral norms attest the reality of a universal moral order, but they do not give a reliable account of this moral order. They nevertheless play a secondary role in preserving social order, and societies are judged by God on how they live up to their own standards.

Distinctive Reformed Emphases
Reformed theology affirms a polarity but not an antithesis between

law and gospel. It is commonly said that the second face of the gospel is the law, and the second face of the law is the gospel. The gospel is the content of the law, and the law is the form of the gospel (Barth). A believer is not released from the imperatives of the law but is now obliged and empowered to obey these imperatives. In Reformed thought the person of faith stands "under grace but also under judgment, under the promise but also under the demand, under the gospel but also under the law."[8] There is not a separation but a correlation between law and gospel. The antithesis is between the law of God as God intended and the human misunderstanding of the law, which is manifested in legalism and rigorism.

In Reformed theology the law is a means to salvation—but only when united with the gospel. Psalm 19:7-8 is often cited: "The law of the LORD is perfect, reviving the soul. . . . The commands of the LORD are radiant, giving light to the eyes" (NIV). The law saves by directing us to the gospel, by relaying the message of the gospel to us. The law by itself does not save but only condemns. It is when Christ speaks to us through the law, it is when we perceive the law through the lens of the gospel, that we are convicted of sin and assured by the promise of the gospel.

Reformed theology takes strong exception to grounding ethics simply in the spirit of love. For the Reformed fathers "ethics was grounded not upon love but upon obeying the commandments as *God's* commandments. The Law keeps its place beside the Gospel as another, a second, reality, equally true and commanding and necessary because the one God stands behind both, because the one Holy Spirit imparts both to men."[9]

Calvin insisted that the gospel too is a sword that slays. The gospel brings judgment as well as grace because it introduces us to the majesty and holiness of God as well as to his infinite mercy. Indeed, God's mercy can be understood and appreciated only in light of his severity toward human sin. Correspondingly, the horror of sin can be apprehended only in light of God's grace and mercy revealed in Jesus Christ.[10]

In the mainstream of Reformed tradition there is one covenant, a covenant of grace, but it has two dimensions or stages—one of preparation, the other of fulfillment. The covenant that God makes with his people in the Old Testament is a preparation for the covenant he consummates in Christ. The Christian church is the new covenant form of the people of God. While in Reformed history allusion was sometimes made to a covenant of works, this is best understood as a legalistic misunderstanding of the covenant of God's grace. The covenant that God made with both Abraham and Moses is based on his unconditional and unmerited love, but this covenant is not fulfilled until its beneficiaries, the people of God, walk according to the way of holiness.

Reformed theology is reluctant to suggest that the gospel abrogates the law. Romans 10:4 has often been a subject of controversy in the history of Christian thought: "Christ is the end of the law so that there may be righteousness for everyone who believes" (NRSV). The word for "end" is *telos*, which generally signifies purpose or completion rather than termination. Yet in its immediate and wider context it can be seen as both termination and completion,[11] because Christ does bring an end to the law as an independent way to salvation.[12] Christ is both the negation and the fulfillment of the Mosaic law. Christ overthrows the law of sin and death in order to clear the way for the law of spirit and life (Rom 8:2).

The law is overturned by the gospel, and yet a new imperative standing in continuity with the original divine imperative proceeds from the gospel. Reinhold Niebuhr recognizes that "a higher than the traditional law is implied in the gospel."[13] Barth calls this the "law of grace" and the "law of freedom." It signifies the paradoxical unity of obligation and permission.

Love and Law

Reformed theology readily acknowledges an abiding tension between love as law and love as grace. Love is both an obligation and a gift that transcends the sense of duty. When we are liberated by the grace that comes to us through both law and gospel, we are only too happy to obey the imperatives of the law. As the psalmist exclaims, "I shall run the course made known in your commandments, for you set free my heart" (119:32 REB).

Co-opting a phrase from Nicolas Berdyaev, Reinhold Niebuhr refers to the ethics of the gospel as "the morality beyond morality."[14] Yet even here, Niebuhr says, law is not completely transcended. When we are freed from legal demands, we nonetheless set out on a new course of obedience—no longer to legal claims but to a holy person.

This notion of the kingdom of God transcending the claims and codes of legal morality is also evident in Barth. "The Kingdom of God has its beginning on the other side of the Cross, beyond all that is called 'religion' and 'life,' beyond conservatism and radicalism, physics and metaphysics; on the other side of morals and of that which is beyond morality."[15] In Barth's view the kingdom of God is not a new world order bringing another set of mandates and obligations but the invasion of an entirely new reality into the structures of human existence, infusing them with the motivating power of love.

With Barth, Ellul, Bonhoeffer and Brunner, I propose an ethics of divine command, but this is the divine command in unity with the divine promise. Love goes beyond the prescriptions of law, but at the same time love fulfills the imperative of law (cf. Mt 5:17; Rom 13:10). Love liberates us from the burden of the law and empowers us to keep the command embodied in law.

To reduce the Christian life to agape (as Nygren does) is to disregard the claims of God's law upon the believing community. God is both love and holiness, and his law proceeds from both. Agape does not cancel the claims of *nomos* (law), but it places *nomos* on a new foundation. Agape is not simply sacrificial love but also holy love. Love leads us to respect the holy law of God as deserving of our fidelity and adherence. But now under grace we adhere to God's commandment not to make ourselves acceptable before God but to show our gratefulness for what God has already done for us in Jesus Christ.

An ethics of the divine command is at the same time an ethics of grace. When we strive to obey the law of God we witness to the gospel fact that salvation comes by grace and grace alone. We are justified and also sanctified only by grace because our works are invariably mixed with motives that are less than pure. Even as Christians we sin in our morality as well as in our immorality. But we can proceed to do good works because, although inevitably falling short of God's glory, they are covered by the perfect righteousness of Christ and thus rendered pleasing in God's sight.

As Christians we are still under the command of God, but this command must now be seen as a permission as well. This paradoxical fact is attested in Matthew 14:28-29. Peter asks to be commanded to come to Jesus in the water, and Jesus says "Come." The command of our Lord fulfills the innermost yearnings of our being and sets our will free to act according to both God's perfect will and our deepest existential need.

Call to Discipleship

Reformed theology has always endeavored to tie the gift of God's unfathomable grace with the call to discipleship under the cross. If grace is not united with discipleship it becomes cheap. Just as grace cost God the life of his own Son, so it must also cost us our lives—our reputation, our self-esteem, sometimes even our health—in the service of the gospel.

The gospel is an evangelical indicative, but an indicative that implies an imperative. This inseparability is seen in Mark 2:1-12, where Jesus heals the paralytic: "Your sins are forgiven" and "Stand up and take your mat and walk" (NRSV). Which is law and which is gospel? They both announce the good news, but a command is also involved.

As Christians we are enjoined to be rich in good works (1 Tim 6:17-19), but our motivation is not to make ourselves acceptable before God or to earn the favor of God. We cannot move God to grant us the treasure of his salvation, but we can deepen our appreciation and hope for this treasure that is assured to us through faith. The

Heidelberg Catechism rightly reminds us that our commitment to a life of service is to be based on gratitude for what God has already done for us in Jesus Christ.[16] And there are other biblical motivations for following Christ: the fear of God, the love of God, the desire to glorify God. Paul confesses that it is "the love of Christ" that "urges us on" (2 Cor 5:14 NRSV).[17]

In delineating the rationale for the Christian life we should heed seriously the biblical dictum that being is prior to action. We must be in Christ before we can act in harmony with his will. This truth is underlined by Paul: "We have not ceased praying for you and asking that you may be filled with the knowledge of God's will in all spiritual wisdom and understanding, so that you may lead lives worthy of the Lord, fully pleasing to him" (Col 1:9-10 NRSV). Jesus makes this same point when he contends that good fruit can come only from a good tree (Lk 6:43-45). Once we are converted into salt and light by God's grace we must sprinkle our salt and let our light shine before others so that they may see our good works and give glory to our Father in heaven (Mt 5:14, 16 NRSV).

Reformed theology emphasizes the need not only for faith but also for obedience. Faith does not simply produce obedience but encompasses obedience. Barth makes this very clear: "There has to be a recognition, an acceptance, an acknowledgment, a respecting, a bowing down. This is why there has to be faith and obedience. This is why expressly there has to be knowledge and action, not just sinking and vanishing, not just stillness and passivity, not just a 'feeling of absolute dependence.'"[18]

To preach grace without sounding the call to holiness is to settle for a truncated gospel. The whole counsel of God embraces both the divine promise of unmerited grace and the divine mandate to live out a vocation to service and holiness. We preach the gospel to comfort the afflicted and the law to afflict the comfortable (Luther). But we also preach both law and gospel to challenge the forgiven sinner to lead a life that redounds to the glory of God.

The Ultimate Criterion

The ultimate criterion for Christian faith is the gospel-law or the law-gospel. I affirm the chronological priority of the law of God on the plane of history (cf. Jn 1:17) but the ontological priority of the gospel (cf. Jn 1:3-5, 9). God's grace precedes God's commandment and also empowers us to fulfill what is commanded. Augustine put this tersely: "Give what you command, and command what you will."[19]

The gospel-law is the divine commandment in its unity with the divine promise. It is neither a universal principle nor a narrative but an event. It is a word of personal address that comes to us through the witness of Scripture and church tradition. It is both a structure of meaning and an act that is laden with meaning.

I uphold a divine command ethic over the justice-love ethic now being promulgated in mainline churches.[20] The latter confounds the rational search for justice with the concrete will of the almighty God. It denies the disjunction between human justice and agape—the sacrificial, paradoxical love of the cross. It also ignores the infinite qualitative distinction between human virtue and divine holiness.

There is no law of creation proceeding to the gospel of redemption (as Braaten, Tillich and Pannenberg claim), but there is a law of creation illumined by the gospel of redemption. The universal moral law does not furnish a point of contact with the gospel of free grace, but this gospel opens our eyes to the reality of a moral order embedded in the cosmos.

I affirm one covenant of grace that unites both Old and New Testaments, prophetic and apostolic history. The grace of God revealed in Christ is a new form of the old covenant made with Abraham and then with Moses. Some Reformed theologians of the past have even recognized a covenant of grace before history, an "eternal pact between the Father and the Son whereby the Father commissioned the Son to be the Savior and gave him a people."[21]

I acknowledge that there are dangers in the gospel-law order as well as in the law-gospel order. The law must not be reduced simply to a dimension of the gospel. Nor does the law by itself prepare the way for the reception of the gospel. Even Barth, who was convinced of the inseparability of law and gospel, nevertheless insisted that there is an infinite distance between them.[22] The law is a tutor that leads us to the gospel but only because grace infuses the law and illumines it. The law is not an independent propaedeutic to the gospel; yet as the righteous hand of God it leads us to the gospel but only in the power of the grace that comes from the gospel.

Again, I wish to affirm the priority of grace over works, the divine promise over the divine command, the truth of the gospel over the prescriptions of the law. The Decalogue itself begins with the announcement of grace: "I am the Lord your God, who brought you out of the land of Egypt, out of the house of slavery; you shall have no other gods before me" (Ex 20:2-3 NRSV). The command follows the declaration of God's mercy.

The commandments in the Bible, particularly the Decalogue and the Sermon on the Mount, should be regarded as road signs that set us on the straight and narrow way. But we should remember that it is only Christ who gives us the power and vision to walk according to the road signs. It is only in the light of Christ that we are enabled to appreciate the full meaning of the road signs, particularly as they bear on our lives in the here and now.

The implications of the gospel-law order are many. Apologetics is not to precede dogmatics but is to be fully incorporated in the dogmatic task. Faith does not stand alone but produces a life of obedience. Repentance is not prior to faith as its logical ground but flows out from faith. In our preaching we do not first try to drive people into a consciousness of sin through the use of the law, but we call people to repentance on the basis of both law and gospel. In pastoral care self-knowledge does not come before God-knowledge, but we know ourselves only in the light of God's incomparable mercy revealed in the cross of Christ. The meaning of the cross precedes and undergirds the examination of the self. The assurance of pardon comes before as well as after the confession of sins.

I think the most comprehensive order, the one that does most justice to the entire biblical witness, is gospel-law-gospel. We are awakened to the seriousness of the law and the gravity of our sins when we hear the gospel of free grace through the atoning sacrifice of Jesus Christ on the cross. The gospel then directs us to the law as a guide for the Christian life. But in reminding us of our sin the law sends us back to the gospel for the grace and consolation it provides. The divine promise precedes the commandment, but the commandment in turn precedes the fulfillment of the promise.

In reassessing the relation of law and gospel we must steer clear of the peril of moralism or legalism on the one hand and that of antinomianism on the other. We are neither justified nor sanctified by works of the law, but we are not released from the obligation to do good works out of fidelity to Jesus Christ. We are justified by *grace* alone but for *holiness* alone, and this means that we are to live out a vocation made possible by grace that gives glory to God. Only those who are fully committed to the Christian life are permitted to confess that they are justified solely by grace *(sola gratia)*. Only those who have done all to honor God and help their neighbor can claim that God's grace covers their sin and secures them for heaven.

·NINE·

THE LORDSHIP
OF CHRIST IN
THEOLOGICAL
HISTORY

Therefore let all Israel be assured of this: God has made this Jesus,
whom you crucified, both Lord and Christ.
ACTS 2:36 NIV

There is not one square inch of the entire creation about which
Jesus Christ does not cry out, "This is mine! This belongs to me!"
ABRAHAM KUYPER

He [Jesus Christ] is the Lord humbled for communion with man
and likewise the Servant exalted to communion with God.
KARL BARTH

If the Creator were only the author of the existence of the world
and could not achieve lordship over it, we could not call him truly
God or indeed Creator in the full sense of the word.
WOLFHART PANNENBERG

Christ the Lord has to be proclaimed anew
in the face of all the lords of this world.
JACQUES ELLUL

The controversy over the lordship of Christ revolves around several theological issues. Among these is the relation between
the natural lordship of Christ and his redeeming lordship. Is

Christ lord of humanity by creation alone or also by redemption? Is his redeeming lordship restricted to the community of faith? Is Christ Lord of all but Savior only of some?

A closely related issue is whether the kingdom of Christ is already realized in the people of faith, or whether it is a future reality that will bring the curtain down on world history. Does the kingdom of God or of Christ arise out of history, or does it break into history from the beyond? Does the Bible teach a prophetic or an apocalyptic eschatology?

This brings us to the complex relationship between the church and the kingdom. Is the church an embodiment of the kingdom or only its anticipatory sign? Does the state serve or impede the kingship of Christ? Is the kingdom being realized outside as well as inside the sphere of faith?

Of special interest today is whether human beings have a positive role in the realization of the kingdom of God in history. Are we only passive recipients of God's grace, or can we prepare the way for his grace? Can we collaborate with the Spirit of God in bringing in the kingdom, or do we merely celebrate and proclaim a kingdom that is God's own and exclusive work? Does the battle for human justice advance the kingdom of God, or does it merely foster a yearning for this kingdom?

We also have to ask whether it is appropriate to include in our eschatology the millennial promise of God's kingdom being realized on earth as well as the hope of heavenly glory. Is the interim kingdom of Christ already an accomplished reality, or will it be inaugurated at his second advent? Does the Christian hope contain a millennial dimension, or is it exclusively otherworldly?

Another pertinent question is whether there is a kingdom of evil arrayed against the kingdom of Christ. Is there a spiritual adversary of God and Christ who presently rules this world and who resists the encroachment of the kingdom of Christ? Is Christ sovereign over this evil power, or will he become sovereign over all things at a later time?

Finally, it behooves us to explore how the kingly role of Christ interacts with his prophetic and priestly roles. Is he first prophet and priest and then king, or is his kingship reflected and carried forward in his prophetic and priestly ministry?

New Testament Views

Already in the New Testament one can detect a tension between realized and apocalyptic eschatology. On the one hand, the kingdom is depicted as a mustard seed or a leaven that is secretly at work penetrating the whole of reality (Mt 13:31-32). On the other, it is envisioned as a new reality that breaks into history and brings it to a close (Mt 6:10; 25:31-46). The kingdom is now in the midst of believers (Lk 17:21 RSV), but it will encompass the whole of humanity in a climactic event at the end of history. Christ is even now lord of the powers, for by his cross and resurrection victory they have been dethroned (Mt 12:29; Mk 3:27; Lk 10:18; Col 2:15). Yet other passages speak of a continuing conflict between Christ and the devil that will not be resolved until his coming again in power and glory at the end of time (Eph 5:8-17; 1 Pet 5:8-10). These tensions indicate not necessarily contradictions but instead varying emphases that reflect the paradox of the "already" and the "not yet." Christ is already present among us, but he is not yet lord of our lives. He rules *over* all, but he is not yet *in* all (Eph 1:10).

Jürgen Moltmann and Ernst Käsemann sense a conflict between Paul and the theology expressed in Ephesians and Colossians (which they claim are post-Pauline).[1] They allege that these two epistles envisage Christ's lordship over the world as already initiated and the cosmic powers as already subjugated, whereas for Paul we do not yet possess the glory of the resurrection and are saved by hope. The cosmic lordship of Christ is indeed powerfully expressed in Ephesians: "He has put all things under his feet and has made him the head over all things for the church, which is his body, the fullness of him who fills all in all" (Eph 1:22-23). Christians are also portrayed as already raised up with Christ and seated with him in heavenly places (2:6). Yet there is another strand in this letter: those who continue in sin do not have "any inheritance in the kingdom of Christ and of God" (Eph 5:5 NRSV; cf. 4:17-24). Colossians is emphatic that "every power and authority in the universe is subject to him as head" (2:10 REB); yet we are enjoined to "put to death" those parts of us "which belong to the earth" (3:5 REB). This tension between the "already" and the "not yet" runs through the Pauline epistles. It is also conspicuous in Hebrews: "In putting everything under him, God left nothing that is not subject to him. Yet at present we do not see everything subject to him" (2:8 NIV; cf. 10:13).

Augustine and Aquinas

In the fifth century Augustine offered a systematic exposition of the role of the kingdom of God in history in his much acclaimed *City of God*.[2] Two cities—the city of the world and the city of God—are graphically depicted in ineradicable conflict with one another, reflecting the dichotomy between two loves—the love of self and the love of God. The city of the world, which is under the immediate control of the devil, includes not only the secular state but also unbelieving segments within the institutional church. The city of God denotes the company of true believers, the elect, who work in the state as well as serve in the church. God is sovereign over both cities, but his kingship is hidden in the city of the world.

Scholars still debate the enigmatic relationship between kingdom and church in Augustine's theology. It seems that for him the church is the historically visible form of the kingdom of God. Yet the church is not the perfected kingdom (the kingdom of glory) but the kingdom in the making, the "kingdom of militancy." He can say that "the church even now is the kingdom of Christ and the kingdom of heaven"; yet this must be taken to mean that the church now functions as the temporal vessel or matrix of the kingdom. He distinguishes the temporary "inn" of the church from the permanent "home" of the kingdom. The church without spot or wrinkle (Eph 5:27; 2 Pet 3:14) is the church in its eschatological fulfillment, not the church as it struggles in history. The kingdom of Christ is not a future millennial kingdom but the rulership of Christ as it is effected through the prophetic and sacramental mediation of the church.

Thomas Aquinas (d. 1274) also stoutly affirmed the lordship of Christ over all of creation and history. This lordship—revealed and confirmed in his glorious resurrection from the dead and ascension into heaven—is not restricted to his divinity but includes his humanity as well: "The Father has not only subjected all of creation to Christ as he is God, to whom everything is subject from eternity, but also to his humanity."[3] This does not mean that Christ is Savior of all, for those who remain in unbelief are made to serve Christ as unwilling servants rather than sons and daughters. In his exaltation "Christ exercises a supreme fullness of power over the entire universe."[4]

The kingdom of grace instituted by Christ does not contravene the kingdom of nature, which encompasses the whole of humanity by virtue of creation. Grace fulfills and elevates nature just as grace will be fulfilled in the coming kingdom of glory when Christ will be in and through all things (Eph 1:23). The new law of Christ does not overthrow the natural law written into the order of nature but validates and illumines this law. Yet while grace does not contradict nature, it does uproot human sin. The kingdom of grace converts sinful human beings into regenerate and holy persons consecrated to the glory of God. The world is altered insofar as sanctified men and women bring a new scale of values to bear upon their secular work.

Unlike Augustine, who saw the state as a necessary evil based on collective interest, Thomas envisioned the state in a much more positive light: as created and sanctioned for the economic and social well-being of humanity. Because the divine law goes beyond natural law, the state should ideally receive guidance from the church in the realization of an order of peace and justice that will reflect the goodness and mercy of God. Thomas allowed for the possibility of a Christian state far more than Augustine, who was inclined to view the state as belonging to the fallen society of the world *(civitas terrena).*[5]

Thomas has been criticized for his heavy reliance on natural law in his philosophy of the state. Christ's coming simply brings light to bear upon natural law, but it does not inaugurate a new order in which the righteousness of the kingdom of God is now the norm for human justice.[6] Christian faith, it seems, reinforces the existing order of things rather than introduces into the human situation a revolutionary dynamic that presses for human liberation and equality on all levels. What Thomas achieved was a Christ-culture synthesis in which cultural values and hopes are fulfilled in an order of existence above this world rather than disrupted and transformed by a creative and redeeming force breaking into this world from the beyond.

While acknowledging the "appealing greatness" of the synthesist belief that God's rule "is established in the nature of things, and that man must build on the established foundations," H. Richard Niebuhr judiciously warns:

> A synthesist who makes the evanescent in any sense fundamental to his theory of the Christian life will be required to turn to the defense of that temporal foundation for the sake of the superstructure it carries when changes in culture threaten it. It is logical that when a synthetic answer has been given to the problem of Christ and culture, those who accept it should become more concerned about the defense of the culture synthesized with the gospel than about the gospel itself. . . . The tendency toward cultural conservatism seems endemic in [this] school.[7]

Luther and Calvin

Following in the tradition of Augustine's *City of God,* Luther postulated two kingdoms: the kingdom of God and the kingdom of the world, the former directed by Christ, the latter by the devil. Yet these two kingdoms are not equal, for God or Christ is lord over both, directing the kingdom of the world by his left hand and the kingdom of heaven by his right. His alien work is to slay and punish (Is 28:21); his proper work is to save and heal. His alien work is in the service of his proper work just as the kingdom of the world is made to serve the kingdom of heaven. The Christian lives in two realms, but Christ is lord over both. Yet fulfilling one's secular duties is not the same as living out one's spiritual vocation. The kingdom of the world necessitates coercion; the kingdom of God demands suffering love.

Contrary to popular academic opinion, Luther did not identify the kingdom of the world with the state. The state was instituted as a dike against sin, the church to proclaim the righteousness of the kingdom. Yet because the kingdom of darkness has infiltrated both the state and the institutional church, the Christian must struggle against the devil in both areas—temporal and spiritual. The state is under the law of God, the church under the gospel.

The history of the world is marked by an unremitting conflict between God and the devil, a conflict decisively settled in the cross and resurrection victory of Jesus Christ, yet destined to continue until the devil and the kingdoms of the world are brought into complete subjection to Jesus Christ. Luther looked forward to a cataclysmic denouement at the end of history in which all peoples would acknowledge the kingship of Christ. The world will groan in travail until Christ comes again and sets up the kingdom that shall have no end—the kingdom of glory.

Luther's two-kingdom theory has been criticized for encouraging acquiescence to social injustice, for limiting the demands of the gospel to the church, thereby creating the impression that the state is solely under the rule of force. It is true that a number of German Lutheran theologians used this theory to justify a tacit accommodation to the Nazi regime. On the other hand, Bishop Berggrav of Norway found in Luther's theory a powerful rationale for opposing the Nazis, since Christ is lord over both realms and the law of God is higher than the laws of the state.[8]

Calvin also believed in two kingdoms engaged in perpetual warfare, but he envisaged state and church in close relationship united in the battle against the kingdom of evil. His ideal was a holy community in which every area of life would be brought under the direction of the revealed law of God, though he never identified this community with the holy city, the new Jerusalem, that is to come down from heaven. Neither church nor state is the kingdom of God, but both can be made to serve this kingdom.

There are both postmillennial and amillennial strains in Calvin. Christ is even now the lord of the nations, but his kingdom at the same time advances in history as people accept the Christian message. Calvin entertained the hope of the kingdom of God gradually seizing power and triumphing over many of the bastions of wickedness within history. Yet the kingdom of God does not find its fruition in history or in the form of earthly power.[9] The community of faith will not inherit the kingdom of the earth until Christ comes again and completes his work of purification and redemption. The eschaton does not mean for Calvin the dissolution of the earth (as for Luther) but its renovation and transfiguration.

While there is a noticeable theocratic strain in Calvin, this is not to be confounded with an ecclesiocracy. Calvin insisted not on the rule of the church over secular life but on the need to bring all aspects of life under the rule of God. And the criterion was not natural law as such but always the law given in revelation, the law illumined by the gospel. Despite his careful attempt to draw clear-cut lines between church and state, Calvin opened the door to the vision of a holy commonwealth in which the state is guided by biblical if not Christian principles. Whereas Lutheranism must be on guard against privatism and ghettoism, Calvinism has to struggle against triumphalism and clericalism.

Like Augustine, Calvin virtually identified the church and the kingdom of God, although he was thinking not of the church as an earthly institution but of the invisible church—the company of the elect from the beginning of history. The kingdom is both historical and transhistorical: its field of operation is within history, but it is directed to life with God in eternity.

Liberal Theology

Reflecting the influence of both Pietism and Romanticism, Friedrich

Schleiermacher (d. 1834) envisioned the kingdom of Christ as essentially spiritual, quite distinct from the kingdom of the world. Christ does not govern the world but commands only "the forces of redemption implanted in the Church."[10] The world is the realm where God rules. The kingdom of grace is not the kingdom of power, but neither is it restricted to the institutions of religion. "There is no stage of purity and perfection which does not belong to Christ's Kingdom."[11] One critic complains, "Christ is no longer the main actor in the dramatic history of world salvation; he is the inspiration of a community of souls."[12]

The kingdom of God advances in history as people become sensitized to the things of the spirit. The triumph of the kingdom is at the same time the forward movement of civilization—the ennobling of individual and social human life. Redemption does not mean a new creation but the stimulation and fulfillment of humanity's creative potential.

A similar position was enunciated by Wilhelm Herrmann (d. 1922), teacher of both Barth and Bultmann:

> Jesus certainly claimed, as was expected of the Messiah, that He would establish the Kingdom of God among men, and that He would thereby make the world complete. But there is no trace of political hopes, no summons to the use of force. The decisions to which he compels men concern their own inner life; for by the Kingdom of God he means God's true lordship over personal life, especially in men's own souls, and in their communion one with another.[13]

Perhaps more than any other German theologian, Albrecht Ritschl (d. 1889) made the kingdom of God a paramount motif in theology. The kingdom represents the supramundane ideal of spiritual and moral perfection that can nevertheless be partially realized within history. The Christian is summoned to the vocation of lordship over the world, and this means bringing the chaotic forces of nature under the dominion of spirit. Christ is the bearer of divine lordship and founder of the divine kingdom, but his kingdom must be carried forward in history by those who follow the ideals he taught and embodied. Ritschl called for united human action motivated by universal love to advance the kingdom of God in the world. Our ultimate standing in the kingdom depends on "the goodness and the rounded completeness of the life-work" we achieve in our moral vocation.[14]

Ritschl laid the foundations for the social gospel (Walter Rauschenbusch, Washington Gladden, Shailer Mathews), which sought to usher in the kingdom of God through political action in the service of human equality and justice. The kingdom was portrayed as a new social order based on the dignity and worth of the human person. In contrast to Ritschl the social gospellers believed that the kingdom of God could be fully realized on earth.

The Contemporary Scene

In palpable reaction against the utopianism of much of the older liberal theology, Reinhold Niebuhr depicted the kingdom of God as the new reality of suffering love that impinges on history but never becomes fully incarnate in history. It is not a supernatural realm above history but "the eternal dimension in which history moves."[15] It is not restricted to the community of faith but signifies the free movement of the Spirit in all communities that are open to the transcendent. It appears in history "in every great judgment and in every new level of community."[16] It is "always coming but it is never here," in that it is a moral ideal only imperfectly reflected in the vicissitudes of history. It is not a kingdom in some other world but "the picture of what this world ought to be."[17]

Niebuhr saw Christ as the symbol of the kingdom of God in time rather than the ruler of world history.[18] It is the Father who symbolizes the divine rule over history; the Son represents the divine presence within history. The cross of Christ is the revelation of the fact that "the final power of God over man is derived from the self-imposed weakness of his love."[19] The triumph of the power of the powerlessness of love takes place at the edge of history in the crucifixion of a holy life, but it never takes root within history because social structures necessitate the imposition of coercive power. Christians can set up signs and symbols of the kingdom of God, but this kingdom "transcends all the struggles of history."[20]

Like Niebuhr, Karl Barth stressed the transcendent character of the kingdom of God but insisted that it is also a dynamic force within history, though always remaining the creative and transformative work of God. Barth conceived of the kingdom as a wholly new reality in history that cannot be merged or united with any existing kingdom or social structure. The kingdom of God stands in "radical antithesis" to all human kingdoms as well as to "the sphere of Satan."[21]

Following church tradition Barth postulated three modes of the kingdom of God: nature, grace and glory. He associated creation with the kingdom of nature, reconciliation with the kingdom of grace and redemption with the kingdom of glory. Whereas the first two are present now, the kingdom of glory is primarily future. Yet, he insisted, we cannot separate them: they are all the one kingdom of the Lord Jesus Christ. Barth hailed Jesus in both his humanity and his divinity as the king of all the nations of the world, although this kingship is not universally recognized. The kingdom of darkness is a pseudokingdom that claims to have power but has actually been divested of its power not only in the cross and resurrection victory of Christ but already at creation.

For Luther's apocalyptic eschatology Barth substituted a christological eschatology. Jesus Christ is already king and the powers have been subjugated, though they fight on through the strength of deception. Instead of a spiritual kingdom in juxtaposition with a temporal kingdom, Barth spoke of the one kingdom of Christ with two dimensions: church and state. The civil community is the outer circle and the Christian community the inner circle of the kingdom of God. Their common center is Jesus Christ—God incarnate, crucified and risen. For Barth the state is based not on natural law or on the rule of force made necessary by sin but on the justice of God revealed in Jesus Christ. Barth introduced the concept of a "political service of God," which consists in the proclamation of Christ's lordship over all of life.

Jürgen Moltmann has taken vigorous exception to Barth's theory of the royal kingship of Christ on the grounds that it emphasizes the "already" at the expense of the "not yet."[22] While Jesus Christ is indeed king, his kingship is not yet realized in a world where the powers of darkness still subjugate humanity, where injustice still reigns, where people are still oppressed and exploited. Christ's lordship is not a universal reality but a possibility that is being realized as Christians dedicate themselves to the cause of justice in what is still an unjust world. Christ will not enter his glorious reign until all earthly lordships, authorities and powers are destroyed, but this will not happen until the eschaton, "when the lordship of the crucified one becomes the lordship of God."[23]

Christ now rules, according to Moltmann, but he rules as the crucified one—not over the world but in its midst. He rules by serving, he redeems through suffering. "The unity of the risen and the crucified one," he maintains, "is grasped neither by a two kingdoms doctrine nor by the doctrine of the kingly lordship of Christ, but only by an eschatological Christology, a Christology 'from ahead.'"[24] This world is not yet the kingdom of God but the battleground and construction site for the kingdom, which will come to earth from God himself.

Moltmann advocates a political theology dedicated to advancing the kingdom through social action and suffering, nonviolent love. We can cooperate with the Spirit of God in humanizing oppressive social structures, though it is only God who justifies the sinner and creates faith. A political theology does not wish "to politicize the church," but it does want "to Christianize church politics and the political involvement of Christians."[25]

Whereas Moltmann offers a theology of hope, a great many Latin American theologians have spearheaded a theology of liberation that often endorses violent revolution as the only recourse for oppressed and exploited peoples.[26] Breaking with the Augustinian and Thomistic traditions, liberation theologians see the church not as the historical form of the kingdom of God but as a springboard for the kingdom. The church is called not to be the kingdom but to serve the kingdom. The kingdom is a new social situation where people can live together as brothers and sisters. It is a new social order that can be partially realized through political action, even social revolution.

In liberation theology God is not so much the lord of history as the transformer of history. He is not an all-powerful king towering above history but "the power of the future," or "the courage to struggle" or "the dynamic of history." The God of liberation theology "is neither all-powerful nor a powerless sufferer. Rather, God is portrayed as one who must contend with strong and stubborn evil. God suffers, but in confrontation, not in acquiescence."[27]

The kingdom of God is not a spiritual realm apart from history but the goal of history. We ourselves can do much to actualize this goal by identifying with the poor and the oppressed. "Going to God means making God real in history; it means building up God's kingdom here and now."[28] Showing its indebtedness to Marxist philosophy, liberation theology envisages a "kingdom of freedom" arrayed against a "kingdom of necessity." Our hope is in "the horizon of freedom" rather than the personal return of Christ. We look forward not to a heaven beyond history but to the possibility of this world becoming the new heaven of God. The whole of humanity is a "latent church" moving toward a human fullness (Segundo). The greatest danger to faith is not the demonic absolutizing of political programs but callous indifference toward the needs of the poor and a preoccupation with worldly comforts at the expense of others. Our task as Christians is not to wait for God to act but to rise up and fulfill the divine mandate to ensure justice and freedom for all peoples, especially for those who are the victims of imperialism, colonialism and a rapacious capitalism.

Still more drastic is the reinterpretation of the lordship of Christ in New Age theology and philosophy. Christ is portrayed as the eros of the universe rather than the lord of the universe. Or he is the "reason" and "mind" of the cosmos rather than the ruler of the cosmos (Matthew Fox). He is the energy that rejuvenates the universe rather than the power that controls the universe. We may speak of him as lord but only in the sense of "one who makes the universe go around."[29] Instead of the infinite-personal God of traditional Christian faith, New Agers uphold the evolutionary creative force that is realizing itself in conjunction with the strivings of a humanity seeking to be reborn. Jesus is the paradigm of heroic manhood who shows us how to draw upon the energy of the cosmic Christ within us.

Jesus as Lord and Victor

The contemporary scene, rife as it is with heretical misunderstandings, challenges us to reappropriate the insights of the biblical revelation concerning the kingdom of God, clarified and illumined in varying degrees in the catholic tradition of the church. While it is a mistake to draw a bifurcation between the reign of the Father and the reign of the Son (as does Schleiermacher and to a lesser extent Reinhold Niebuhr), we can nevertheless affirm that the rule of both Father and Son has several dimensions. Even at creation Christ was already ruler, for the whole universe was created in him and for him (Col 1:16-20). "Every power and authority in the universe is subject to him as head" (Col 2:10 REB). Paul declares that the creative and redemptive work of Christ embraces "all things, whether on earth or in heaven" (Col 1:20). God or Christ is called the *pantokrator* (ruler of all things) in Revelation 1:8; 4:8; 11:17; 15:3; 16:7, 14; 19:6, 15; 21:22. Yet the lordship of Christ will not achieve its goal in the redemption of humanity until the eschaton, when he shall return the kingdom to the Father (1 Cor 15:24). Not until then will we be afforded "full and free admission into the eternal kingdom of our Lord and Saviour Jesus Christ" (2 Pet 1:11 NEB; cf. 2 Tim 4:18).

I concur with church tradition that it is appropriate to differentiate the kingdoms of power, grace and glory. Both God and Christ are lord over all of them,[30] yet these kingdoms are not coextensive. The kingdom of grace is the new reality of reconciliation and redemption, which enters human history in the life, death and resurrection of Jesus

Christ. This kingdom is destined to include the whole of the kingdom of nature, but its efficacy depends on the degree to which a sinful humanity acknowledges Christ as king and lord. Paul says that Christ has "rescued us from the power of darkness and transferred us into the kingdom of his beloved Son, in whom we have redemption, the forgiveness of sins" (Col 1:13-14 NRSV). But the reference is to the community of faith, not to the whole of creation. All things are now subject to Christ, but not all things are subject to Christ willingly. The powers of the world still continue their hostile defiance of Christ's lordship even while they remain under his authority. The author of Revelation exults, "Sovereignty over the world has passed to our Lord and his Christ, and he shall reign for ever!" (Rev 11:15 REB). But this was envisaged as an eschatological event that was to happen momentarily or at least very shortly.

Jesus Christ as "very God of very God" is already ruler over all creation, but he rules with a "rod of iron" (Ps 2:9; Rev 2:27; 12:5; 19:15). He is also king and lord of the church, but here he rules from the cross and through the Word. He *will* rule as the king of glory—when every knee shall bow and tongue confess that he is indeed "King of kings and Lord of lords" (1 Tim 6:15; Rev 17:14; 19:16). Whereas power is imposed, grace is offered and enacted; glory is received and celebrated. His alien work is the rule of his wrath; his proper work is the rule of his love. Not until the eschaton will we be able to perceive the paradoxical unity between these two modes of divine rule. Then we shall come to know in a concrete way that the wrath of God is actually a form of his love, that his alien work serves his proper work, that creation is for the sake of redemption, that the warrior king is at the same time the prince of peace.

Since Jesus came to inaugurate the kingdom, it is appropriate in the period of his earthly ministry to speak of the kingdom dawning upon the world. At the resurrection and Pentecost the kingdom of Christ was established as a concrete reality in the world, but it remains hidden. It works secretly as the yeast in the loaf (Lk 13:20-21) or the seed in the ground (Mt 13:1-9). At the coming again of Christ the kingdom will be consummated, and the old creation will be transfigured into a new heaven and a new earth.

We now live in the interim kingdom—between the resurrection and the second advent. This is the millennial kingdom, though the glory of the millennium is still ahead of us, for Christ's rule will not become visible until he comes again.[31] His return in glory and his final conquest over the powers of evil will prepare the way for the eternal kingdom of God.

Instead of holding that both church and state belong to the one kingdom of grace (as do Barth, Oscar Cullmann and Dietrich Bonhoeffer), I prefer to speak of the kingdom of grace as penetrating both church and state through the impact of the community of true believers. As Christians permeate the state as a leaven, the state is brought within the sphere of redemptive history. The state is the arena or field of redemption; the church is the historical sign and means of redemption. The kingdom is the hidden reality of God's providential and redemptive rule within both church and state.

The two orders of creation and redemption remain distinct, yet overlap like two intersecting circles. The overlapped area is the so-called interim kingdom where Christ's reign is fully established, but this reign continues to take in more and more territory. This is a moving, not a static, picture. The redemptive activity of Christ has already penetrated the order of creation and is slowly but surely surging forward to bring all of creation under his sway (Eph 1:22-23 REB).[32] Christ is Savior only in the order of redemption, but redemption is the goal and climax of creation. What I am proposing is not a triumphalism of the church but a triumphalism of the kingdom. The institutional church may falter and fall, but the kingdom of God—the invisible church—continues to move forward even when appearances may be to the contrary.

Clinton Morrison makes an interesting albeit not altogether satisfactory distinction between Christ's lordship and victory.[33] The lordship of Christ extends over all of creation, but the victory of Christ takes place only in the community of faith. In my view, the victory of Christ is twofold: his cross and resurrection triumph over the principalities and powers, and the implementation of this triumph by the Holy Spirit in both church and world. The powers of darkness were indeed disarmed by the resurrection victory of Christ (Col 2:15), but they continue to fight on the basis of a lie—that they still possess real power. His victory is objective and cosmic as well as subjective and existential. We must not minimize the decisive role of faith through the power of the Spirit, but neither should we obscure or downplay the reality of Christ's universal triumph over sin, death and the devil in his cross and resurrection.

Instead of Barth's royal lordship of Christ, Moltmann's crucified lordship and Schleiermacher's spiritual lordship, I affirm a progressive lordship whereby the victory of Christ is carried forward into history through the outpouring of the Holy Spirit. Christ's rule is manifested not only in the victory of suffering love—his rule by his right hand—but also in the overthrow of the powers of the world by the sword—his rule by his left hand. Christ's redemption becomes real for us only through the paradoxical love of the cross received by faith, but his lordship is already effected over the powers of the world by virtue of his cross and resurrection triumph. These powers are now made to serve his conquering kingdom even when they remain openly hostile to him.

Our role as Christians is to spread the good news of the kingdom of God through the proclamation of the word and the witness of vicarious love. It behooves us also to remind the secular powers that the state is under the law of God, that its mission is to secure order and to implement justice in the secular realm. The kingdom of God does not yet include the state, but the state in its efforts to enforce justice in society can witness to the coming of the kingdom, even when God and his law are not publicly or consciously acknowledged. We should steer clear of an ecclesiocracy in which the church tries to gain control of the state, but we should be open to the vision of a christocracy in which the state moves more and more under the lordship of Christ. We should not entertain any notion of establishing a truly Christian state, for this is an exclusively eschatological reality; yet we should diligently strive for a just state, one that defends the rights of the poor and oppressed, one that upholds human dignity and equality in the light of the transcendent criterion of the law and the gospel.[34]

While both church and state are ruled by Christ, the church is also destined to rule with Christ (Eph 2:6). People of faith participate now, however, not in his magisterial power but in his ministerial power. We have been made a "Kingdom of Priests" in order to serve God the Father (Rev 1:6 NJB), but this is a spiritual vocation that excludes the goal of worldly power. We conquer not by the sword but by the power of the powerlessness of love. Our weapons are the "helmet of salvation" and "the sword of the Spirit, which is the word of God" (Eph 6:17 NRSV). If we suffer with him now we shall reign with him in glory (Rom 8:17; 2 Tim 2:12; 1 Pet 4:13).

Christocracy in the evangelical sense does not mean that the church obtrusively tries to force its convictions on the state or nation. "Its true meaning is that the Church announces what it believes to be the word of Christ for the world, but that it does not use any other means of persuasion than the truth of its message."[35] This is a christocracy that relies not on the power of the sword but on "the prophetic means of the word and the priestly means of prayer and leaves it to the King himself to make these means effective."[36]

As Christians we cannot bring in the kingdom but we can witness to it. We can be instruments in its realization, but this depends wholly on the discretion of the Holy Spirit, who works in his own time and way (1 Tim 6:13-15 REB). We can perhaps hasten its coming by our prayers, though this, too, rests solely on the free action of God. Barth is right that even the best human action cannot be identified with God's action; yet God may work in conjunction with human action, God may use human action to prepare the way for his own redeeming action. The apostle says that we should "look forward to the coming of the day of God, and work to hasten it on" (2 Pet 3:12 REB). While we cannot create the kingdom, we can set up signs and parables of the kingdom. We can announce the coming of the kingdom and call people to be ready for Christ's appearing. We cannot build the kingdom, but we can serve the kingdom with the aid of the Spirit, who leads us to proclaim and demonstrate the power of the new age as we seek to make the world the theater of God's glory.

·TEN·

THE FINALITY OF CHRIST

I am the way, and the truth and the life;
no one comes to the Father, but by me.

JOHN 14:6

There is no salvation through anyone else; in all the world
no other name has been granted to mankind
by which we can be saved.

ACTS 4:12 REB

A Gospel which is not exclusive will never include the world,
for it will never master it.

P. T. FORSYTH

True religion can consist only in the fact that our trust is not in
"religion" at all, but wholly and solely in the divine mercy
which meets us in God's revelation.

EMIL BRUNNER

Jesus Christ, as he is testified to us in Holy Scripture,
is the one Word of God, whom we are to hear,
whom we are to trust and obey in life and in death.

BARMEN DECLARATION

There are times in which the only way to keep alive the
nonvindictive, nonjudgmental, self-sacrificing witness of Jesus
Christ is to stand with rude dogmatism on the rock that is Jesus
Christ, condemning all compromise as the work of the AntiChrist.

RONALD GOETZ

With the rise of neo-Protestant theology in the early nineteenth century and neo-Catholic theology somewhat later, a new theological paradigm has emerged into prominence that seriously calls into question the exclusivistic claims of the Christian faith in its traditional forms. This paradigm has been facilitated by the encounter of the church with Romanticism, with its emphasis on individuality, pluralism and relativism. It was Schleiermacher who exulted in the plurality of the modern world: "Let none offer the seekers a system making exclusive claim to truth, but let each man offer his characteristic, individual presentation."[1] Interestingly, Schleiermacher indicated a preference for pagan Rome over Christian Rome because of its toleration of a variety of religions.

The history of religions school associated with such illustrious names as Ernst Troeltsch, Hermann Gunkel and Johannes Weiss also paved the way for modern relativism and pluralism. Troeltsch articulated the theory of historicism, which holds that all ideas and values are conditioned by historical and sociological forces. For him there is no final revelation: the Divine Life within history always manifests itself in new and peculiar individualizations. Truth is polymorphous in that ultimate reality is necessarily apprehended in a variety of ways, all of which have some claim to validity.[2]

The emerging philosophy of pragmatism gave additional impetus to the slide toward relativism and pluralism. William James, who has had an unmistakable influence on both process theology and New Age theology, advanced the notion of a pluralistic universe, which denies a unitary, overarching criterion of meaning and allows for the coexistence of conflicting religious claims: "The divine can mean no single quality, it must mean a group of qualities, by being champions of which in alternation, different men may all find worthy missions."[3]

More recently, with the rise of the theology of religions, the uniqueness and particularity of Christian revelation has been further called into question. Paul Knitter says that we need to "recognize the possibility that other 'saviors' have carried out . . . for other people" the redemptive work which as Christians we know in Jesus Christ.[4] For Knitter the common ground of religion exists in the struggle to liberate the oppressed peoples of the world. Eugene C. Bianchi upholds a

"Christian polytheism" that allows for other savior figures besides Christ: "In our fuller confrontation with other religions, we will have to mitigate earlier claims about Jesus. There may be ways of maintaining the uniqueness of his mediatorship for believers, but we will have to recognize other mediators, ancient and contemporary, of God to man."[5] Hans Küng, who perhaps stands closer to the center of Christian faith, nevertheless contends that a person "is to be saved within the religion that is made available to him in his historical situation. Hence it is his right and his duty to seek God within that religion in which the hidden God has already found him."[6] Calling for a "global religious vision" John Hick avers that it is no longer necessary "to insist . . . upon the uniqueness and superiority of Christianity; and it may be possible to recognize the separate validity of the other great world religions, and both to learn from them and enable them to learn from the Christian tradition."[7]

This pluralistic vision is further articulated by Hick, Knitter, Gordon Kaufman, Langdon Gilkey, Marjorie Hewitt Suchocki and a number of other theologians in *The Myth of Christian Uniqueness.*[8] The authors advocate going beyond *inclusivism,* which sees Christ as the fulfillment of the world religions, to *pluralism,* which abandons any claim to finality for Christ and Christianity. Every religion, according to this new view, is shaped by a particular cultural ethos and speaks to needs and questions peculiar to that ethos. No religion can justifiably make absolutist claims in the light of the incredible diversity of religious expression uncovered by historical science, but every religion has a claim to uniqueness.

I see Christianity as both radically exclusive and incontrovertibly inclusive in that it upholds Jesus Christ as the only way to salvation, but this claim goes out to all peoples, irrespective of race, nationality, religious affiliation or ethnic background. All are called to have a role in the denouement of the kingdom of God. An inclusivism that regards other religions as salvific and their faithful adherents as incipiently or implicitly Christian or even as worthy models of devotion invariably leads to a corrosive pluralism, which sees other religions as having independent validity. Pluralism in turn leads back to a syncretistic inclusivism, since it gives rise to a desire to find what unites us in our diversity, even if this is only a general quest for truth.

The ascendancy of the new theological orientation can be described in various ways. Samuel Moffett, veteran Presbyterian missionary to Korea, views the nineteenth century as the age of missions, the early and middle part of the twentieth as the age of ecumenism, and the present period as the age of religious pluralism. New Agers describe this last stage as the "Age of Aquarius"—marked by the celebration of the intuitive over the cerebral. Some of the devotees of the new spirituality urge the cultivation of a holocentric over a theocentric perspective: we begin with a vision of the whole of reality that overcomes the antithesis between divinity and humanity. Whatever images are used, it cannot be doubted that an exclusive monotheism is being challenged and in many cases supplanted by a religious pluralism that borders on syncretism.

Whereas Jesus Christ was once the focal point of theology (in the heyday of neo-orthodoxy), we have entered a period when our religious unity is to be found simply in the experience of a divine presence that takes multitudinous forms. This presence is variously called the Higher Self, the World Spirit, the Life Force, the Real and the Creative Surge. A materialistic metaphysics has been edged out by a panpsychism that envisages the universe or nature as a great thought (James Jeans, Fritjof Capra).[9] A holistic vision has taken the place of the dualism of Descartes's era; humanity and nature are now treated as dimensions of a cosmic unity. The utter transcendence of God is either outrightly denied or seriously compromised.

This is not to discount the many voices within the Christian community that retain the traditional focus. Conservative evangelicals like Carl Henry, Millard Erickson, Harold Netland, Michael Horton, Daniel Clendenin and Ronald Nash strongly contend for a biblical supernaturalism over the reigning naturalism and idealism that distinguish the new cultural paradigm. Those who look back to the theology of crisis (associated with Karl Barth, Emil Brunner, Hendrik Kraemer) stoutly insist on the uniqueness of the Christian revelation in the face of the many other claims to definitive revelation.[10] Neo-Lutherans like Carl Braaten uphold a christocentric over a purely theocentric theology in the area of interreligious dialogue.[11] Eastern Orthodox theologians like Alexander Schmemann lament the drift toward relativism and syncretism and call the ecumenical movement back to its original purpose: the unity and the renewal of the church of Jesus Christ. Schmemann observes that while the original goal of the ecumenical movement was organic unity in Christ, the new goal appears to be "the smooth functioning of pluralistic society," having little to do with "the fundamental Christian values of unity, faith and truth."[12]

Despite a discernible reaction to the swing toward pluralism and relativity, one cannot deny that the new cultural paradigm, which is antagonistic toward any claim to exclusive truth, now holds sway over most of the nations of the Western world. This is also true for the nations of Eastern Europe, including the former Soviet Union, which are resolutely abandoning the inflexible dogmas of Marxist socialism for freedom, autonomy and individuality, although Marxism continues to be a force to reckon with when united with nationalistic aspirations. If one considers the reigning mentality in academic religious circles today, one must conclude that there has been a paradigmatic shift of immense proportions from a theology of transcendence to a theology of radical immanence. A dogmatic stance has been eroded in favor of relativism and mysticism. Heresy as a valid theological concern is now out of fashion, although heresy in fact is stronger than ever. Orthodoxy too is not a burning issue, not even a worthy theological goal. Perhaps one reason for this shift is that conceptual revelation is no longer seriously considered a valid criterion for faith and practice. Martin Marty has adroitly suggested that henotheism is coming to prevail over monotheism: people still worship at the altar of the traditional god but increasingly allow for the possibility of the truth and salvific efficacy of other gods.

The new trends in biblical criticism also foster a relativistic mentality. Structuralism finds the meaning of the text in the literary form that the text embodies; questions of historical reliability and ontological truth are conveniently left to the historians and philosophers, respectively. Reader-response criticism (Edgar V. McKnight) finds the meaning of the text in the subjective response of the interpreter, thus opening the door to a thoroughgoing relativism. For the deconstructionist the literary structures are changing because language is fluid; there is consequently no solid text with which the interpreter can work. Paul Ricoeur, who is both a structuralist and a narrative theologian, describes the Bible as a salvific religious poem that throws light upon the human predicament. Most of the new biblical critics generally regard the notion that the Bible gives infallible information concerning the will and purpose of God for the world as a relic of an outmoded dogmatism.

Christ in the New Theologies

The soundness of any particular theological school or position is finally measured by how it stands on Jesus Christ. Needless to say, the Christ of Chalcedonian orthodoxy is in palpable eclipse in most circles except those of the old Roman Catholicism, confessional evangelicalism and Eastern Orthodoxy.

In the older liberalism Jesus Christ was no longer the Word made flesh, the preexistent Son of God in human garb, but now the "moral ideal" (Ritschl), or the "mediator of God-consciousness" (Schleiermacher) or a prophetic figure in which the redeeming power of God is made manifest (Herrmann). For Troeltsch our faith is not in Jesus but in the God that Jesus revealed and proclaimed.

With its drastic reinterpretation of God, process theology must also see Jesus in an entirely new light. He is envisioned as a prophetic genius whose power lies in the supreme ideal that he actualized (Alfred North Whitehead). Or he is the supreme act of God in the world (David Griffin). Or "the omega point of evolution" (Pierre Teilhard de

Chardin). Or a high point in the creative process, though not necessarily the highest (Henry Nelson Wieman). Or for John Cobb, who welcomes the new religious pluralism, though not without reservations, "the image of creative transformation."[13]

Existentialist theology discerns in Jesus a person through whom we make contact with the New Being (Tillich) or the unconditional (Bultmann). He is sometimes portrayed as the paradigm of authentic selfhood. Tillich acknowledges Christ as the final revelation but not the only revelation. Like Schleiermacher he looks forward to the time when a new global religion (which he calls "the Religion of the Concrete Spirit") will supplant institutional Christianity.[14]

In liberationist circles Jesus is a social revolutionary, a martyr for righteousness, or the historical personification of liberating love. In his life and death the power of revolutionary love is released into the world, thereby making it possible to continue the ongoing struggle for peace and social justice.[15]

Narrative theologians like George Lindbeck will confess Jesus as Lord, but they tell us that this is not an ontological truth but an intrasystematic truth.[16] It has relevance to the community of faith, but not necessarily to peoples of other religious traditions and cultural heritages. Theology is descriptive of the language and thought world of a particular community of faith. Theologians must avoid introducing into the public arena ontological truth claims, lest they transpose theology into simply another philosophy of religion and involve us in questionable apologetics.

Finally, serious attention should be given to what I call neomysticism, now a dominant force in both the theology of religions and the New Age movement. Marcus Borg launches a third quest for the historical Jesus in his *Jesus: A New Vision* and reinterprets Christ as a renowned psychic and spiritual master whose ministry was authenticated by his exorcisms and healings.[17] Matthew Fox describes Jesus as the historical symbol of Mother Earth who is daily crucified and resurrected.[18] The new mystics see God not as the receptacle of the world's values (the process view) nor primarily as the matrix of the world's possibilities (as in feminist theology) but as the eruption of creative power from the world's depths.

The common thread in most of the new theologies is a denial of Jesus Christ as the very God himself, as a divine person in two natures. Instead we are directed to a Christ who is the decisive realization of human possibilities or the embodiment of some eternal value or ideal. The new heresies verge toward either an ebionitic interpretation of Christ (beginning with his humanity) or a docetic interpretation (beginning with an abstract idea of Christ). In countering the new theologies we need to stand in perceptible continuity with the ancient councils. Christ is first of all not the maturation of the human spirit, or the mirror of a transcendent ideal or the flower of humanity, but the incarnation of the preexistent Word of God, the second person of the Trinity: in Christ we encounter the very God himself.

A Reaffirmation of Biblical Christianity

Against the new theologies Christians faithful to the biblical revelation must again affirm what Brunner aptly called the scandal of particularity: the inexplicable fact that God became man at one point in history, that God revealed himself among one particular people in history, the Jews, and that his revelation in this people and in this person is definitive and final. God revealed himself once for all times in this particular event or series of events attested and mirrored in the Bible. For Schleiermacher the superiority of Christianity lies primarily in its freedom from exclusivity. In the catholic evangelical theology that I uphold, the superiority of Christianity lies in its willingness to be continually purified and reformed in the light of the one great revelation of God in Jesus Christ, which cannot be duplicated or renewed but can be heralded and obeyed.

If we were to focus simply on the *particularity* of the biblical revelation, we could then be justly accused of fostering an insular or parochial form of religion. But as biblical Christians we must also emphasize the scandal of *universality:* that this one revelation is intended for all, that Christ's salvation goes out to all, including the outsider and the sinner. The kingdom of God seeks to embrace not only the people of Israel, not only people of faith but the whole world, including the enemies of faith, though the pathway into the kingdom is only through faith and repentance. Christ died not for the righteous but for sinners, he justifies not the godly but the ungodly. The fellowship he inaugurates is one based on sin rather than holiness (Nygren) in that it is consummated on our level. We enter this fellowship through the confession of sin, not through progress toward holiness. At the same time, the other part of the dialectic must also be maintained: we remain in this fellowship only by leaving sin behind us and moving toward holiness. God's love goes out to sinners, but it does not leave us in our sins: it turns us toward a new life and a new future.

As evangelical Christians we are challenged to reclaim the biblical message that Jesus Christ is God incarnate and that he came into this world to deliver a lost humanity from its bondage to sin, death and the devil. Jesus is indeed our example as well as our Savior, but his mission was first to save and then to lead.

Evangelical Christianity is focused on hearing, not seeing. The kingdom of God is not a visible reality but an invisible one that makes its way in the world through the proclamation of the gospel (cf. Lk 17:20-21). The new theologies speak of imaging God in order to make him real for human experience.[19] Evangelical theology reaffirms the commandment against graven images (Ex 20:4; Deut 5:8) and extends this to a prohibition against mental images of God as well. Because the true God is incomprehensible and invisible, because he infinitely transcends all sight and understanding, he cannot be made known until he makes himself known. And God has made himself known fully and decisively in this one person, Jesus Christ. All other revelations and illuminations are simply clarifications and reaffirmations of this one incomparable revelation in human history. We make contact with Christ only through hearing the gospel about Christ, which we encounter in the Bible and also in the proclamation and ministrations of the church (cf. Rom 10:14-17; 1 Cor 1:21). Luther observed, "In order to see God we must learn to put our eyes into our ears." This indeed is the biblical way, and all other ways lead to obfuscation and deception.

Some of the new theologies calling for liturgical renewal are inclined to envisage the church as a continuation of the incarnation, and the Eucharist as a mystical reenactment of Christ's atoning sacrifice. But in a biblical, Reformed theology the church is at best a sign and witness of the incarnation. The sacrament is a proclamation and commemoration, not a repetition or extension, of Christ's sacrifice.

Neither is the world an extension of the incarnation (as Teilhard de Chardin and New Age theology would have us believe). Instead the world is the arena in which the incarnate Christ advances, the battleground on which the kingdom of God overcomes and utterly defeats the kingdom of evil. Barth rightly reminds us, however, that it is not the Christian community that brings in the kingdom of God but God alone through the work of his Spirit. To be sure, God sometimes uses us but often despite our own efforts and purposes. Our task is to witness to what he has done and is now doing to create a new world free from oppression and exploitation.

A biblical, evangelical theology will also emphasize the crucial role of the Bible as the primary witness to God's self-revelation in Jesus Christ and the primary means by which this revelation breaks through the barrier of sin to bring light and hope to a distraught humanity. The Bible is not the light itself (as in fundamentalism); nor is it a window to a transcendent light (as in much Christian mysticism); nor is it primarily a lens through which we see light in the world (as in narrative theology). Instead it is a prism by which the light of God shines on us. We see but partly; we know but not fully. The Bible is neither opaque to its object (as in mysticism) nor transparent (as in rationalism) but translucent (as in catholic evangelical theology).

Revelation too needs to be reappraised if evangelical Christians are to regain the ground lost by the mainstream of theology in the past several decades. Too long we have made the mistake of identifying God's revelation with the propositional content of the Bible. The result has been that revelation becomes the property of the church, for what we apprehend directly we possess. But neither should we go the way of liberal theology by conceiving of revelation as an experience of the creative power of the universe (Schleiermacher) or as a breakthrough into a higher consciousness (Gregory Baum). I am also unhappy with Pannenberg's redefinition of revelation as the light we glean from the unfolding of history rather than an event that breaks into history from above.

I would define revelation as the movement of God into a particular human history, namely, the personal history of Jesus Christ, and the self-communication of God to his people through both the events surrounding Jesus Christ and the inspired witness to these events, which constitutes Holy Scripture. Revelation includes the experiential and the conceptual, but it goes beyond these: it basically concerns the self-disclosure of the very reality of the living God in the person of his Son. When we know this God we come to know the meaning of divine holiness and divine love. We also receive the mandate to proclaim the mighty deeds of a loving, holy God to the world. Revelation happened in the divine-human encounter that we see in the life history of Jesus, but it happens ever again as the Spirit of God awakens us to the significance of this encounter for our lives here and now.

Because revelation in biblical understanding indicates an authentic unveiling of the mystery of the divine presence and reality, I deem it more appropriate to refer to a "general awareness of God" than to "general revelation" when dealing with God's light in nature and universal history. What we can gain on our own from these extrabiblical sources is not genuine knowledge of God but only an anticipatory intimation of God's love and judgment. Theologians who build on general revelation are also ineluctably led to construct a natural theology, which is always a dead-end road. God's universal light is invariably misinterpreted and distorted because of human sin, which clouds our cognitive capabilities as well as binding our will to powers hostile to God. I fully agree with Gregory of Nyssa that "we cannot see God in nature, but we can try to see nature in God."

Barth has been helpful in his conception of "little lights" and "other true words" that the Christian is able to discern in nature and in other religions by virtue of the one great light of Christ that makes these lesser lights and words intelligible and credible. In his later writings Barth alluded to a third circle of witnesses outside the Bible and the church that magnify the name of Christ and testify to his goodness. But only people of faith by virtue of the opening of their eyes to the revelation of the glory of God in Jesus Christ can validly assess these other words and lights, which always constitute something alien and discordant in the systems and credos of the world of unbelief.[20]

This brings us again to the enigmatic relationship between Christianity and the great world religions. I think we would do well to emphasize today that while Christianity is indeed one of the world religions, it must be sharply differentiated from all other religions in terms of its origin and goal.[21] Biblical Christianity affirms that the Christian religion is founded on a unique revelation of God to humankind in the person of Jesus Christ and that this religion is a sign and witness to God's self-revelation. Christianity as a revelation must be distinguished from Christianity as an empirical religion, but the former can be perceived only through the eyes of faith. It is permissible to compare Christianity as an empirical phenomenon with other religions, but it must be judged theologically on the grounds of its unique foundation, which lies outside the confines of a phenomenological analysis of religion. The world religions should be treated not as ways to salvation but as pointers to salvation, since the revelation of God in Jesus Christ fulfills as well as negates the deepest spiritual aspirations of humankind. The non-Christian religions should not be categorically or uniformly repudiated as agencies of damnation, but they should be regarded as signs of contradiction, for their conceptions of God unfailingly conflict with God's disclosure of himself in Jesus Christ. We should be accepting of people of all religions but surely not of all religious claims and practices.

Barth was right to see the Christian revelation as bringing about the abolition of religion, but it is an abolition that at the same time purifies and restores the human yearnings for fellowship with God. In this sense it is possible to speak of a true religion, a religion that points beyond itself to the Word of God, which stands in judgment over all religious and moral striving.[22]

As opposed to an ecclesiocentric view of religion in which salvation is tied to the rites and creeds of the church and a purely theocentric view which sees all religions as pathways to God, I propose with Barth, Kraemer, Braaten and others a christocentric view of religions, which acclaims Jesus Christ as both their fulfillment and their negation. This is not religious imperialism or churchly triumphalism but a humble acknowledgment that salvific truth is the property of no particular religion and that the redemption of religion entails looking beyond all outward forms and credos to the living God himself, who judges the sinful craving for power in the religions and who directs peoples of every faith to his once-for-all intervention for a sinful world in the person of Jesus Christ.

Hans Küng recommends weighing the validity of the various religions in the light of a general ethical criterion that he calls "the spirit of Jesus Christ" or simply "humanization."[23] But this is to subordinate the truth claims of the various religions to an ethical metaphysic ostensibly drawn for the most part from the Enlightenment. Evangelical Christianity insists that the truth of the religions is to be found in their openness to and congruity with the Christ revelation. Because this revelation overturns the idols of the religious imagination of all peoples, including Christians, the pathway to the regeneration of the religions lies in the personal transformation of religious and not so religious people by the power of the gospel of the cross.

Finally, it is incumbent on biblical Christians to affirm once again that the mission of the church is the evangelizing of the world and the equipping of the saints for the arduous life of discipleship under the cross. To reconceive the church's mission as the self-development of oppressed peoples or the civilizing of backward peoples is to move away from New Testament Christianity to a vague humanitarianism that has its roots in the Renaissance and Enlightenment.

The liberation theologian Frederick Herzog is typical of the avant-garde mentality when he interprets the Christian mission as "the radical risk of sharing corporate selfhood with the wretched of the earth" rather than "an attempt to impose strange dogmas upon other men not Christian. . . . It is not at all conversion of . . . heathen to the Christian religion, but the surrender of the private middle-class self."[24] This position is shared by Jürgen Moltmann, who at the eighth ecumenical World Mission Conference at Bangkok (1973) advocated salvation in and through economic justice, political freedom and cultural change.[25]

It is fashionable in the circles of neo-Protestant theology to assert that the mission of the church is not to bring Christ to the peoples of the world but to find Christ already among them, for Christ is presently ministering to them in a hidden way.[26] Or it is said that the world is the church in its latency, and our mission is to transform the latent church into the manifest church (Tillich). Those who live up to the highest within them are labeled "anonymous Christians" (Karl Rahner).

It is important to make a distinction between the spiritual and cultural mandates of the church. The first concerns the proclamation of the gospel to lost sinners, which must take priority over everything else on the church's agenda. But the church also has the mandate of reclaiming the life and thought of the culture for the gospel, and this it does through its teaching and serving ministry. The church must never become a political lobby, but it must preach the whole counsel of God—the law and the gospel—and this means that its message will have far-reaching political and social implications. It is up to individual Christians as citizens of the state to apply the teachings of the church to the political arena. The church as a church points directions but must take care not to propose political solutions, though there may be rare occasions when this is necessary.

The proclamation of the church to the world also involves exposing the fallacies of the world's self-interpretations and therefore requires offering a credible apologetic defense of the faith. But this is an apologetics in the service of the kerygmatic proclamation. It is an apologetics that forms an integral part of dogmatics. It is dogmatics in conversation with the ideologies and philosophies that dominate the world's structures. Theology is not simply *descriptive*, as narrative theology would have it, but also *prescriptive*. The Christ we proclaim is Lord over the culture as well as over the church.

The mission of the church is to herald the coming kingdom of God, but the church must never mistake itself for the kingdom or confuse its own actions with the actions of God in realizing his kingdom. We as Christians can prepare the way for the kingdom, but God in his own time and way brings in the kingdom. We can manifest and demonstrate its power, but we cannot build or perfect it. The task of the church is a modest one: to wait, pray and hope for the coming of the kingdom, to witness to and acclaim God's redeeming and sanctifying work; but the church must never confuse its work with God's work or its righteousness with divine righteousness. The church can create parables and signs of the kingdom, but it cannot extend or fortify the kingdom through its own power and strategy. Biblical Christians could never say with the philosopher Hegel: "The Kingdom of God is coming, and our hands are busy at its delivery."[27] God builds his kingdom through his own power and initiative, but he enlists us as coworkers in making the promise of the kingdom known to the world.

An Emerging Confessional Situation

Theologians of various persuasions are beginning to speak of a new confessional situation, a *status confessionis*, as the church finds itself engulfed in a crisis concerning the integrity of its message and the validity of its language. The many attempts today to resymbolize God and to reconceive Christ are signs that people of faith may be called again to battle for the truth, to engage in a new *Kirchenkampf* (church struggle).

The problem of theological authority has become especially acute, since it would seem that cultural experience is supplanting the biblical witness as the ruling criterion for faith and practice. An emerging neognosticism locates truth in the alteration of consciousness rather than in an event in sacred history.[28] The philosopher Schopenhauer, a favorite of many New Agers, has declared that we are justified neither by faith nor by works but by knowledge. Tillich's contention that self-discovery is God-discovery betrays a gnostic mentality. When Carl Jung asserts, "I do not believe, I know," he is placing his trust in intuitive knowledge over historical revelation.

In feminist circles there is a call for a new canon and a Third Testament that would drastically alter the foundations of the faith. Rosemary Ruether pleads for augmenting the canon with writings that manifest a sensitivity to the concerns of women and other oppressed peoples. She recommends including tracts drawn from goddess religions, Gnosticism and marginal Christian traditions often deemed heretical.[29]

The new mood in the culture was strikingly anticipated by Ralph Waldo Emerson, one of the mentors of the new spirituality: "Man is weak to the extent that he looks outside himself for help. It is only as he throws himself unhesitatingly upon the God within himself that he learns his own power and works miracles."[30] The motto of the New Age is struggle, growth and freedom as opposed to the biblical motto: faith, repentance and service.

The loss of transcendence is especially disconcerting when we consider the theological options today. There seems to be a confluence of various theological movements (liberationist, feminist, neomystical, process) toward a religion of radical immanence in which human experience and imagination preempt biblical revelation as the measuring rod for truth.

That real heresy is now a problem in the church is attested by the frequent attempts to downgrade the Old Testament. Johann Semler, one of the first German theologians to apply the historical-critical method of the study of Scripture, described the Old Testament as "a collection of crude Jewish prejudices diametrically opposed to Christianity."[31] Complaining that the Old Testament promotes a legalistic type of thought, Schleiermacher recommended that it be ranked as a mere appendage to the New Testament.[32] Radical feminists see the Old Testament as incurably patriarchal and the Sky Father, the supposed god of the Old Testament, as an obstacle to women's liberation.[33] Existentialist and process theologians view large parts of the Bible as mythological and have assigned themselves the task of translating what they consider basically poetry into a modern ontology. There is some sentiment in liberationist circles to deemphasize the Jewish matrix of Scripture out of a commitment to the rights of Palestinians.

What is ominous is that the new theologies, which are for the most part aligned with ideological movements, are seeking to revamp the worship practices of the church, notably through the production of radically altered prayer books and hymnals.[34] Father language for God is being drastically curtailed and new symbols for God are being offered: the infinite depth and ground of all being, the creative process, the Womb of Being, the Primal Matrix, the pool of unlimited power, the New Being, the power of being, the Eternal Now and so on. Try praying to one of these!

In November 1989 the Anglican Church in New Zealand introduced a prayer book that not only eliminated allegedly sexist language but dropped most references to Zion and Israel. It was explained that a prayer manual was needed to offer texts more relevant to the Maoris and South Pacific Islanders. Wendy Ross, president of the New Zealand Jewish Council, protested: "The only precedent for this was the German church during the Nazi era that wanted to de-Judaize the Scriptures. We don't have copyright because [the psalms] are too old,

JESUS CHRIST: SAVIOR & LORD

but it is our ancient and sacred literature and we don't like having it distorted. . . . We regard the removal of the words Zion and Israel in most cases as profoundly anti-Jewish."[35]

Such activities should remind us of the close parallels between the religious situation today and the situation of the church in Germany in the later 1920s and 1930s. The so-called German Christians represented that segment within the German church that sought to accommodate to the rising ideology of National Socialism. Hitler was hailed as a new Messiah, and the election that brought the Nazis to power was celebrated as an act of God. The German Christians were especially intent on combating the idea that revelation was limited to biblical times: it continues, they said, throughout human history—in every culture and race. The religious intuitions of the German people were deemed equal (if not superior) in authority to the insights of the Bible. Scripture was reinterpreted through the lens of the *Volksgeist* (the spirit of the Germanic people). A concerted attempt was made to purge the Bible of Judaic expressions like "Zion" and "Hallelujah." They preferred to speak of the people of God instead of the people of Israel. Interestingly, in some radical circles God was conceived of androgynously and referred to as Father-Mother.

The German Christians enlisted in their support some of the leading theologians and biblical scholars, among them Gerhard Kittel, the erudite New Testament scholar; Emanuel Hirsch, a Kierkegaard scholar; and Paul Althaus, a renowned Luther scholar. Others beguiled at least for a time by the new ideology were Friedrich Gogarten, a former student of Troeltsch; Rudolf Otto, well-known historian of religion; Werner Elert; Otto Weber; and Heinrich Bornkamm. The respected Catholic theologian Karl Adam, who later broke decisively with the Nazis, gave this tribute to Hitler at the time of his meteoric rise to power: "Now he stands before us as the one for whom the voices of our poets and sages called, as the liberator of the German genius, who took the blindfold from our eyes and—through all the political, economic, social and confessional veils—let us again see and love the one essential: our unity of blood, our German self, the *homo Germanus.*"[36]

It was against the German Christian compromise that the Confessing Church movement emerged with its vigorous attack on natural theology and its bold reaffirmation of the uniqueness of the revelation of Jesus Christ and the authority of the Scriptures. In the words of the Barmen Declaration, drawn up primarily by Barth:

> Jesus Christ, as he is testified to us in the Holy Scripture, is the one Word of God, whom we are to hear, whom we are to trust and obey in life and in death. We repudiate the false teaching that the church can and must recognize yet other happenings and powers, images and truths as divine revelation alongside this one Word of God, as a source of her preaching.[37]

This statement does not rule out the possibility that God may communicate his light and truth in various ways, but it does insist that the church is bound in its proclamation to the definitive and incomparable revelation given in Jesus Christ. In the fourth article the church is urged to take care not to accommodate its message to prevailing ideological and political winds.

As in prewar Germany, there is currently in the nations of the West a resurgence of interest in the occult, a growing openness to Eastern religions and the rise of a naturistic mysticism. Pluralism is celebrated as something good in its own right; the destructive or demonic side of religion is conveniently overlooked. An inclusivistic mentality regards with disdain any appeal to a particular revelation or any absolutist claim to religious truth. The most that we can achieve is a "relative absoluteness" in which our religious way becomes only one among others, though through dialogue we can gain some further intimation of the infinite mystery that hovers over all religions.[38]

The god of pluralism and inclusivism can be a jealous god; whatever does not fit into a pluralistic or globalistic agenda is condemned as backward and provincial. Theological seminaries in the mainline churches today are remarkably open to including Buddhists and Hindus on their staff but are conspicuously reluctant to invite scholars identified with either the old Catholicism or the evangelical side of Protestantism.

The battle today is between the historical Christian faith with its confession of the reality of a supernatural God and the uniqueness of Jesus Christ and the new spirituality, which embraces most of the recent theological and religious movements. It is the difference between a biblical monotheism and a naturalistic panentheism, between a catholic evangelicalism and neomysticism and neognosticism. One side defends both the particularity of divine revelation and the universality of its claims and mission; the other champions an inclusivistic or global vision.

Class conflict is also an important factor in this growing cleavage. Those who constitute the so-called new class—upwardly mobile professionals, teachers and social workers—are open to an inclusivistic and relativistic worldview, for it lends moral sanction to their growing affluence.[39] On the other hand, those identified with the older business and farming interests are more likely to defend traditional moral values and religious claims. The New Age movement could aptly be called a royal theology, for it justifies the privileged status of the upper middle and upper classes by its doctrine of karma, in which social status is determined by merits or demerits accumulated in previous states of existence. Shirley MacLaine, one of the gurus of this movement, argues that "if you're poor or unemployed—you have only yourself to blame. You have victimized yourself by not living up to your potential."[40] The key to changing society, they say, lies in a transformation of consciousness.

Against this view biblical Christianity insists that the key to changing the world is the atoning death and glorious resurrection of Jesus Christ and the outpouring of the Holy Spirit at Pentecost. The world can be changed because it already has been changed through the miraculous intervention of the living God into human history. The powers of darkness have already been defeated, and therefore the future of the human race is not bleak but filled with hope and promise.

A truly just society is dependent not on experiments in social engineering, not on the cultivation of a global consciousness, not on an amalgamation of the world religions, but on a universal acknowledgment of the reality of the holy and living God of the Scriptures and acceptance of the message that he has acted decisively and irrevocably for the salvation of the human race through the life, death and resurrection of Jesus Christ. The hope of humanity rests on the kingdom of God, which is now at work in our midst, and on its consummation through the coming again of Jesus Christ in power and glory when his universal lordship will be revealed for all to see and the fruits of his redemption will be assured to all who repent and believe.

In its witness the church should not press for a return to a monolithic society in which church and state work together to ensure a Christian civilization, for such an undertaking would only draw the church away from its redemptive message and blur the lines between church and world. Neither should the church withdraw from society and cultivate little bastions of righteousness that strive to preserve the ethical and religious values handed down from the past. Instead, the church should witness to the truth of the gospel in the very midst of society in the hope and expectation that this truth will work as the leaven that turns society toward a higher degree of justice and freedom. The church cannot build the kingdom of righteousness, but it can serve this kingdom by reminding the world that there is a transcendent order that stands in judgment over every worldly achievement and that the proper attitude of leaders of nations is one of humility before a holy God and caring concern for the disinherited and the oppressed.

Notes

Chapter 1: Christ in Dispute

[1]Burton L. Mack, *The Lost Gospel: The Book of Q and Christian Origins* (San Francisco: HarperCollins, 1993), p. 10. Also see his *Who Wrote the New Testament?* (San Francisco: HarperCollins, 1995).

[2]See Pheme Perkins, "Jesus Before Christianity: Cynic and Sage?" (a review of Mack's *Lost Gospel*), *Christian Century* 110, no. 22 (1993):749.

[3]John Dominic Crossan, *The Historical Jesus: The Life of a Mediterranean Jewish Peasant* (San Francisco: HarperCollins, 1991), pp. 421-22. Also see his *Jesus: A Revolutionary Biography* (San Francisco: HarperCollins, 1994), p. 198.

[4]Cf. Geza Vermes, *Jesus the Jew: A Historian's Reading of the Gospels* (Philadelphia: Fortress, 1981), pp. 69, 90, 224; *Jesus and the World of Judaism* (Philadelphia: Fortress, 1984), p. 10; and his *The Religion of Jesus the Jew* (Minneapolis: Fortress, 1993), pp. 73, 206-7.

[5]See Marcus J. Borg, *Jesus: A New Vision* (San Francisco: Harper & Row, 1987); and his *Jesus in Contemporary Scholarship* (Valley Forge, Penn.: Trinity Press International, 1994).

[6]See Johannes Weiss, *Jesus' Proclamation of the Kingdom of God*, trans. and ed. Richard Hyde Hiers and David Larrimore Holland (Philadelphia: Fortress, 1971); and Albert Schweitzer, *The Quest of the Historical Jesus*, trans. W. Montgomery (1910; reprint, New York: Macmillan, 1959).

[7]See John P. Meier, *A Marginal Jew: Rethinking the Historical Jesus*, vol. 2: *Mentor, Message and Miracles* (New York: Doubleday Anchor, 1994).

[8]See Ben Witherington III, *The Christology of Jesus* (Minneapolis: Fortress, 1990). Witherington accepts the thesis of Birger Gerhardsson and Rainer Riesner that the disciples passed on the Jewish tradition in much the same way as other Jewish students passed on the precepts of their teachers. Not surprisingly he finds that "the alleged chasm between the speech event of the historical Jesus and the post-Easter speaking about Jesus probably never existed" (p. 15). Also see Witherington, *Jesus the Sage: The Pilgrimage of Wisdom* (Minneapolis: Fortress, 1994), and his *The Jesus Quest* (Downers Grove, Ill.: InterVarsity Press, 1995).

[9]See William R. Farmer, *The Gospel of Jesus: The Pastoral Relevance of the Synoptic Problem* (Louisville: Westminster/John Knox, 1994).

[10]See N. T. Wright, *Who Was Jesus?* (Grand Rapids: Eerdmans, 1993), and his *Jesus and the Victory of God* (Minneapolis: Fortress, 1996). Also sharply critical

of the Jesus Seminar is Luke Timothy Johnson, *The Real Jesus* (San Francisco: HarperCollins, 1996), pp. 1-56, 141-77. The Jesus Seminar, associated with such names as John Dominic Crossan, Marcus Borg, Robert Funk, James M. Robinson and Walter Wink, is a self-selected consortium of academics who are trying to forge a new understanding of the historical Jesus. See Robert Funk et al., *The Five Gospels: The Search for the Authentic Words of Jesus* (New York: Macmillan, 1993).

[11]Witherington, *Jesus the Sage*, p. 385.

[12]Farmer, *Gospel of Jesus*, pp. 177-201.

[13]Wright, *Jesus and the Victory of God*, pp. 29-82, 109-12, 658-60.

[14]See esp. Stanley J. Grenz, *Theology for the Community of God* (Nashville: Broadman & Holman, 1994), pp. 398-405.

[15]John Hick, "Jesus and the World Religions," in *The Myth of God Incarnate*, ed. John Hick (Philadelphia: Westminster, 1977), p. 183.

[16]John Hick, *The Metaphor of God Incarnate: Christology in a Pluralistic Age* (Louisville: Westminster/John Knox, 1993), p. 105. Hick allows that the "myth" of the incarnation has a historical basis in the perception of a "human life lived in faithful response to God," but he excises from this life all reference to the miraculous and supernatural.

[17]See John Macquarrie, *Principles of Christian Theology* (New York: Charles Scribner's Sons, 1966), pp. 225-32, and his *Jesus Christ in Modern Thought* (1990; reprint, Philadelphia: Trinity Press International, 1991), pp. 78-81, 120-21, 200.

[18]See Borg, *Jesus: A New Vision*, pp. 32-34, 57-75.

[19]Crossan, *Jesus: A Revolutionary Biography*, pp. 75-95.

[20]See C. S. Lewis, *Miracles* (New York: Macmillan, 1947).

[21]Elsa Tamez gives a creative reinterpretation of justification through the eyes of the marginalized and dispossessed in her *Amnesty of Grace: Justification by Faith from a Latin American Perspective*, trans. Sharon H. Ringe (Nashville: Abingdon, 1993). She sees justice and solidarity at the core of justification.

[22]See chap. 8 in this book.

[23]Friedrich Schleiermacher, *The Christian Faith*, ed. H. R. Mackintosh and J. S. Stewart, 2 vols. (New York: Harper & Row, 1963), 1:64.

[24]Joseph A. Bracken, *The Triune Symbol: Persons, Process and Community* (Lanham, Md.: University Press of America, 1985), p. 49.

[25]*The Sermons of Henry Ward Beecher* (New York: J. B. Ford, 1872), 4:32.

[26]See my extensive discussion of Bultmann in Bloesch, *Holy Scripture* (Downers Grove, Ill.: InterVarsity Press, 1994), pp. 223-54.

[27]Macquarrie, *Jesus Christ in Modern Thought*, pp. 164-66, 306-7, 383-86.

[28]Jürgen Moltmann, *The Way of Jesus Christ*, trans. Margaret Kohl (San Francisco: HarperCollins, 1990), p. 55.

[29]Jürgen Moltmann, *The Crucified God*, trans. R. A. Wilson and John Bowden (New York: Harper & Row, 1974), p. 192.

[30]Moltmann, *Way of Jesus Christ*, p. 43.

[31]Wolfhart Pannenberg, *Systematic Theology*, trans. Geoffrey W. Bromiley (Grand Rapids: Eerdmans, 1994), 2:387.

[32]Jon Sobrino, *Christology at the Crossroads*, trans. John Drury (Maryknoll, N.Y.: Orbis, 1978), pp. 369-70.

[33]Leonardo Boff, *Jesus Christ Liberator* (Maryknoll, N.Y.: Orbis, 1978), p. 275.

[34]John Howard Yoder, *The Politics of Jesus* (Grand Rapids: Eerdmans, 1972), p. 63.

[35]For Rebecca D. Pentz's criticisms of the modern focus on God as Friend, see Pentz, "Can Jesus Save Women?" in *Encountering Jesus*, ed. Stephen T. Davis (Atlanta: John Knox, 1988), pp. 105-7.

[36]Cited in *United Voice: Episcopalians United* 6, no. 6 (1994):1, 4.

[37]Pierre Teilhard de Chardin, *Christianity and Evolution*, trans. René Hague (New York: Harcourt Brace Jovanovich, 1971), p. 158.

[38]Pierre Teilhard de Chardin, *The Divine Milieu*, trans. Bernard Wall (New York: Harper & Bros., 1960), pp. 89-139.

[39]Bracken, *Triune Symbol*, p. 93.

[40]Ibid.

[41]Ibid., p. 95.

[42]Peter C. Hodgson, *Winds of the Spirit* (Louisville: Westminster/John Knox, 1994), p. 261.

[43]Ibid.

[44]Ibid., p. 262.

[45]Paul F. Knitter, "Toward a Liberation Theology of Religions," in *The Myth of Christian Uniqueness*, ed. John Hick and Paul F. Knitter (Maryknoll, N.Y.: Orbis, 1987), p. 190.

[46]Hick, *Metaphor of God Incarnate*, p. 162.

[47]See ibid., pp. 140-43.

[48]Jacques Dupuis, *Jesus Christ at the Encounter of World Religions*, trans. Robert R. Barr (Maryknoll, N.Y.: Orbis, 1991), pp. 242-47. Cf. John P. Keenan, *The Meaning of Christ: A Mahāyāna Theology* (Maryknoll, N.Y.: Orbis, 1989); and S. J. Samartha, *One Christ—Many Religions: Toward a Revised Christology* (Maryknoll, N.Y.: Orbis, 1991). A strikingly different position stressing the particularistic claims of faith is given by Daniel B. Clendenin in his *Many Gods, Many Lords: Christianity Encounters World Religions* (Grand Rapids: Baker, 1995).

[49]Worthy books by conservative evangelicals on christology include Leon Morris, *The Atonement: Its Meaning and Significance* (Downers Grove, Ill.: InterVarsity Press, 1983); I. Howard Marshall, *Jesus the Saviour* (Downers Grove, Ill.; InterVarsity Press, 1990); David F. Wells, *The Person of Christ*

(Westchester, Ill.: Crossway, 1984); and Millard J. Erickson, *The Word Became Flesh* (Grand Rapids: Baker, 1991). Also see David Parker's helpful disquisition, "Jesus Christ: Model Man of Faith, or Saving Son of God?" *Evangelical Quarterly* 67, no. 3 (1995):245-64.

Chapter 2: The Plight of Humanity

[1]On the impact of Enlightenment rationalism on evangelicalism see Mark A. Noll, *The Scandal of the Evangelical Mind* (Grand Rapids: Eerdmans, 1994), pp. 83-107.

[2]Emil Brunner, *The Mediator,* trans. Olive Wyon (Philadelphia: Westminster, 1947), p. 144.

[3]Kant is one of the few philosophers to discern the inexplicable presence of radical evil in the human heart, but he was not able to assimilate this insight into his system. On Kant's explication of radical evil see his *Religion Within the Limits of Reason Alone,* trans. Theodore M. Greene and Hoyt H. Hudson (1934; rev. ed., New York: Harper & Bros., 1960), pp. 15-138. See Brunner's discussion of Kant in *Mediator,* pp. 127-31.

[4]Reinhold Niebuhr, *The Contribution of Religion to Social Work* (New York: Columbia University Press, 1932), p. 66.

[5]See discussion by G. Stählin and W. Grundmann in *Theological Dictionary of the New Testament,* ed. Gerhard Kittel and Gerhard Friedrich, trans. and abridged by Geoffrey W. Bromiley (Grand Rapids: Eerdmans, 1985), pp. 48-49.

[6]See Frederick Copleston, *A History of Philosophy* (1946; reprint, Garden City, N.Y.: Doubleday Image, 1985), 1:208.

[7]Plato *Protagoras* 330c3ff.

[8]See Copleston, *History of Philosophy,* 1:332-50.

[9]Paul Tillich, *The Courage to Be* (London: Nisbet, 1952), p. 17.

[10]Richard Crouter, introduction to *On Religion: Speeches to Its Cultured Despisers,* by Friedrich Schleiermacher, ed. and trans. Richard Crouter (New York: Cambridge University Press, 1988), p. 53.

[11]See Bruce J. Nicholls, "Hinduism," in *The World's Religions,* ed. Norman Anderson, rev. ed. (London: Inter-Varsity Press, 1975), p. 145.

[12]Quoted in Huston Smith, *The World's Religions,* rev. ed. (San Francisco: HarperCollins, 1991), p. 99. See Richard Viladesau and Mark Massa, eds., *World Religions* (New York: Paulist, 1994), p. 81.

[13]*The Dhammapada,* in David Manning White, ed., *The Search for God* (New York: Macmillan, 1983), p. 258.

[14]Cited in Leslie Lyall, "Confucianism," in *The World's Religions,* ed. Norman Anderson, rev. ed. (London: Inter-Varsity Press, 1975), p. 222.

[15]Josef van Ess, "The Image of God and Islamic Mysticism, the Image of Man and Society," in *Christianity and the World Religions,* by Hans Küng et al., trans. Peter Heinegg (Garden City, N.Y.: Doubleday, 1986), p. 77.

[16]Ibid., p. 78.

[17]Bruce B. Lawrence, "Sin, Muslim Concept," in *Abingdon Dictionary of Living Religions,* ed. Keith Crim (Nashville: Abingdon, 1981), p. 694.

[18]Michael Fishbane, "Judaism," in *Abingdon Dictionary of Living Religions,* p. 386.

[19]J. H. Hertz, ed., *The Pentateuch and Haftorahs* (1936; 2d ed. London: Soncino, 1960), p. 484.

[20]See the discussion in John Hick, *Evil and the God of Love* (New York: Harper & Row, 1966), pp. 217-24.

[21]See Stuhlmacher's discussion of Augustine's exegesis of Rom 5:12 in Peter Stuhlmacher, *Paul's Letter to the Romans,* trans. Scott J. Hafemann (Louisville: Westminster/John Knox, 1994), p. 86.

[22]According to Philip Schaff, the leading idea in semi-Pelagianism is "that divine grace and the human will jointly accomplish the work of conversion and sanctification, and that ordinarily man must take the first step." Schaff, *History of the Christian Church* (1889; reprint, Grand Rapids: Eerdmans, 1981), 3:858. "The Pelagian system has really no place for the ideas of redemption, atonement, regeneration, and new creation. It substitutes for them our own moral effort to perfect our natural powers, and the mere addition of the grace of God as a valuable aid and support" (p. 815).

[23]For Augustine and the Reformers disordered desire or the tinder of sin is to be viewed as sin itself. See the discussion in Wolfhart Pannenberg, *Systematic Theology,* trans. Geoffrey W. Bromiley (Grand Rapids: Eerdmans, 1994), 2:239-45.

[24]See Luther, *On the Bondage of the Will,* trans. J. I. Packer and O. R. Johnston (Old Tappan, N.J.: Revell, 1957).

[25]See *Luther's Works,* trans. George V. Schick, ed. Jaroslav Pelikan (St. Louis: Concordia, 1958), 1:162.

[26]See the discussion in Hick, *Evil and the God of Love,* pp. 225-41.

[27]Friedrich Schleiermacher, *The Christian Faith,* ed. H. R. Mackintosh and J. S. Stewart, 2 vols. (New York: Harper & Row, 1963), 1:288.

[28]See H. R. Mackintosh, *Types of Modern Theology* (London: Nisbet, 1937), pp. 83-84.

[29]See Søren Kierkegaard, *The Concept of Dread,* trans. Walter Lowrie (Princeton, N.J.: Princeton University Press, 1957); *The Sickness unto Death,* trans. Walter Lowrie (Princeton, N.J.: Princeton University Press, 1941); and Martin J. Heinecken, *The Moment Before God* (Philadelphia: Muhlenberg, 1956).

[30]For an illuminating discussion of Kierkegaard's understanding of despair see Heinecken, *Moment Before God,* pp. 183-224. Also see Edward John Carnell, *The Burden of Søren Kierkegaard* (Grand Rapids: Eerdmans, 1965), pp. 78-81, 121, 125, 146, 151-52.

[31]See Emil Brunner, *Man in Revolt,* trans. Olive Wyon (New York: Charles Scribner's Sons, 1939), esp. pp. 123-67; and his *The Christian Doctrine of*

Creation and Redemption, trans. Olive Wyon (Philadelphia: Westminster, 1952), pp. 89-132.

[32]Brunner, *Christian Doctrine of Creation and Redemption,* p. 109.

[33]Paul Tillich, *Systematic Theology,* 3 vols. (Chicago: University of Chicago Press, 1951-63), 2:67.

[34]Ibid., p. 56.

[35]Ibid., p. 34.

[36]See Reinhold Niebuhr, *The Nature and Destiny of Man,* 2 vols. (New York: Charles Scribner's Sons, 1941), 1:178-264.

[37]Karl Barth, *Church Dogmatics,* trans. G. W. Bromiley, ed. G. W. Bromiley and T. F. Torrance (Edinburgh: T. & T. Clark, 1958), 4(2):415-16.

[38]Ibid., pp. 403-4.

[39]Dietrich Bonhoeffer, *Creation and Fall,* trans. John C. Fletcher (New York: Macmillan, 1959); *The Cost of Discipleship,* trans. R. H. Fuller, rev. ed. (London: SCM, 1959); *Ethics,* ed. Eberhard Bethge, trans. Neville Horton Smith (New York: Macmillan, 1955); and *Letters and Papers from Prison,* ed. Eberhard Bethge, trans. Reginald Fuller and Frank Clarke, rev. ed. (New York: Macmillan, 1972).

[40]See Terrence Reynolds, *The Coherence of Life Without God Before God: The Problem of Earthly Desires in the Later Theology of Dietrich Bonhoeffer* (Lanham, Md.: University Press of America, 1989).

[41]Ibid., pp. 98-99.

[42]Wolfhart Pannenberg, *Anthropology in Theological Perspective,* trans. Matthew J. O'Connell (Philadelphia: Westminster, 1985), p. 57.

[43]Ibid., p. 123.

[44]Ibid., p. 58.

[45]Ibid., p. 134.

[46]Ibid., p. 110.

[47]In his *Systematic Theology* vol. 2 Pannenberg still emphasizes self-fixation as the core of sin but directly relates it to unbridled desire, anxiety, pride and unbelief (see pp. 251-53).

[48]Pannenberg, *Anthropology in Theological Perspective,* p. 152.

[49]For my further discussion of Pannenberg, see pp. 42, 43, 47.

[50]See Donald Bloesch, *A Theology of Word & Spirit* (Downers Grove, Ill.: InterVarsity Press, 1992), pp. 61-66. Also see nn. 29 and 30 in this chapter. My earlier discussion in *Theology of Word & Spirit* focuses on Kierkegaard's understanding of the relationship between faith and reason.

[51]See Gustaf Aulén, *Christus Victor,* trans. A. G. Hebert (New York: Macmillan, 1951), pp. 56, 67, 108.

[52]Stuhlmacher, *Paul's Letter to the Romans,* p. 169.

[53]See Kierkegaard, *Concept of Dread,* pp. 41-46.

[54]For my earlier discussion of Niebuhr on sin and temptation see Bloesch, *Essentials of Evangelical Theology* (San Francisco: Harper, 1978), 1:96. In my opinion the dictum that temptation presupposes sin needs to be somewhat qualified, for if temptation were rebuffed at the outset it would remain external to the human subject who in this case would be unscathed by sin (as we can see in the example of Jesus Christ). If, on the other hand, temptation is seriously entertained this indicates that sin is already present within us. What makes humanity vulnerable to temptation is that humanity stands in the grip of sin.

[55]Pannenberg, *Systematic Theology*, 2:250-52.

[56]While Tillich insisted that ontological anxiety belongs to finitude itself and not to the distortion of finitude, he did not sufficiently consider that ontological anxiety in the matrix of fallen human existence contains a destructive as well as a creative element and therefore needs to be redeemed. *Systematic Theology*, 1:191-94.

[57]Pannenberg, *Systematic Theology*, 2:249-50.

[58]Joseph A. Fitzmyer, The Letter to the Romans," in *The New Jerome Biblical Commentary*, ed. Raymond E. Brown, Joseph A. Fitzmyer and Roland E. Murphy (Englewood Cliffs, N.J.: Prentice-Hall, 1990), p. 846.

[59]Pannenberg suggests that we should think not so much of the fall of an original couple as a fall of primeval humanity, which takes place in various stages and events (*Systematic Theology*, 2:263).

[60]Because unbelief or hardness of heart is a perverseness that has no basis in reason, it has the characteristics of folly and absurdity.

[61]Fear in its essence is a state of apprehensiveness that engulfs a person's whole being and therefore leads directly to spiritual death. It includes the reaction to specific threats as well as a state of uneasiness about life in general (as in anxiety or dread). It is not to be confounded with reverential fear or awe, which is a wholesome and necessary element in Christian life and worship. On the debilitating effects of fear and how it invariably leads to flight—an evasion of personal responsibility—see Peter C. Hodgson, *Winds of the Spirit* (Louisville: Westminster/John Knox, 1994), pp. 218-19, 224-29. Cornelius Plantinga Jr. also discusses this aspect of sin in his *Not the Way It's Supposed to Be: A Breviary of Sin* (Grand Rapids, Mich.: Eerdmans, 1995), pp. 173-97. While profoundly indebted to Søren Kierkegaard, I also appreciate Wolfhart Pannenberg's insight that dread or anxiety is a product of sin and not simply its precursor. See my discussion of the subject in this chapter, pp. 42-43.

[62]Both self-deprecation and self-exaltation are forms of egocentrism, since the focus is on the self rather than on God or neighbor. The Bible teaches self-surrender, which sets us free for repentance—turning from our absorption in

self—and for obedience—serving God and neighbor in self-giving love.

[63]Some liberationists include as social sin humanocentrism and heterosexism, but the Bible clearly teaches the precedence of humanity over the animal world and heterosexuality as the norm for sexual behavior. We who are humans should not flaunt our superiority over the animal creation, however, for we are commanded to care for the animals. Nor should we as heterosexuals take pride in our sexual orientation or routinely discriminate against those who are afflicted in this manner. This is not to imply that the church is free to bless homosexual unions or to ordain avowed, practicing homosexuals to any of its ministries.

[64]See Rosemary Radford Ruether, *To Change the World: Christology and Cultural Criticism* (New York: Crossroad, 1981); *Sexism and God-Talk: Toward a Feminist Theology* (Boston: Beacon, 1983); Elisabeth Schüssler Fiorenza, *In Memory of Her* (New York: Crossroad, 1983); Judith Plaskow, *Sex, Sin and Grace: Women's Experience and the Theology of Reinhold Niebuhr and Paul Tillich* (Washington, D.C.: University Press of America, 1980); Elizabeth A. Johnson, *She Who Is* (New York: Crossroad, 1992); Leonardo Boff, *Jesus Christ Liberator* (Maryknoll, N.Y.: Orbis, 1978); Enrique D. Dussel, *Ethics and the Theology of Liberation* (Maryknoll, N.Y.: Orbis, 1978); Gustavo Gutiérrez, *A Theology of Liberation* (Maryknoll, N.Y.: Orbis, 1973); José Míguez Bonino, *Doing Theology in a Revolutionary Situation* (Philadelphia: Fortress, 1975); and Marjorie Hewitt Suchocki, *The Fall to Violence: Original Sin in Relational Theology* (New York: Continuum, 1994).

[65]We might also include social isolation, sickness, lawlessness and war. Sickness is a product of our sinful condition, but we must be careful not to view all sickness as a result of specific sin. War can be considered the epitome and lethal culmination of sin. See Donald G. Bloesch, "The Folly of War," in his *Freedom for Obedience* (San Francisco: Harper & Row, 1987), pp. 287-319.

[66]I have already noted Tillich's views on this subject (see p. 37). Pannenberg's position is remarkably similar. He believes that it is only death as separation from God that is the result of sin. Death itself follows from our finitude. See his *Systematic Theology,* 2:265-75. Interestingly C. S. Lewis in the first two volumes of his space trilogy argues that for those in the other planetary kingdom death is an occasion for being welcomed into the presence of the Creator. Because there is no sin among this people there is also no fear of death. See Lewis, *Out of the Silent Planet* (New York: Macmillan, 1952), p. 79; *Perelandra* (New York: Macmillan, 1951), pp. 116-17.

[67]Stuhlmacher, *Paul's Letter to the Romans,* p. 86.

[68]Ibid., p. 112.

[69]Fitzmyer, "Letter to the Romans," p. 845.

[70]Gerhard von Rad, *Genesis,* trans. John H. Marks, Old Testament Library (Philadelphia: Westminster, 1961), p. 92.

[71]Emil Brunner, *Revelation and Reason,* trans. Olive Wyon (Philadelphia: Westminster, 1946), pp. 383-84.

[72]I acknowledge a natural law and universal norms, but these cannot be a solid basis for order and justice in society because sin irremediably clouds our reasoning. Natural law can be dependable only when illumined by divine revelation. See my conversation with Carl Henry and Carl Braaten in *First Things* 52 (April 1995):3-4.

[73]I here concur with Ted Peters, who warns against an ideological agenda dictating theological understanding. See Peters, *Sin: Radical Evil in Soul and Society* (Grand Rapids: Eerdmans, 1994), pp. 173-75.

[74]While Luther was much closer to biblical truth than was Erasmus in their celebrated debate over free will, he nevertheless went too far in his *Bondage of the Will* when he portrayed the sinner as a helpless automaton in the hands of either God or the devil. Luther was indeed right to uphold the sovereignty of grace in our redemption, but he was wrong in espousing a monergism of grace. Grace alone saves from sin, but grace makes us active in responding to the offer of salvation, and apart from this response salvation is not yet realized. The biblical position is neither monergism (in which God does all) nor synergism (in which God does part and we do part) but the paradox that God does all—but in and through human effort—and that we do all—in and through divine grace.

God's grace precedes, arouses and acts within human decision in order to accomplish its goal. Apart from grace we are severely disadvantaged because of the all-pervasive corrupting impact of sin in human life, but we are still responsible for our deliberations and actions. Grace brings us both divine pardon and the power to believe and obey. Divine grace alone works an ontological change within us, but we are then moved by the Spirit to ratify and confirm God's regenerating work, thereby bringing his salvific plan for our lives to completion.

[75]For the Reformers concupiscence is itself sin and not merely the tinder of sin (as in the developing Catholic view). See note 23 in this chapter.

[76]Pannenberg, *Systematic Theology,* 2:252.

[77]Ibid.

[78]*Catechism of the Catholic Church* (United States Catholic Conference, 1994), no. 388, p. 98.

[79]Ibid., no. 387, p. 97.

[80]Cited in Smith, *World's Religions,* p. 109.

[81]See *Catechism of the Catholic Church,* no. 1855, p. 454.

[82]Niebuhr, *Nature and Destiny of Man,* 1:219-27.

[83]Bonhoeffer, *Ethics*, p. 65.

[84]Luther became severely critical of those who upheld justification as sheer imputation without the corresponding new creation worked within us by the Spirit of God, who thereby unites us with Christ. See Jaroslav Pelikan, *The Christian Tradition* (Chicago: University of Chicago Press, 1984), 4:154-55. Philip Watson contended that for Luther justification includes "participation in Christ's victorious strife against sin and all evil; it means that God in Christ still comes, through the Spirit, to dwell with sinners and to continue in their hearts and lives His redeeming work." Watson, *Let God Be God! An Interpretation of the Theology of Martin Luther* (London: Epworth, 1947), p. 171. For my later discussion of Luther see note 74 in this chapter.

[85]This is not an implied criticism of Luther, who at least on one occasion used this kind of language, since his intention was that we should go forward boldly in our Christian walk even though our actions will invariably involve sin. Luther counseled obedience to Christ without being immobilized by the fear of being a sinner. Yet his counsel has often been appealed to as an excuse for continuing in sin. See my discussion in Bloesch, *Freedom for Obedience*, p. 213.

[86]See Bonhoeffer, *Cost of Discipleship*, pp. 35-83.

[87]Bonhoeffer, *Ethics*, p. 350.

Chapter 3: The Mystery of the Incarnation

[1]Karl Barth, *Church Dogmatics*, trans. T. H. L. Parker et al., ed. G. W. Bromiley and T. F. Torrance (Edinburgh: T. & T. Clark, 1957), 2(1):616.

[2]*Saint Ambrose: Theological and Dogmatic Works*, trans. Roy L. Deferrari (Washington, D.C.: Catholic University of America Press, 1963), p. 233.

[3]See Nels F. S. Ferré, *Christ and the Christian* (New York: Harper & Bros., 1958), pp. 111-13, 197-99, 213-15.

[4]Clement of Alexandria, cited in Geoffrey W. Bromiley, *Historical Theology: An Introduction* (Grand Rapids: Eerdmans, 1978), p. 134.

[5]"The Athanasian Creed," in *The Creeds of Christendom*, ed. Philip Schaff (1877; reprint, New York: Harper & Bros., 1919), 2:69.

[6]Quoted in G. C. Berkouwer, *The Person of Christ*, trans. John Vriend (Grand Rapids: Eerdmans, 1954), p. 94.

[7]Heinrich Heppe, ed., *Reformed Dogmatics*, rev. ed. Ernst Bizer, trans. G. T. Thomson (London: Allen & Unwin, 1950), p. 419.

[8]For Bruce M. Metzger's trenchant defense of the traditional translation of Romans 9:5 see his "Punctuation of Rom. 9:5," in *Christ and Spirit in the New Testament*, ed. Barnabas Lindars and Stephen S. Smalley (Cambridge: Cambridge University Press, 1973), pp. 95-112.

[9]Throughout the New Testament the risen Christ is referred to as *kyrios*, a posi-

tion equal to that of God. See W. Foerster, "κύριος in the New Testament," in *Theological Dictionary of the New Testament,* ed. Gerhard Kittel and Gerhard Friedrich, trans. and ed. Geoffrey Bromiley (Grand Rapids: Eerdmans, 1965), 3:1086-94.

[10]See Charles A. M. Hall, *With the Spirit's Sword: The Drama of Spiritual Warfare in the Theology of John Calvin* (Richmond, Va.: John Knox, 1968), pp. 87-88, 104.

[11]On the various kinds of union see Heppe, *Reformed Dogmatics,* pp. 431-32.

[12]See the discussion in Barth, *Church Dogmatics,* trans. G. T. Thomson and Harold Knight, ed. G. W. Bromiley and T. F. Torrance (Edinburgh: T. & T. Clark, 1956), 1(2):163-65.

[13]Ibid., p. 162.

[14]For Mackintosh's criticisms of John of Damascus see H. R. Mackintosh, *The Doctrine of the Person of Jesus Christ,* 2d ed. (Edinburgh: T. & T. Clark, 1913), p. 222.

[15]See François Wendel, *Calvin,* trans. Philip Mairet (London: Collins, 1963), p. 220.

[16]Bromiley, *Historical Theology,* p. 354.

[17]Jaroslav Pelikan, *The Christian Tradition* (Chicago: University of Chicago Press, 1971), 1:174.

[18]Robert I. Moore, *The Origins of European Dissent* (New York: St. Martin's, 1977), p. 150.

[19]Mary Baker Eddy, *Science and Health with Key to the Scriptures* (1875; reprint, Boston: First Church of Christ, Scientist, 1934), p. 46.

[20]See I. C. Sharma, *Cayce, Karma and Reincarnation* (New York: Harper & Row, 1975), p. 140.

[21]*Meditations of Maharishi Mahesh Yogi* (New York: Bantam, 1968), pp. 123-24.

[22]See G. C. Berkouwer, *The Second Vatican Council and the New Catholicism,* trans. Lewis B. Smedes (Grand Rapids: Eerdmans, 1965), p. 244. Cf. Heiko Oberman, *The Harvest of Medieval Theology* (Grand Rapids: Eerdmans, 1967), pp. 313-14.

[23]Cf. Gustaf Aulén, who writes that "the Divine will wholly dominated the human life of the Word of God." *Christus Victor,* trans. A. G. Hebert (New York: Macmillan, 1951), pp. 33-34. Aulén is here setting forth what he believes to be Irenaeus's position, but he obviously identifies with it.

[24]See Pelikan, *Christian Tradition,* 1:251-56.

[25]Cited in Dietrich Bonhoeffer, *Christ the Center,* trans. John Bowden (New York: Harper & Row, 1960), p. 81.

[26]Malcolm Furness, *Vital Doctrines of the Faith* (Grand Rapids: Eerdmans, 1974), p. 22.

[27]Ibid.

[28]See the discussion in Berkouwer, *Person of Christ,* pp. 273-74.

[29]Quoted by Donald M. Baillie, *God Was in Christ* (New York: Charles Scribner's Sons, 1948), p. 61.

[30]Quoted in G. C. Berkouwer, *The Conflict with Rome,* trans. David H. Freeman (Philadelphia: Presbyterian & Reformed, 1958), p. 304.

[31]Thomas O'Meara, *Loose in the World* (New York: Paulist, 1974), p. 76.

[32]For my further discussion see pp. 189-91.

[33]Friedrich Schleiermacher, *The Christian Faith,* ed. H. R. Mackintosh and J. S. Stewart, 2 vols. (New York: Harper & Row, 1963), 1:63. One critic contends that for Schleiermacher "Jesus . . . is the Divine centre or reservoir of power which can rouse and vivify the God-consciousness already present." H. R. Mackintosh, *Types of Modern Theology* (London: Nisbet, 1937), p. 95.

[34]Friedrich Schleiermacher, *On Religion: Speeches to Its Cultured Despisers,* trans. John Oman (New York: Harper & Row, 1958), pp. 6, 242, 248-50.

[35]Interestingly Bonhoeffer classifies both Schleiermacher and Ritschl as docetists. *Christ the Center,* p. 83.

[36]Emil Brunner, *The Mediator,* trans. Olive Wyon (Philadelphia: Westminster, 1947), p. 346.

[37]See ibid., p. 343.

[38]See Barth, *Church Dogmatics,* 1(2):160-61.

[39]See Baillie, *God Was in Christ,* pp. 114-18.

[40]Ibid., pp. 147-51. Baillie affirms the preexistence of the Son of God but not the preexistence of Jesus as the Christ.

[41]See J. A. T. Robinson, *The Human Face of God* (Philadelphia: Westminster, 1973).

[42]Ibid., p. 204.

[43]Ibid.

[44]Ibid., p. 239.

[45]Paul Tillich, *Systematic Theology,* 3 vols. (Chicago: University of Chicago Press, 1951-63), 2:148.

[46]Paul Tillich, *The Interpretation of History,* trans. N. A. Rasetzki and Elsa L. Talmey (New York: Charles Scribner's Sons, 1936), p. 265.

[47]Wolfhart Pannenberg, *Jesus—God and Man,* trans. Lewis L. Wilkins and Duane A. Priebe (Philadelphia: Westminster, 1968), pp. 132-33.

[48]Wolfhart Pannenberg, *Systematic Theology,* trans. Geoffrey W. Bromiley (Grand Rapids: Eerdmans, 1994), 2:34, 113, 122-24.

[49]Personal letter from Kenneth Hamilton, Jan. 23, 1974. Also see Hamilton, *Words and the Word* (Grand Rapids: Eerdmans, 1971), pp. 105-6.

[50]Pannenberg, *Systematic Theology,* 2:389-96.

[51]Bonhoeffer, *Christ the Center,* p. 92.

[52]Ritschl can legitimately be classified as both ebionitic and docetic, since for

him Jesus is both the historical founder of Christianity and the exemplar of abiding values. See n. 35.

[53]Walter Rauschenbusch, *A Theology for the Social Gospel* (New York: Macmillan, 1917), p. 154.

[54]Glenn R. Bucher, "Liberation, Male and White: Initial Reflections," *Christian Century* 91, no. 11 (1974):312-16.

[55]See Klaas Runia, "A 'New' Christology Challenges the Church," *Christianity Today* 18, no. 7 (1974):6.

[56]O'Meara, *Loose in the World*, p. 71.

[57]See note 11, p. 260.

[58]Karl Barth, *The Humanity of God*, trans. John Newton Thomas (Richmond, Va.: John Knox, 1960), p. 46.

[59]Pelikan, *Christian Tradition*, 1:227.

[60]On how Reinhold Niebuhr tries to reconcile Jesus' perfection with the reality of his temptation see *Nature and Destiny of Man*, 2 vols. (New York: Charles Scribner's Sons, 1951), 2:70-95. Niebuhr is unable to affirm the sinlessness of Jesus as sacred tradition has understood this. For my earlier discussion see chapter 2, "The Plight of Humanity," note 54.

[61]*Luther's Works*, ed. Jaroslav Pelikan (St. Louis: Concordia, 1963), 26:288.

[62]Baillie, *God Was in Christ*, p. 152.

[63]Schaff, *Creeds of Christendom*, 3:680.

[64]P. T. Forsyth, *The Church and the Sacraments* (1917; 4th ed., London: Independent Press, 1953), p. 83.

[65]P. T. Forsyth, "Does the Church Prolong the Incarnation?" *London Quarterly Review* 133 (1920):212.

[66]P. T. Forsyth, *Positive Preaching and the Modern Mind* (1907; 3d ed., London: Independent Press, 1949), p. 124. Cf. "The true key to Christ's person is in His work. It lies not in a miraculous manner of birth, nor in a metaphysical manner of two co-existent natures, but in a moral way of atoning experience" (p. 242).

[67]R. C. Moberly was emphatic that Christ was not "a man only, amongst men." "His relation to the human race is not that He was another specimen, differing, by being another, from everyone except Himself. His relation to the race was not a differentiating but a consummating relation. He was not generically, but inclusively, man." Moberly, *Atonement and Personality* (London: John Murray, 1909), p. 86. I would caution that we must not lose sight of the fact that Jesus Christ was also a particular man. As a particular human he was at the same time representative humanity.

[68]For compelling reasons why we should not use the neologism "Godself" in theological discourse see Donald D. Hook and Alvin F. Kimel Jr., "The Pronouns of Deity: A Theolinguistic Critique of Feminist Proposals," *Scottish*

Journal of Theology 46, no. 3 (1993):314-15.

[69]*Forum Letter* 22, no. 9 (1993):3.

[70]While there is one name, there are various forms of this name, and "Jesus Christ" is one of these.

[71]See Robert W. Jenson, "The Father, He, . . ." in *Speaking the Christian God: The Holy Trinity and the Challenge of Feminism,* ed. Alvin F. Kimel Jr. (Grand Rapids: Eerdmans, 1992), pp. 95-109.

[72]See my discussion in Donald G. Bloesch, *Is the Bible Sexist? Beyond Feminism and Patriarchalism* (Westchester, Ill.: Crossway, 1982), pp. 61-83.

[73]See *The New Testament and Psalms: An Inclusive Version,* ed. Victor Roland Gold, Thomas L. Hoyt, Sharon H. Ringe, Susan Brooks Thistlethwaite, Burton H. Throckmorton Jr. and Barbara Withers (New York: Oxford University Press, 1995).

[74]See Donald G. Bloesch, *The Battle for the Trinity: The Debate over Inclusive God-Language* (Ann Arbor, Mich.: Servant, 1985), pp. 69-87.

[75]For a trenchant critique of the Oxford University inclusive version of the New Testament and Psalms see Gail R. O'Day, "Probing an Inclusive Scripture," *Christian Century* 113, no. 21 (1996): 692-94. On the deletion of references to "Jews" in the Fourth Gospel, the author applauds the attempt of the editors to counter anti-Jewish bias, but she complains that they have "slightly overshot their goal. By completely eliminating any reference to Judaism, they have given an oddly ahistorical, culturally disembodied twist to John's narrative" (p. 694).

Chapter 4: The Virgin Birth

[1]See, e.g., Stanley J. Grenz, *Theology for the Community of God* (Nashville: Broadman, 1994), pp. 409-23; and René Laurentin, *The Truth of Christmas, Beyond the Myths,* trans. Michael J. Wrenn et al. (Petersham, Mass.: St. Bede's Publications, 1985).

[2]See David Friedrich Strauss, *The Life of Jesus Critically Examined,* trans. George Eliot, ed. Peter C. Hodgson (1892; reprint, Philadelphia: Fortress, 1972), pp. 119-90.

[3]John Hick, "Jesus and the World Religions," in *The Myth of God Incarnate,* ed. John Hick (Philadelphia: Westminster, 1977), p. 184.

[4]John Shelby Spong, *Born of a Woman* (San Francisco: HarperCollins, 1992), p. 45.

[5]Quoted in James Orr, *The Virgin Birth of Christ* (New York: Charles Scribner's Sons, 1921), p. 17.

[6]Cited in Robert Glenn Gromacki, *The Virgin Birth* (Nashville: Nelson, 1974), p. 189.

[7]Ibid.

[8]See Karl Barth, *Church Dogmatics,* trans. G. T. Thomson and Harold Knight, ed. G. W. Bromiley and T. F. Torrance (Edinburgh: T. & T. Clark, 1956), 1(2):172-202.

[9]Alan Richardson, *An Introduction to the Theology of the New Testament* (New York: Harper & Bros., 1958), pp. 175-76.

[10]Alan Richardson, "Virgin Birth," in *A Dictionary of Christian Theology,* ed. Alan Richardson (Philadelphia: Westminster, 1969), p. 357.

[11]Thomas Boslooper, *The Virgin Birth* (Philadelphia: Westminster, 1962), p. 186.

[12]Raymond E. Brown, *The Virginal Conception and Bodily Resurrection of Jesus* (New York: Paulist, 1973), pp. 47-68. Also see p. 37.

[13]Ibid., p. 39.

[14]Ibid., p. 40.

[15]Wolfhart Pannenberg, *Jesus—God and Man,* trans. Lewis L. Wilkins and Duane A. Priebe (Philadelphia: Westminster, 1968), p. 146.

[16]Brown, *Virginal Conception,* p. 45.

[17]Eduard Schweizer, *The Good News According to Matthew,* trans. David E. Green (Atlanta: John Knox, 1975), pp. 34-35.

[18]Ibid., p. 34.

[19]J. Kenneth Grider, *A Wesleyan-Holiness Theology* (Kansas City, Mo.: Beacon Hill, 1994), pp. 320-21.

[20]See Richard A. Horsley, *The Liberation of Christmas: The Infancy Narratives in Social Context* (New York: Crossroad, 1989); Jane Schaberg, *The Illegitimacy of Jesus: A Feminist Theological Interpretation of the Infancy Narratives* (San Francisco: Harper & Row, 1987); René Coste, *The Magnificat: The Revolution of God* (Quezon City, Philippines: Claretian Publications, 1988); Rosemary Radford Ruether, *Mary—The Feminine Face of the Church* (Philadelphia: Westminster, 1977); Leonardo Boff, *The Maternal Face of God* (San Francisco: Harper & Row, 1987); Edward Schillebeeckx and Catherina Halkes, *Mary Yesterday, Today, Tomorrow* (New York: Crossroad, 1993); Edward Luther Kessel, *The Androgynous Christ: A Christian Feminist View* (Portland: Interprint, 1988); Els Maeckelberghe, ed., *Desperately Seeking Mary: A Feminist Appropriation of a Traditional Religious Symbol* (Kampen, Netherlands: Kok Pharos, 1991); and Elisabeth Schüssler Fiorenza, *Jesus: Miriam's Child, Sophia's Prophet* (New York: Continuum, 1994), pp. 163-90, 232-40. Some of the above books focus on the virginity of Mary rather than on the virgin birth of Jesus.

[21]Schaberg, *Illegitimacy of Jesus.* See esp. pp. 195-99.

[22]Ibid., p. 8.

[23]Ibid.

[24]Ibid., p. 12.

[25]Ibid., p. 179.

[26]Interestingly, British Methodist theologian Gordon Wakefield does not regard

Jesus' possible illegitimacy as wholly outside the bounds of Christian speculation: "The other alternative that Christ's birth was illegitimate shocks our
sense of morality, and makes us feel . . . that he is less than perfect man. But
is this necessarily so? Dare we limit God to our standards of respectability?
May not this be one more instance of the weak things of the world confounding the morally mighty?" Gordon S. Wakefield, "The Virgin Mary in
Methodism," in *Mary's Place in Christian Dialogue,* ed. Alberic Stacpoole
(Wilton, Conn.: Morehouse-Barlow, 1982), p. 156. He goes on to acknowledge
that this may be "vain speculation" (p. 157).

[27]Brown, *Virginal Conception,* p. 62.

[28]Paul K. Jewett, *The Ordination of Women* (Grand Rapids: Eerdmans, 1980), pp.
52-53.

[29]Wakefield, "The Virgin Mary in Methodism," p. 157.

[30]Ibid.

[31]For an insightful analysis of the views of Luther and Calvin on Mary, includ-
ing her perpetual virginity, see Thomas A. O'Meara, *Mary in Protestant and
Catholic Theology* (New York: Sheed & Ward, 1966), pp. 111-45. Also see
Gottfried Maron, "Mary in Protestant Theology" (trans. David Cairns), in *Mary
in the Churches,* ed. Hans Küng and Jürgen Moltmann, English ed. Marcus
Lefébure (New York: Seabury, 1983), pp. 40-47.

[32]Interestingly in his *The Seat of Wisdom,* trans. A. V. Littledale (New York:
Pantheon, 1962), Louis Bouyer appeals to the respected Protestant exegete
John Albert Bengel in support of the view that these words of Mary show that
she intended to keep her virginity (p. 37). See Bengel's *Gnomon of the New
Testament,* trans. Charlton T. Lewis and Marvin R. Vincent (Philadelphia:
Perkinpine & Higgins, 1862), 1:386.

[33]Recent scholarship shows that a semimonastic movement existed within
Judaism, and therefore the ideal of celibacy was not wholly foreign to the Jews
at that time. See Joseph A. Fitzmyer, "The Dead Sea Scrolls," in *Harper's Bible
Dictionary,* ed. Paul J. Achtemeier (San Francisco: Harper & Row, 1985), pp.
915-17.

[34]On the other hand John McHugh claims that the evidence indicates the brothers of Jesus were younger than he, since they are depicted as still living at
home. See *The Mother of Jesus in the New Testament* (London: Darton,
Longman & Todd, 1975), pp. 244-51.

[35]The Lutheran-Catholic task force concluded that Mary the mother of James,
Joses and Joseph (Mk 15:40; Mt 27:56) is probably not the mother of our Lord,
and therefore James, Joses, Judas and Simon in Mk 6:3 are likely not the blood
brothers of Jesus. See *Mary in the New Testament,* ed. Raymond E. Brown, Karl
P. Donfried, Joseph A. Fitzmyer and John Reumann (Philadelphia: Fortress,
1978), pp. 68-72.

[36]John McHugh suggests that Jesus may have had foster brothers and sisters in that another Mary and her children seemed to be closely associated with the holy family. *Mother of Jesus*, pp. 234-54. One reputable Catholic biblical scholar, John Meier, takes the opposing view, maintaining that the New Testament evidence supports the belief that Jesus had real brothers and sisters. John P. Meier, *A Marginal Jew: Rethinking the Historical Jesus*, vol. 1: *The Roots of the Problem and the Person* (New York: Doubleday, 1991), pp. 318-32.

[37]*Mary in the New Testament*, p. 153.

[38]See David Scaer, *Christology* (Fort Wayne, Ind.: International Foundation for Lutheran Confessional Research, 1989), p. 38.

[39]According to the Lutheran-Catholic task force on Mary in the New Testament, Jesus' father is not mentioned in Mark "because he is dead. This is the simplest and most satisfactory explanation of the absence of Joseph in 3:31-35 and also 6:1-6." See *Mary in the New Testament*, p. 64.

[40]See Hans von Campenhausen, *The Virgin Birth in the Theology of the Ancient Church*, trans. Frank Clarke, Studies in Historical Theology 2 (Naperville, Ill.: Allenson, 1964), pp. 47-49.

[41]Keith Weston, "Mary: An Evangelical Viewpoint," in *Mary's Place in Christian Dialogue*, ed. Alberic Stacpoole (Wilton, Conn.: Morehouse-Barlow, 1982), p. 160.

[42]Douglas Edwards, *The Virgin Birth in History and Faith* (London: Faber & Faber, 1943), p. 25.

[43]Klaas Runia, "Conceived by the Holy Spirit, Born of the Virgin Mary," *Christianity Today* 19, no. 5 (1974):6.

[44]Some scholars speculate that Luke's genealogy is more true to history and Matthew's is the product of theological interpretation. Both genealogies trace Davidic descent through Joseph.

[45]Richard Longenecker, "Whose Child Is This?" *Christianity Today* 34, no. 18 (1990):27.

[46]Midrash is basically a commentary on Scripture that expands the meaning of the text by relating it to Jewish tradition. This type of biblical interpretation occurs frequently in rabbinic literature.

[47]Brown, *Virginal Conception*, pp. 19, 54-55. According to Brown, while it is possible that some sources for the infancy narratives were "folkloric or non-historical . . . other sources or items of tradition came down from genuine family memories" (p. 55).

[48] Joseph A. Fitzmyer, *The Gospel According to Luke I—IX*, Anchor Bible (Garden City, N.Y.: Doubleday, 1981), p. 309.

[49]Ben Witherington III, "Birth of Jesus," in *Dictionary of Jesus and the Gospels*, ed. Joel B. Green and Scot McKnight (Downers Grove, Ill.: InterVarsity Press, 1992), p. 63.

[50]According to S. MacLean Gilmour, "If pre-Christian motifs helped to shape the

Lukan story, they have not been documented." "Luke," in *Interpreter's Bible*, ed. G. A. Buttrick (Nashville: Abingdon, 1952), 8:48.

[51]Ibid., pp. 57-58. W. F. Albright and C. S. Mann regard the account of the visit of the magi as "broadly historical," holding that "there is nothing in the least improbable about magi traveling from Babylon west, or indeed anywhere else in the Mediterranean world. They would find welcome audiences anywhere, from royal courts to market places." *Matthew*, Anchor Bible (Garden City, N.Y.: Doubleday, 1971), pp. 15-16.

[52]Orr, *Virgin Birth of Christ*, pp. 88-90.

[53]John Knox, *Jesus Lord and Christ* (New York: Harper & Bros., 1958), p. 253.

[54]Brown, *Virginal Conception*, p. 66.

[55]William Childs Robinson, "The Virgin Birth—A Broader Base," *Christianity Today* 17, no. 5 (1972):7.

[56]Jaroslav Pelikan, *The Christian Tradition* (Chicago: University of Chicago Press, 1971), 1:287-88.

[57]Robinson, "Virgin Birth," p. 7.

[58]See Boslooper, *Virgin Birth*, pp. 28-33.

[59]J. Gresham Machen, *The Virgin Birth of Christ* (New York: Harper & Bros., 1930), p. 293. In the older tradition the prophecy in Is 7:10-17 refers directly to the virgin birth of Jesus. A defense of this position is found in Edward J. Young, *The Book of Isaiah* (1965; 2d ed., Grand Rapids: Eerdmans, 1972), 1:277-95; and Harry Rimmer, *The Magnificence of Jesus* (Grand Rapids: Eerdmans, 1943), pp. 124-28.

[60]J. Ridderbos, *Isaiah*, trans. John Vriend, Bible Student's Commentary (Grand Rapids: Zondervan, 1985), p. 87.

[61]Ibid.

[62]John N. Oswalt argues convincingly against Hezekiah's being the subject of the Isaiah child prophecies. He sees no allusion, however, to a virgin birth in the much debated passage in Is 7. See Oswalt, *The Book of Isaiah: Chapters 1—39*, New International Commentary on the Old Testament (Grand Rapids: Eerdmans, 1986), pp. 212, 227, 245. Young is also averse to identifying Immanuel with Hezekiah. Young, *Book of Isaiah*, 1:289.

[63]See R. B. Y. Scott, "Isaiah," in *Interpreter's Bible* (Nashville: Abingdon, 1956), 5:219. Also see Hugo Gressmann, *Der Messias* (Göttingen: Vandenhoeck & Ruprecht, 1929), pp. 235-42; E. Hammershaimb, "The Emmanuel Sign," in his *Some Aspects of Old Testament Prophecy from Isaiah to Malachi* (Copenhagen: Rosenskilde, 1966), pp. 9-28; and M. E. W. Thompson, "Isaiah's Sign of Immanuel," *Expository Times* 95, no. 3 (1983):67-71.

[64]Albright and Mann, *Matthew*, p. 8.

[65]See Dale Moody, *Spirit of the Living God* (Philadelphia: Westminster, 1968), pp. 46-48. Also see Benedict T. Viviano's commentary on Matthew in *The New*

Jerome Biblical Commentary, ed. Raymond E. Brown, Joseph A. Fitzmyer and Roland E. Murphy (Englewood Cliffs, N.J.: Prentice-Hall, 1990), p. 635.

[66]See Machen, *Virgin Birth,* pp. 297-311; and Charles Gore, *Dissertations on Subjects Connected with the Incarnation* (New York: Charles Scribner's Sons, 1895), pp. 61-63.

[67]Boslooper, *Virgin Birth,* pp. 189-94, 219-20.

[68]*Mary in the New Testament,* pp. 91-92, 124.

[69]See *New Jerusalem Bible,* p. 1201 n. 2.

[70]*Mary in the New Testament,* pp. 150-51. One should note that the authors of this book are not convinced that Matthew or Luke derived their information from Mary.

[71]Avery Dulles, "The Challenge of the Catechism," *First Things* no. 49 (1995):51.

[72]The tendency to defend the virgin birth of Christ on the basis of science and empirical evidences betrays a capitulation of evangelicalism to modernity.

[73]One should note that in the Jewish ethos betrothal was the first step in marriage. When Jesus was born Mary was already legally bound to Joseph.

[74]See pp. 94-97.

[75]Wilbur M. Smith, *The Supernaturalness of Christ* (Boston: W. A. Wilde, 1940), p. 92.

[76]C. A. Briggs argued that "a parthenogenesistic explanation of the virgin birth is an indirect denial of conception by the Holy Spirit alone." See Boslooper, *Virgin Birth,* p. 159.

[77]Kessel, *Androgynous Christ,* p. 25.

[78]Quoted in Paul Althaus, *The Theology of Martin Luther,* trans. Robert C. Schultz (Philadelphia: Fortress, 1966), p. 160.

[79]Boslooper, *Virgin Birth,* p. 124.

[80]Jaroslav Pelikan, *The Riddle of Roman Catholicism* (Nashville: Abingdon, 1959), pp. 131-32.

[81]Ibid., p. 137.

[82]Richardson, "Virgin Birth," *Dictionary of Christian Theology,* p. 357.

[83]Søren Kierkegaard, *Journals and Papers,* ed. and trans. Howard V. Hong and Edna H. Hong (Bloomington, Ind.: Indiana University Press, 1967), 1:124.

[84]Richardson, "Virgin Birth," p. 357. Emil Brunner is among those who discern the imprint of an ascetic spirituality on the virgin birth stories. See Brunner, *Dogmatics,* trans. Olive Wyon (Philadelphia: Westminster, 1952), 2:355.

[85]See pp. 82-83.

[86]Brunner, *Dogmatics,* 2:355; Nels F. S. Ferré, *Christ and the Christian* (New York: Harper & Bros., 1958), pp. 99-101.

[87]Cf. Emil Brunner, *The Mediator,* trans. Olive Wyon (Philadelphia: Westminster, 1947), pp. 322-27; and Reinhold Niebuhr, *The Nature and Destiny of Man,* 2 vols. (New York: Charles Scribner's Sons, 1951), 2:72-73.

[88]See Rudolf Bultmann, *Theology of the New Testament,* trans. Kendrick Grobel, 2 vols. (New York: Charles Scribner's Sons, 1951-55), 1:50, 131, 177; 2:30.

[89]See Longenecker, "Whose Child Is This?" p. 28. Like Longenecker I would not discount an apologetic element in these stories (particularly Matthew's version), but their overall purpose is to announce Jesus as the Messiah of Israel, not to present a rational proof for Jesus' deity or his preexistence, which they do not actually affirm.

[90]Scaer, *Christology,* p. 35.

[91]Frances Young, "A Cloud of Witnesses," in *The Myth of God Incarnate,* ed. John Hick (Philadelphia: Westminster, 1977), p. 47.

[92]Rosemary Radford Ruether, *Sexism and God-Talk* (Boston: Beacon, 1983), p. 154.

[93]Geddes MacGregor, *Dictionary of Religion and Philosophy* (New York: Paragon House, 1989), p. 647. For the salient emphases in MacGregor's thought see his *Gnosis* (Wheaton, Ill.: Theosophical Publishing House, 1979).

[94]Carl Jung, *Psychology and Religion: West and East,* trans. R. F. C. Hull (New York: Pantheon, 1958), p. 6.

[95]Nels F. S. Ferré, *The Christian Understanding of God* (New York: Harper & Bros., 1951), p. 192.

[96]Some Catholic spiritual writers urge us to go first of all to Mary in order to gain what we desire. "Whoever desires graces must go to Mary; whoever goes to Mary is sure to obtain what he desires." St. Alphonsus Maria de Liguori, *The Glories of Mary* (Baltimore: Helicon, 1963), 2:57. Cf. St. Louis De Montfort: "If we fear to go directly to Jesus Christ, our God, whether because of His infinite greatness, or because of our vileness, or because of our sins, let us boldly implore the aid and intercession of Mary, our Mother. She is good, she is tender, she has nothing in her austere and forbidding, nothing too sublime and too brilliant." *True Devotion to Mary,* trans. Frederick William Faber (1941; rev. ed., Bay Shore, N.Y.: Montfort, 1954), p. 62.

[97]See "The Church," in *The Documents of Vatican II,* ed. Walter M. Abbott (Chicago: Association Press and Follett, 1966), pp. 9-106.

[98]Ibid., pp. 89-90.

[99]Interestingly Pope John Paul has warned against "unhealthy extremes" in the veneration of Mary and reaffirmed the Second Vatican Council admonition "to abstain from all false exaggeration" in Marian devotion. See "Pope Warns of Overdevotion to Mary," *Christian Century* 113, no. 3 (1996):72.

[100]Karl Prümm, *Der Christliche Glaube und die altheidnische Welt* (Leipzig: Jakob Hegner, 1935), 1:285-333.

[101]See Geoffrey Ashe, *The Virgin* (London: Routledge & Kegan Paul, 1976); and Stephen Benko, *The Virgin Goddess: Studies in the Pagan and Christian Roots of Mariology* (Leiden: Brill, 1993). Also see E. O. James, *The Cult of the Mother-Goddess* (New York: Barnes & Noble, 1959), pp. 192-260; and Michael P.

Carroll, *The Cult of the Virgin Mary* (Princeton, N.J.: Princeton University Press, 1986).

[102]Benko, *Virgin Goddess*, p. 264.

[103]Ibid., p. 4.

[104]Jaroslav Pelikan, *Mary Through the Centuries: Her Place in the History of Culture* (New Haven, Conn.: Yale University Press, 1996). See esp. pp. 8-21, 222-23.

[105]Benko, *Virgin Goddess*, p. 202.

[106]Ibid., p. 256.

[107]For the right meaning and translation of this phrase see Raymond E. Brown, *The Birth of the Messiah* (Garden City, N.Y.: Doubleday Image, 1979), pp. 326-27; and John Macquarrie, *Mary for All Christians* (Grand Rapids: Eerdmans, 1991), p. 72.

[108]In Giovanni Miegge, *The Virgin Mary* (Philadelphia: Westminster, 1956), p. 112.

[109]Ibid., p. 113.

[110]In his *Magnificat* (1521) Luther held that Mary was without sin. See *Luther's Works*, ed. Jaroslav Pelikan (St. Louis: Concordia, 1956), 21:327. At one time he contended that Mary was purified from the womb and at another that she was made pure at the birth of Jesus. His later position was that only Christ's birth was wholly pure. See O'Meara, *Mary in Protestant and Catholic Theology*, pp. 116-19.

[111]See Miegge, *Virgin Mary*, p. 104.

[112]One should note that the first two of the three modern thinkers eventually converted to Roman Catholicism.

[113]Ashe, *Virgin*, p. 200.

[114]Von Campenhausen, *Virgin Birth*, p. 43.

[115]Irenaeus declared that "as by her disobedience the virgin Eve was the cause of death for herself and for the human race, so the obedient virgin became a cause of salvation for herself and the human race." *Adversus Haereses* 3.22.3. See Miegge, *Virgin Mary*, p. 134.

[116]Cited by Paul Evdokimov in his "Holiness in the Orthodox Tradition," in *Man's Concern with Holiness*, ed. Marina Chavchavadze (London: Hodder & Stoughton, 1970), p. 163.

[117]See Schillebeeckx and Halkes, *Mary Yesterday, Today, Tomorrow*, p. 28.

[118]These include W. Goosens and H. Lennerz. See Miegge, *Virgin Mary*, p. 156.

[119]See Leonardo Boff, *The Maternal Face of God*, trans. Robert R. Barr and John W. Diercksmeier (San Francisco: Harper & Row, 1987), pp. 154, 159-63.

[120]See René Laurentin, *The Question of Mary*, trans. I. G. Pidoux (New York: Holt, Rinehart & Winston, 1965), p. 87; and Miegge, *Virgin Mary*, p. 189.

[121]Laurentin, *Question of Mary*, p. 25.

[122]Quoted in Walther von Loewenich, *Modern Catholicism*, trans. Reginald H.

Fuller (New York: St. Martin's, 1959), p. 196.

[123]In Liguori, *Glories of Mary,* 1:145.

[124]Ibid., p. 126.

[125]Ibid., p. 125.

[126]Francis Fernandez, *In Conversation with God* (London: Scepter, 1990), 3:279-80.

[127]Ashe, *Virgin,* pp. 198-99.

[128]Laurentin, *Question of Mary,* p. 25.

[129]Ibid., p. 63.

[130]Schillebeeckx, *Mary Yesterday, Today, Tomorrow,* p. 18.

[131]Ibid., p. 29.

[132]Elizabeth A. Johnson, *She Who Is* (New York: Crossroad, 1992), p. 129.

[133]Richard Rohr, "The Church Without Mary," in *Mary, the Spirit and the Church,* ed. Vincent P. Branick (New York: Paulist, 1980), p. 19.

[134]Hans Asmussen, *Maria, die Mutter Gottes* (Stuttgart: Evangelisches Verlagswerk, 1951), p. 61. Translation by O'Meara, *Mary in Protestant and Catholic Theology,* p. 322.

[135]In O'Meara, *Mary in Protestant and Catholic Theology,* p. 324.

[136]Ibid., p. 323.

[137]Ibid., p. 143.

[138]Ibid., pp. 143-44.

[139]Martin Luther, Christmas homilies of 1523 and 1529. Cited in Ralph Martin, *The Catholic Church at the End of an Age* (San Francisco: Ignatius, 1994), p. 175. Also see Max Thurian, *Mary, Mother of the Lord, Figure of the Church,* trans. Neville B. Cryer (London: Faith Press, 1963), pp. 172-73.

[140]John Macquarrie makes a not wholly credible attempt to ground all of the Marian doctrines in Scripture. See his *Mary for All Christians.*

[141]One should note that the central prayer in the well-known Catholic devotion, the rosary, is the "Hail Mary."

[142]Bonhoeffer is helpful in his claim that "we can encounter others only through the mediation of Christ." Dietrich Bonhoeffer, *Life Together,* trans. Daniel W. Bloesch (Minneapolis: Fortress, 1996), pp. 43-44.

[143]See Thurian, *Mary,* pp. 13-19, 176-88.

[144]See John Breck, "Mary: Mother of Believers, Mother of God," *Pro Ecclesia* 4, no. 1 (1995):105-11.

[145]One critic, Michael Carroll, maintains that Eastern Orthodoxy is not as prone as Roman Catholicism to develop an independent Mariology, since its fidelity to the *theotokos* (Mary as the God-bearer) subordinates Mariology to christology. Carroll, *Cult of the Virgin Mary,* pp. 17-21. He points out that Orthodoxy tends to reject those doctrines, such as the immaculate conception, that pos-

tulate Mary having a higher nature than other mortals. While most Orthodox accept the assumption of Mary as a pious opinion, they tend not to regard it as an essential dogma of the faith.

[146]Cf. Rosemary Radford Ruether: "This understanding of Mary as type of the church of liberation does not stereotype Mary as representative only of women or 'feminine' passive attributes, but rather makes the liberated woman of the poor the inclusive model for the whole church, for both women and men, for both those lifted up from oppression and those who must give up unjust wealth and power to enter God's reign." Ruether, "Mary in U.S. Catholic Culture," *National Catholic Reporter* 31, no. 15 (1995):17.

[147]Note that Catholic theologian Ralph Martin fully affirms *ecclesia semper reformanda* in his *Catholic Church at the End of an Age,* pp. 133-34.

[148]For my earlier discussion see Donald G. Bloesch, *Holy Scripture* (Downers Grove, Ill.: InterVarsity Press, 1994), pp. 255-77.

[149]David Strauss (as well as several others mentioned here) can be claimed both by those who appreciate the role of myth in the Bible and by those who see it as a problem in biblical interpretation. Strauss regarded myth as a corrective to the older scientific, rationalist approach to Scripture, but at the same time he averred that acceptance of myth in the Bible constitutes a rejection of its historical claims. One can make a case that Strauss believed myth to belong to an age in the past, and the task now is to assess the significance of the biblical myth in a scientific age. See James P. Mackey, *Jesus, the Man and the Myth* (New York: Paulist, 1979), pp. 30-34.

[150]Cited in "David Friedrich Strauss," in *Westminster Dictionary of Church History,* ed. Jerald C. Brauer (Philadelphia: Westminster, 1971), p. 790. See Strauss, *Life of Jesus Critically Examined.*

[151]See Rudolf Bultmann, "New Testament and Mythology," in *Kerygma and Myth,* ed. Hans-Werner Bartsch, trans. Reginald H. Fuller (London: SPCK, 1953), 1:1-44, 191-211.

[152]Uta Ranke-Heinemann, *Putting Away Childish Things,* trans. Peter Heinegg (San Francisco: HarperCollins, 1994).

[153]Karl Barth, *Church Dogmatics,* trans. J. W. Edwards et al., ed. G. W. Bromiley and T. F. Torrance (Edinburgh: T. & T. Clark, 1958), 3(1):81-94. While Barth was adamant that Christian faith cannot be dissolved into myth, he was staunch in his insistence that theology is free to make use of mythical language, which forms a part of the ancient worldview. See Gary Dorrien, "The 'Postmodern' Barth? The Word of God as True Myth," *Christian Century* 114, no. 11 (1997):338-42.

[154]On Campbell's appraisal of biblical myth see Joseph Campbell, ed., *Myths to Live By* (New York: Viking, 1972), pp. 4-5, 12, 88-89, 96-97.

[155]Bernard F. Batto, *Slaying the Dragon: Mythmaking in the Biblical Tradition* (Louisville: Westminster/John Knox, 1992), p. 173.

[156]Ibid., p. 12. Batto distinguishes carefully between *mythopoeic*, which pertains to the shaping of a mythical vision of reality, and *mythopoetic*, which refers to the mode of language in which transhistorical reality is described.

[157]See C. S. Lewis, "Myth Became Fact," in his *God in the Dock* (Grand Rapids: Eerdmans, 1970), pp. 63-67; and his *Miracles: A Preliminary Study* (New York: Macmillan, 1947), pp. 131-58, 161 n. 1. One should note that Lewis held that the Christian narrative has a different style from pagan myths and legends. See Lewis, "Modern Theology and Biblical Criticism," in his *Christian Reflections* (London: Geoffrey Bles, 1967), p. 155.

[158]See C. Stephen Evans, "The Incarnational Narrative as Myth and History," *Christian Scholar's Review* 23, no. 4 (1994):387-407, esp. 403-4. Evans rightly points out that Lewis's appraisal of myth is not unequivocally positive (p. 396).

[159]John Polkinghorne, *Reason and Reality* (Philadelphia: Trinity Press International, 1991), p. 33.

[160]Bultmann, "New Testament and Mythology," pp. 10-11.

[161]Batto, *Slaying the Dragon,* p. 10.

[162]See the critiques of Bultmann's position in *Kerygma and Myth,* 1:45-190. Also see Bloesch, "Rudolf Bultmann: An Enduring Presence," in *Holy Scripture,* pp. 223-54.

[163]Emil Brunner, *Revelation and Reason,* trans. Olive Wyon (Philadelphia: Westminster, 1946), p. 406.

[164]Brunner, *Mediator,* pp. 378-79.

[165]Ibid., p. 378.

[166]Ibid., p. 391.

[167]Ibid., p. 377.

[168]See Wolfhart Pannenberg, "The Later Dimensions of Myth in Biblical and Christian Tradition," in his *Idea of God and Human Freedom,* trans. R. A. Wilson (Philadelphia: Westminster, 1973), pp. 1-79.

[169]Ibid., p. 69.

[170]Ibid., p. 72.

[171]Ibid., p. 74.

[172]Ibid., p. 61.

[173]Wolfhart Pannenberg, *Systematic Theology,* trans. Geoffrey W. Bromiley (Grand Rapids: Eerdmans, 1991), 1:187.

[174]Pannenberg, *Idea of God and Human Freedom,* p. 79.

[175]Ibid., p. 76. Also see Hugo Rahner, *Greek Myths and Christian Mystery,* trans. Brian Battershaw (New York: Harper & Row, 1963). Both Pannenberg and Rahner fail to mention in this context the infiltration of the faith by the

mythology of the Great Mother. The church fathers tried to contain this mythology but could not dispel it. See my discussion on pp. 108-16.

[176]Cf. Avery Dulles's definition of myth as "a symbolic narrative which deals with events attributed to super-human, personalized agencies. These events, unfolding in a time above that of our experience, are conceived as having a profound influence on the typical occurrences familiar to us." *Myth, Biblical Revelation and Christ* (Washington, D.C.: Corpus, 1968), p. 11. While acknowledging a residue of myth in the Bible, Dulles maintains that it is purified myth. He concurs with Heinrich Schlier's assertion: "In daring to take over the language of myth the New Testament shows that Jesus Christ is the end, not only of the Law, but of myth besides" (p. 23). Note that these essays were originally published in Dulles, *Revelation and the Quest for Unity* (Washington, D.C.: Corpus, 1968). See Schlier, "Das Neue Testament und der Mythus," *Hochland* 48 (1956):201-12 (see esp. p. 212).

[177]Helmut Thielicke, *The Evangelical Faith,* trans. and ed. Geoffrey W. Bromiley (Grand Rapids: Eerdmans, 1974), 1:84-114.

[178]See Donald Bloesch, "The Self-Revealing God," in his *God the Almighty* (Downers Grove, Ill.: InterVarsity Press, 1995), pp. 59-78.

[179]Pannenberg, *Idea of God and Human Freedom,* p. 46.

[180]Evans trenchantly observes that it is precisely because we live in a "flattened" culture emptied of transcendent meaning that modern people increasingly find myth appealing. Evans, "Incarnational Narrative," pp. 403-4.

[181]A poignant example of symbolic or mythopoetic language that is made to serve historical unfolding and eschatological fulfillment is found in Jesus' words that his followers will eat his flesh and drink his blood (Jn 6:51-58). Bultmann maintained that these words as relayed by an editor have a mythological background in the Hellenistic mysteries in which the food taken in the sacred meal is god himself. Whatever the authorial source or sources of this passage, one cannot deny that its content is radically different from myth, for its focus is on the saving work of Christ at Calvary and the coming of the new age of the kingdom. When the Johannine author identifies the living Christ as the bread of life and interprets the eating of Jesus' flesh and drinking of his blood as an inward participation in the death he was to die on the cross, he is pointing his hearers beyond cultic practices to God's decisive action in history. Many scholars believe that the bread of life discourse in John does have eucharistic allusions, but the sacramental eating and drinking must not be treated magically as in ritualistic and mythological religion. See Rudolf Bultmann, *The Gospel of John,* trans. and ed. G. R. Beasley-Murray (Philadelphia: Westminster, 1971), pp. 218-37; Raymond E. Brown, *The Gospel According to John I—XII,* Anchor Bible (Garden City, N.Y.: Doubleday, 1966), pp. 281-303; and Leon Morris, *The Gospel According to John,* New

International Commentary on the New Testament (Grand Rapids: Eerdmans, 1971), pp. 369-81.

[182]While scholars deem 1 Maccabees as overall historically reliable, 2 Maccabees contains considerable theological interpretation, but this author too is historically competent. See Neil J. McEleney, "1-2 Maccabees," in *The New Jerome Biblical Commentary*, ed. Raymond E. Brown, Joseph A. Fitzmyer and Roland E. Murphy (Englewood Cliffs, N.J.: Prentice-Hall, 1990), pp. 421-25.

[183]Immanuel Kant is helpful in his distinction between the reality that appears to us (the phenomenal) and the reality as it exists in itself (the noumenal). From my perspective visions of the divine or of celestial spirits belong to the phenomenal realm, not the noumenal. Such visions, however, may place us in contact with the noumenal. To see the face of God is to have direct access to the noumenal, which is not a possibility while we still dwell in the realm of sin and death. In contrast to Kant I contend that the noumenal became incarnate in the phenomenal in Jesus Christ, but the noumenal continues to remain veiled in Jesus Christ even in its unveiling.

[184]The text teaches not only the solidarity of Christ with Old Testament believers but their joining with Christ in his resurrection and ascension into heaven. Cf. Eph 4:8.

[185]Jesus himself contradicted the ancient mythology concerning demons by associating demonic possession with the power of sin and by positing a spiritual head of the forces of darkness—the fallen angel Satan or the devil. See my discussion in *Holy Scripture*, p. 358.

[186]See W. M. Schmidt, "Mythos in Alten Testament," *Evangelische Theologie* 27 (1967):246, quoted in Pannenberg, *Idea of God and Human Freedom*, p. 27.

[187]This is why the language of Scripture is best described as *confessional* rather than mythological. Or it is confessional before it is mythological. For other terms that aptly describe the language of faith see p. 131 and n. 192 on 276.

[188]One can say that the Bible is a mixture of history remembered and prophecy historicized. It is neither bare history nor abstract reflection.

[189]In my judgment the Bible is on the whole historically reliable, though one must be careful not to read the modern understanding of historical precision into the biblical accounts. Historical reliability is not the same as historical exactness. One must also beware of assigning historicity to stories that are manifestly intended to be taken figuratively or symbolically, though even symbolic tales in the Bible usually have a historical nexus. While the Bible does have an incontrovertible basis in history, this does not make it the authoritative Word of God. The authority of the Bible as the Word of God rests on the content of its witness—the gospel of God's saving work in Jesus Christ—which is revealed by the Holy Spirit as people are exposed to the bib-

lical testimony through reading and hearing.

[190]See Rahner, *Greek Myths and Christian Mystery,* p. 34.

[191]Norman Perrin, *Jesus and the Language of the Kingdom* (Philadelphia: Fortress, 1976), p. 198.

[192]Another term that has been brought into the discussion through ecumenical dialogue is *iconic*—language that points beyond itself to transcendent reality, which cannot be captured in either symbols or concepts. Both of these means of discourse, however, may be used by the Spirit to introduce the believer to deeper levels of meaning that are inaccessible to reason alone. In a theology that purports to be catholic and orthodox, concepts must always be open-ended in the sense of being windows to a higher reality. See Verna E. F. Harrison, "The Relationship Between Apophatic and Kataphatic Theology," *Pro Ecclesia* 4, no. 3 (1995):318-32. In contradistinction to the mystical heritage of the church as we find it in both Roman Catholicism and Eastern Orthodoxy, I see the biblical language not so much as a "ladder of ascent to union with the unknowable God" (Harrison's description of Vladimir Lossky's position, p. 323) as the earthly vehicle by which the Spirit brings the Word of God to human consciousness.

Chapter 5: The Preexistence of Jesus Christ

[1]Adolf von Harnack, *History of Dogma,* trans. Neil Buchanan (1894; reprint, New York: Russell & Russell, 1958), 2:318-32.

[2]This text is not mentioned by Harnack in his discussion of Jesus' preexistence.

[3]In the same chapter the writer complains that "a perishable body presses down the soul, and this tent of clay weighs down the mind with its many cares" (9:15 NJB). This definitely reflects the ethos of Hellenism.

[4]Harnack, *History of Dogma,* 1:319.

[5]Ibid., p. 327.

[6]Ibid., p. 328.

[7]H. R. Mackintosh, *The Doctrine of the Person of Jesus Christ* (New York: Charles Scribner's Sons, 1914), p. 449.

[8]Ibid., p. 450.

[9]Ibid., p. 454.

[10]Ibid., p. 457.

[11]The scholarly consensus is that the Pastoral Epistles were probably written by a disciple of Paul but nonetheless may contain genuine Pauline fragments.

[12]See the discussion in Philip Schaff, *History of the Christian Church* (Grand Rapids: Eerdmans, 1910), 2:558-59.

[13]See Sidney Spencer, *Mysticism in World Religion* (Baltimore: Penguin, 1963), pp. 284-98.

[14]Ibid., p. 286.

[15]Ibid., p. 285.

[16]See the discussion in Charles Hodge, *Systematic Theology* (New York: Charles Scribner's Sons, 1898), 2:423-28.

[17]Ibid., p. 422.

[18]See Adolf von Harnack, *What Is Christianity?* trans. Thomas Bailey Saunders (1957; reprint, Philadelphia: Fortress, 1986), pp. 127-30.

[19]Karl-Josef Kuschel, *Born Before All Time? The Dispute over Christ's Origin,* trans. John Bowden (New York: Crossroad, 1992).

[20]Ibid., p. 493.

[21]Ibid., p. 494.

[22]Ibid., p. 495.

[23]Donald M. Baillie, *God Was in Christ* (New York: Charles Scribner's Sons, 1948), p. 150.

[24]John Knox, *The Humanity and Divinity of Christ* (Cambridge: Cambridge University Press, 1967), p. 106.

[25]Klaas Runia, "A 'New' Christology Challenges the Church," *Christianity Today* 18, no. 7 (1974):7.

[26]See Harry Rimmer, *The Magnificence of Jesus* (Grand Rapids: Eerdmans, 1943), pp. 31-67.

[27]Karl Barth, *Church Dogmatics,* trans. G. W. Bromiley et al., ed. G. W. Bromiley and T. F. Torrance (Edinburgh: T. & T. Clark, 1957), 2(2):145.

[28]Karl Barth, *Church Dogmatics,* trans. Harold Knight et al., ed. G. W. Bromiley and T. F. Torrance (Edinburgh: T. & T. Clark, 1960), 3(2):155.

[29]Ibid., p. 464.

[30]Robert W. Jenson, *Alpha and Omega: A Study in the Theology of Karl Barth* (New York: Nelson, 1963), p. 67. These are Jenson's words.

[31]Barth, *Church Dogmatics,* 2(2):108, 116.

[32]See Karl Barth, *The Humanity of God,* trans. John Newton Thomas and Thomas Wieser (Richmond, Va.: John Knox, 1960).

[33]See *Karl Barth's Table Talk,* ed. John D. Godsey (Edinburgh: Oliver & Boyd, 1963), p. 49. Barth here voices his disagreement with Brunner.

[34]Helmut Thielicke, *Theological Ethics,* trans. John W. Doberstein, ed. William H. Lazareth (Philadelphia: Fortress, 1966), 1:109.

[35]Ibid. See Barth, *Church Dogmatics,* 2(2):59.

[36]Quoted in Wilhelm Vischer, *The Witness of the Old Testament to Christ,* trans. A. B. Crabtree (London: Lutterworth, 1949), p. 153.

[37]Arthur W. Pink, *Gleanings in Joshua,* 4th ed. (Chicago: Moody Press, 1968), p. 141.

[38]Ray S. Anderson, "The Incarnation of God in Feminist Christology: A Theological Critique," in *Speaking the Christian God,* ed. Alvin F. Kimel Jr. (Grand Rapids: Eerdmans, 1992), p. 307.

[39]Harnack, *History of Dogma*, 1:322-23.

[40]Barth, *Humanity of God*, p. 51.

[41]See, e.g., Sallie McFague, *Models of God* (Philadelphia: Fortress, 1987), pp. 61-62.

Chapter 6: Christ's Atoning Sacrifice

[1]This chapter constitutes an elucidation and expansion of themes found in my earlier discussion in Bloesch, *Essentials of Evangelical Theology,* 2 vols. (San Francisco: Harper & Row, 1978-79), 1:148-80.

[2]Karl Barth, *Church Dogmatics,* trans. G. W. Bromiley, ed. G. W. Bromiley and T. F. Torrance (Edinburgh: T. & T. Clark, 1956), 4(1):126-27.

[3]Jaroslav Pelikan, *The Christian Tradition* (Chicago: University of Chicago Press, 1971), 1:153-54, 285-86. Paul Tillich observes that the anxiety of death was nowhere more pronounced than at the end of ancient civilization. See *The Courage to Be* (London: Nisbet, 1952), pp. 53-55.

[4]Pelikan, *Christian Tradition,* 1:235.

[5]This motif was also fueled by the mystery religions in the Hellenistic world.

[6]Raymond B. Blakney, ed. and trans., *Meister Eckhart* (New York: Harper & Bros., 1941), pp. 55, 226.

[7]Cited in Paul Althaus, *The Theology of Martin Luther,* trans. Robert C. Schultz (Philadelphia: Fortress, 1966), p. 222.

[8]G. C. Berkouwer, *The Conflict with Rome,* trans. David H. Freeman (Philadelphia: Presbyterian & Reformed, 1958), p. 209.

[9]Barth, *Church Dogmatics,* 4(1):185.

[10]Arthur B. Crabtree, *The Restored Relationship* (Valley Forge, Penn.: Judson, 1963), p. 46.

[11]P. T. Forsyth is helpful in his distinction between a change of feeling and a change of treatment. "God's feeling toward us never needed to be changed. But God's treatment of us, God's practical relation to us—that had to change." *The Work of Christ* (1910; reprint, London: Independent Press, 1948), p. 105. One can say that God's basic disposition toward us does not change, but God does not view the manner of our life with the same degree of favor or disfavor.

[12]For Barth nothingness includes sin, but it is also wider and deeper than sin.

[13]See Gustaf Aulén, *Christus Victor,* trans. A. G. Hebert (New York: Macmillan, 1951).

[14]John Chrysostom, *Homiliae* IV, 4, col. 41. Cited in *Luther's Works,* trans. Walter A. Hansen, ed. Jaroslav Pelikan (St. Louis: Concordia, 1968), 29:137.

[15]*Luther's Works,* 29:135.

[16]See Herbert Hartwell, *The Theology of Karl Barth* (Philadelphia: Westminster, 1964), pp. 131-41.

[17]See Barth, *Church Dogmatics,* 4(1):486-87.

[18]See Anselm, *Why God Became Man,* trans. Joseph M. Colleran (Albany: Magi, 1969).

[19]Aulén, *Christus Victor,* pp. 81-82.

[20]Cited in François Wendel, *Calvin,* trans. Philip Mairet (London: Collins, 1963), p. 228. See John Calvin, *Institutes of the Christian Religion,* 2.17.1.

[21]Wendel, *Calvin,* pp. 228-29.

[22]See Charles A. M. Hall, *With the Spirit's Sword: The Drama of Spiritual Warfare in the Theology of John Calvin* (Richmond, Va.: John Knox, 1968).

[23]Heinrich Heppe, *Reformed Dogmatics,* ed. Ernst Bizer, trans. G. T. Thomson (London: Allen & Unwin, 1950), p. 473.

[24]Archibald A. Hodge, *The Atonement* (1867; reprint, Grand Rapids: Baker, 1974), pp. 52-53.

[25]See discussion in Aulén, *Christus Victor,* pp. 128-33.

[26]Aulén convincingly shows that the classic theory always contains a subjective dimension, since the objective work of Christ is continued in the work of the Holy Spirit. See *Christus Victor,* p. 150.

[27]Abelard cited Luke 7:47: "Therefore, I tell you, her sins, which are many, are forgiven, for she loved much." In contrast to Abelard, evangelical theology sees the forgiveness of sins as prior to our love for God rather than our love being the basis for divine forgiveness.

[28]Abelard, *Christian Theology,* trans. and ed. J. Ramsay McCallum (Oxford: Blackwell, 1948), p. 84.

[29]See Albrecht Ritschl, *The Christian Doctrine of Justification and Reconciliation,* trans. H. R. Mackintosh and A. B. Macaulay (Clifton, N.J.: Reference Book Publishers, 1966).

[30]Walter Rauschenbusch, *A Theology for the Social Gospel* (New York: Macmillan, 1917), p. 154.

[31]Ibid., p. 273.

[32]Ibid.

[33]Quoted in Wilhelm Niesel, *The Gospel and the Churches,* trans. David Lewis (Philadelphia: Westminster, 1962), p. 138.

[34]William Law, *Selected Mystical Writings,* ed. Stephen Hobhouse (London: Rockliff, 1938), pp. 18, 21, 88-89, 335-36.

[35]Ibid., pp. 155-66.

[36]See Emmy Arnold, ed., *Inner Words* (1963; reprint, Rifton, N.Y.: Plough, 1975), pp. 56, 75-76, 88. A notable evangelical strand of piety is also discernible in Eberhard Arnold and the Bruderhof. Also see *God's Revolution: The Witness of Eberhard Arnold,* ed. John Howard Yoder (Farmington, Penn.: Plough, 1984); and J. Heinrich Arnold, *Discipleship* (Farmington, Penn.: Plough, 1994).

[37]See John Miley, *The Atonement in Christ* (New York: Hunt & Eaton, 1889).

[38]Barth, *Church Dogmatics,* 4(1):172.

[39]Forsyth, *Work of Christ,* pp. 214-15.

[40]P. T. Forsyth, *The Cruciality of the Cross* (1909; 2d ed., London: Independent Press, 1948), p. 99.

[41]Forsyth, *Work of Christ,* p. 159.

[42]P. T. Forsyth, *The Christian Ethic of War* (London: Longmans, Green, 1916), pp. 93-94.

[43]See Anders Nygren, *Essence of Christianity,* trans. Philip Watson (Philadelphia: Muhlenberg, 1961), esp. pp. 89-100.

[44]Forsyth declared that in the cross of Christ we have not only God's love shown in sacrifice but also his holiness secured in judgment. The cross served not only to reconcile a broken humanity to God but also and above all to hallow God's holy name. See his *Justification of God* (1917; reprint, London: Independent Press, 1948), p. 165.

[45]A. E. Garvie, "Placarding the Cross," *Congregational Quarterly* 21, no. 4 (Oct. 1943):348.

[46]See the excellent doctoral dissertation by Leslie Charles McCurdy, "Attributes and Atonement: The Holy Love of God in the Theology of P. T. Forsyth" (University of Aberdeen, 1994).

[47]Menno Simons, "Letter of Consolation to a Sick Saint," in *The Complete Writings of Menno Simons, c. 1496-1561,* trans. Leonard Verduin, ed. John Christian Wenger (Scottdale, Penn.: Herald, 1956), p. 1053.

[48]Forsyth, *Work of Christ,* p. 182. Cf. "It is a matter not so much of substitutionary expiation (which, as these words are commonly understood, leaves us too little committed), but of solidary confession and praise from amid the judgment fires, where the Son of God walks with the creative sympathy of the holy among the sinful sons of men." Ibid., pp. 225-26.

[49]Forsyth made a distinction between punishment and penalty. "A man who loses his life in the fire-damp, where he is looking for the victims of an accident, pays the penalty of sacrifice, but he does not receive its punishment. And I think it useful to speak of Christ as taking the penalty of sin, while I refuse to speak of His taking its punishment." *Work of Christ,* p. 162.

[50]Karl Barth, *Church Dogmatics,* trans. T. H. L. Parker et al., ed. G. W. Bromiley and T. F. Torrance (Edinburgh: T. & T. Clark, 1957), 2(1):399.

[51]Karl Barth, *Church Dogmatics,* trans. G. T. Thomson and Harold Knight, ed. G. W. Bromiley and T. F. Torrance (Edinburgh: T. & T. Clark, 1956), 1(2):308.

[52]See Howard Taylor and Geraldine Taylor, *Hudson Taylor and the China Inland Mission* (1918; reprint, London: China Inland Mission, 1961), pp. 168-83.

[53]See Althaus, *Theology of Martin Luther,* p. 214.

[54]Donald Baillie, *God Was in Christ* (New York: Charles Scribner's Sons, 1948), pp. 157-202.

[55]Quoted by Philip S. Watson, *Let God Be God!* (London: Epworth, 1947), p. 131.

[56]*Works of Martin Luther,* trans. A. T. W. Steinhaeuser (Philadelphia: Holman, 1930), 3:178.

[57]Emil Brunner, *Dogmatics,* trans. Olive Wyon (Philadelphia: Westminster, 1952), 2:337.

[58]Emil Brunner, *The Mediator,* trans. Olive Wyon (Philadelphia: Westminster, 1947), p. 524.

[59]For a more literal translation see *The Heidelberg Catechism with Commentary,* ed. Alan Miller and M. Eugene Osterhaven (Philadelphia: United Church Press, 1963).

[60]Thomas Aquinas, *Summa Theologica,* 3.49.3.3.

[61]Rudolf Bultmann, "New Testament and Mythology," in *Kerygma and Myth,* ed. Hans Werner Bartsch, trans. Reginald H. Fuller (London: SPCK, 1953), 1:7.

[62]Rudolf Bultmann, *Jesus Christ and Mythology* (New York: Charles Scribner's Sons, 1958), p. 72.

[63]John Calvin, *Institutes of the Christian Religion,* ed. John T. McNeill, trans. Ford Lewis Battles, 2 vols. (Philadelphia: Westminster, 1960), 2.16.13 (1:520).

[64]Barth, *Church Dogmatics,* 4(1):229-30.

[65]Ibid., p. 756.

[66]Ibid., p. 751.

[67]Ibid., p. 776.

[68]Ibid., p. 643.

[69]Ibid., p. 330.

[70]Ibid., p. 665.

[71]See Karl Barth, *Church Dogmatics,* trans. G. W. Bromiley, ed. G. W. Bromiley and T. F. Torrance (Edinburgh: T. & T. Clark, 1969), 4(4). In one of his last works, "The Children and Their Father," Barth candidly acknowledges that in the New Testament only those who believe are free to call God their Father. Only these have attained the liberty of the children of God. Yet the New Testament also holds out the hope that all may come to this realization. Barth, *The Christian Life,* trans. G. W. Bromiley (Grand Rapids: Eerdmans, 1981), pp. 49-109. See esp. pp. 84-85.

[72]Abraham Kuyper, *The Work of the Holy Spirit,* trans. Henri De Vries (New York: Funk & Wagnalls, 1900), p. 370.

[73]John Calvin, *Commentary on 1 Timothy,* trans. William Pringle (Edinburgh: Calvin Translation Society, 1856), p. 14.

[74]See John Calvin, *Institutes* 3.24.12; *Corpus Reformatorum,* 40:445-46. See John H. Leith, *John Calvin's Doctrine of the Christian Life* (Louisville: Westminster/John Knox, 1989), p. 138; and William J. Bouwsma, *John Calvin: A Sixteenth-Century Portrait* (New York: Oxford University Press, 1988), p. 172.

[75]See the discussion in R. T. Kendall, *Calvin and English Calvinism to 1649*

(Oxford: Oxford University Press, 1979), pp. 16-18; and Alan C. Clifford, *Atonement and Justification: English Evangelical Theology 1640-1790* (Oxford: Clarendon, 1990), pp. 69-94. Clifford maintains that Calvin treated Christ's death and intercession as inseparable. Just as Christ's death is sufficient for all but efficacious only for some, so he intercedes for all, but he prays for his elect in a special way.

[76]Heppe, *Reformed Dogmatics,* pp. 477-78.

[77]Cited in Hodge, *Atonement,* p. 382.

[78]Ibid., p. 390. Note that Hodge claims to be presenting Calvin's position.

[79]In this discussion we need to bear in mind that Calvin's position and that of later Calvinism are not identical. See Clifford, *Atonement and Justification,* pp. 69-110.

[80]See Philip S. Watson, ed., *The Message of the Wesleys* (New York: Macmillan, 1964), p. 39.

[81]Nicholas Ludwig Count von Zinzendorf, *Nine Public Lectures on Important Subjects in Religion,* trans. and ed. George W. Forell (Iowa City: University of Iowa Press, 1973), p. 68.

[82]See James Daane, *The Freedom of God* (Grand Rapids: Eerdmans, 1973), pp. 14-33, 177-205.

[83]Because "irresistible grace" has been associated with determinism, it might be more felicitous to refer to efficacious grace, invincible grace or triumphant grace.

[84]See Bloesch, *Essentials of Evangelical Theology,* 2:211-34.

[85]For my earlier discussion see Bloesch, *God the Almighty* (Downers Grove, Ill.: InterVarsity Press, 1995), pp. 91-96, 208-11.

[86]Thomas J. J. Altizer, one of the leading proponents of the so-called death of God theology, drew upon both Hegel and Blake in positing a God who incarnated himself in the totality of history. See Altizer, *The Gospel of Christian Atheism* (Philadelphia: Westminster, 1966); Thomas Altizer and William Hamilton, *Radical Theology and the Death of God* (Indianapolis: Bobbs-Merrill, 1966); and Thomas Altizer, *The New Apocalypse: The Radical Vision of William Blake* (East Lansing, Mich.: Michigan State University Press, 1967). For helpful critiques of the death of God theology see Kenneth Hamilton, *God Is Dead: The Anatomy of a Slogan* (Grand Rapids: Eerdmans, 1966); and Jourdain Bishop, *Les Théologiens de "la mort de Dieu"* (Paris: Cerf, 1967).

[87]See Arthur C. Danto, *Nietzsche as Philosopher* (New York: Macmillan, 1965), pp. 191-94.

[88]William C. Placher, *Narratives of a Vulnerable God* (Louisville: Westminster/John Knox, 1994), p. 15.

[89]Ibid., p. 18.

[90]Ibid., p. 21.

⁹¹See Donald G. Bloesch, "Process Theology and Reformed Theology," in *Process Theology,* ed. Ronald H. Nash (Grand Rapids: Baker, 1987), pp. 31-56.

⁹²Alfred North Whitehead, *Process and Reality* (New York: Macmillan, 1929), p. 532.

⁹³See Jürgen Moltmann, *The Crucified God,* trans. R. A. Wilson and John Bowden (New York: Harper & Row, 1974), pp. 200-290.

⁹⁴See the helpful discussion by John Thompson, *Modern Trinitarian Perspectives* (New York: Oxford University Press, 1994), pp. 44-67.

⁹⁵This note is especially prominent in William James. See his *Will to Believe* (1896; reprint, New York: Dover, 1956); *Pragmatism* (1907; reprint, London: Longmans, Green, 1919); and *A Pluralistic Universe* (1907; reprint, Longmans, Green, 1947). James has had a palpable influence on a number of process theologians, including Bernard E. Meland, as well as on the neo-orthodox theologian Reinhold Niebuhr. The impact of James's philosophy can also be discerned in the New Thought and New Age movements.

⁹⁶Hans Urs von Balthasar explores the Christianized meaning of *actus purus* in his *Theology of Karl Barth,* trans. Edward T. Oakes (San Francisco: Ignatius, 1992), pp. 341-43. He quotes from Michael Schmaus (*Katholische Dogmatik,* 1:454), "God's Being is an active, doing Being, purest efficacy, acting by being and being by acting. There is no realm in God that is not loftiest activity, constant deed." In this discussion we must avoid both actualism, which reduces God's being to his act, and essentialism, which confounds God's being with universal static essence.

⁹⁷God experienced our despair in Jesus the man but not in himself. Moreover, this despair was promptly transcended by the joy of the resurrection. A theology of the cross must always be united with a theology of glory if we are to do justice to God's cosmic victory over the powers of sin and death.

⁹⁸For a perceptive critique of the idea of God's timeless knowledge as elucidated by Thomas Aquinas see John C. Moskop, *Divine Omniscience and Human Freedom: Thomas Aquinas and Charles Hartshorne* (Macon, Ga.: Mercer University Press, 1984). While clearly preferring Charles Hartshorne's position over that of Thomas, the author is keenly aware of the difficulties in process theism.

⁹⁹My principal difference with open-view theists is that I believe God is fully knowledgeable and fully in charge of the denouement of history. See my critique of Clark Pinnock et al., *The Openness of God* (Downers Grove, Ill.: InterVarsity Press, 1994), in Bloesch, *God the Almighty,* pp. 254-60.

Chapter 7: Salvation in Evangelical Protestantism

¹*Satisfaction* can be accepted in Christian vocabulary so long as it is subordinated to God's unconditional grace. Too often *satisfaction* presupposes a

legalistic understanding that makes fulfillment of the demands of the law the condition for God's forgiveness. Avery Dulles has this astute comment: "As sometimes presented, satisfaction seems to suggest that God, when he forgives, is not quite willing to forget the past and still insists that the sinner make amends for the evil done. Understood in this way, the requirement of satisfaction seems out of keeping with the loving mercy of God who justifies sinners by pure grace in view of the superabundant satisfaction already rendered by Christ." Dulles, "Justification in Contemporary Catholic Theology," in *Justification by Faith: Lutherans and Catholics in Dialogue VII*, ed. H. George Anderson, T. Austin Murphy and Joseph A. Burgess (Minneapolis: Augsburg, 1985), p. 270.

[2]While terms like *deification* and *divinization* occur frequently in Eastern Orthodoxy and Catholic mysticism, one should note that the dominant view in Orthodoxy is that the Christian participates in the communicable energies of God but not in his essence. See Georgios I. Mantzaridis, *The Deification of Man: St. Gregory Palamas and the Orthodox Tradition*, trans. Liadain Sherrard (Crestwood, N.Y.: St. Vladimir's Seminary Press, 1984). Also see *Salvation in Christ: A Lutheran-Orthodox Dialogue*, ed. John Meyendorff and Robert Tobias (Minneapolis: Augsburg, 1992), pp. 19-20. Theodore Stylianopoulos, professor of New Testament at Holy Cross Greek Orthodox Seminary, contends that words like *deification* should be used with care and that it is more biblical to speak of Christian maturity and growth in grace when referring to the process of purification that characterizes the life of faith. See his "Theology and Spirituality: Biblical and Historical Perspectives," unpublished paper given at a meeting of the Society for the Study of Eastern Orthodoxy and Evangelicalism, Billy Graham Center, Wheaton College, Wheaton, Ill. Oct. 7, 1995.

[3]John Wesley, *A Plain Account of Christian Perfection* (London: Epworth, 1952), p. 47.

[4]Karl Barth, *Church Dogmatics,* trans. G. W. Bromiley, ed. G. W. Bromiley and T. F. Torrance (Edinburgh: T. & T. Clark, 1956), 4(1):128-54.

[5]It should be added, however, that the Anabaptists affirmed a discipleship rooted in justifying and sanctifying grace. Whether Anabaptist theology and spirituality are closer to the Reformation than to the mystical-ascetic tradition of the church continues to be a matter of dispute among scholars. According to Harold S. Bender, Anabaptism represents "the culmination of the Reformation, the fulfillment of the original vision of Luther and Zwingli." Bender, "The Anabaptist Vision," in *The Recovery of the Anabaptist Vision*, ed. Guy F. Hershberger (Scottdale, Penn.: Herald, 1957), p. 37. In his *Anabaptism and Asceticism* (Scottdale, Penn.: Herald, 1974) Kenneth Ronald Davis traces the roots of Anabaptism to the *Devotio Moderna* tradition, which emphasized the pursuit of personal holiness. In his *Concept of Grace in the Radical Reformation*

(Nieuwkoop: B. De Graaf, 1977), Alvin Beachy argues that the Anabaptists understood grace primarily as a transforming divine energy that actually changes human nature. Thomas Finger reminds us that on occasion Anabaptists in South Germany and the Netherlands used terms that suggest an affinity to Catholic and Orthodox spirituality (such as *divinization* and *deification*). See Finger, "Anabaptism and Eastern Orthodoxy: Some Unexpected Similarities," *Journal of Ecumenical Studies* 31, nos. 1-2 (1994): 67-91.

[6]For a powerful defense of the centrality of justification in its juridical meaning throughout the New Testament see John Reumann, *"Righteousness" in the New Testament: "Justification" in the United States Lutheran-Roman Catholic Dialogue* (Philadelphia: Fortress, 1982). Significantly Reumann's findings are for the most part endorsed by the Catholic biblical scholar Joseph A. Fitzmyer in his "Biblical Basis of Justification by Faith: Comments on the Essay of Professor Reumann," in ibid., pp. 193-227.

[7]It is well to note that Luther warned against locating justification and the forgiveness of sins in a bare act of divine imputation. Faith involves a real participation in the righteousness of Christ. See Jaroslav Pelikan, *The Christian Tradition* (Chicago: University of Chicago Press, 1984), 4:153-55. Also see Simo Peura, *"Christus Praesentissimus:* The Issue of Luther's Thought in the Lutheran-Orthodox Dialogue," *Pro Ecclesia* 2, no. 3 (1993):364-71. Peura contends that for Luther justification is a process as well as an act and that it includes both mystical union and deification. Our salvation is based on Christ's alien righteousness; yet this does not remain outside us but enters into us and renews us. I agree that there is a mystical side to Luther, but this is subordinate to his emphasis on justification as declarative and forensic.

[8]See John Calvin, *Institutes of the Christian Religion,* 3.16.1.

[9]The Council of Trent held that a person who is in contact with God's prevenient grace can help to procure justification by cooperating with this prior grace. The Reformers stoutly maintained that justification is an undeserved gift that needs only to be received and acknowledged by the sinner. See "The Canons and Decrees of the Council of Trent," in *The Creeds of Christendom,* ed. Philip Schaff (1877; reprint, New York: Harper & Bros., 1919), 2:92-96.

Eastern Orthodoxy sees salvation in terms of a cooperative endeavor (synergy) between divine grace and human free will. See Christoforos Stavropoulos, "Partakers of Divine Nature," in *Eastern Orthodox Theology,* ed. Daniel B. Clendenin (Grand Rapids: Baker, 1995), pp. 183-92, esp. 189-92. Evangelical Protestants tend to suspect Orthodoxy of semi-Pelagianism, though this may not be entirely fair. According to the Orthodox theologian John Breck, synergy "implies a fundamental (and non-Pelagian) paradox: the initiative is wholly divine, originating and coming to completion within

Trinitarian divine life; yet an appropriate human response is necessary for the appropriation of saving grace." See Breck, "Divine Initiative: Salvation in Orthodox Theology," in *Salvation in Christ, ed.* John Meyendorff and Robert Tobias (Minneapolis: Augsburg, 1992), p. 112. Also see Theodore Stylianopoulos, *The Good News of Christ* (Brookline, Mass.: Holy Cross Orthodox Press, 1991), pp. 26-27.

[10]"Reformed" in this context includes the mainstream Reformation and is therefore roughly equivalent to "evangelical."

[11]Cited in Geddes MacGregor, *Dictionary of Religion and Philosophy* (New York: Paragon House, 1989), p. 548.

[12]Hans Küng, *Justification,* trans. Thomas Collins, Edmund E. Tolk and David Granskou (New York: Nelson, 1964).

[13]Rudolf Ehrlich argues persuasively that Küng still subscribes to the Tridentine understanding of faith as a theological virtue. See Ehrlich, *Rome, Opponent or Partner?* (Philadelphia: Westminster, 1965), pp. 101-205. In later works Küng more fully identifies with the Reformation position and even maintains that Luther was right in his doctrine of *sola fide.* "'Justification' according to the New Testament is not in fact a process of supernatural origin which is understood physiologically and which takes place in the human subject, but is the verdict of God in which God does not impute their sin to the godless but declares them righteous in Christ and precisely in so doing makes them really righteous." *Great Christian Thinkers,* trans. John Bowden (New York: Continuum, 1994), p. 146. Also see Küng, *Christianity: Essence, History and Future,* trans. John Bowden (New York: Continuum, 1995), pp. 531-34. For another significant positive assessment of Luther's doctrine of justification by a Roman Catholic scholar see George H. Tavard, *Justification: An Ecumenical Study* (New York: Paulist, 1983).

[14]I here have difficulty with Arthur Crabtree's position that justification and sanctification are really descriptions of the same act from different perspectives. See Crabtree, *The Restored Relationship* (Valley Forge, Penn.: Judson, 1963), pp. 186-87.

[15]Regin Prenter, "Holiness in the Lutheran Tradition," in *Man's Concern with Holiness,* ed. Marina Chavchavadze (London: Hodder & Stoughton, 1970), pp. 123-44.

[16]Lutheran theologian David P. Scaer says, "Lutherans should be a little uncomfortable with the line in 'Amazing Grace' . . . 'I once was lost but now I am found.' A profound sense of spiritual forsakenness persists as long as the Christian lives. . . . The Christian prays as a lost and condemned sinner" who "does not deserve to be forgiven, but asks that God would receive him for the bitter sufferings and death of God's Son, Jesus Christ." Scaer, "The Law and the Gospel in Lutheran Theology," *Grace Theological Journal* 12, no. 2 (1991):166. Lutherans who stand in the tradition of Pietism would take a

somewhat different view and could also claim Luther for their position.

[17]Since he regarded our original freedom as an endowment of grace, Pelagius could say that we owe everything that is good to God, but he did not believe that we come into the world in bondage to sin and therefore stand in need of redemption from the very beginning. See Philip Schaff, *History of the Christian Church* (1910; reprint, Grand Rapids: Eerdmans, 1981), 3:785-843; and Otto W. Heick, *A History of Christian Thought,* 2 vols. (1965; reprint, Philadelphia: Fortress, 1973), 1:196-213. Robert F. Evans tries to show that Pelagius was not as bereft of biblical insight as tradition suggests. See his *Pelagius: Inquiries and Reappraisals* (New York: Seabury, 1968). Evans is not convincing when he argues that Pelagius is basically a theologian of grace.

[18]On the convergences and divergences between Augustine and Luther see Harry J. McSorley, *Luther: Right or Wrong?* (New York: Newman; Minneapolis: Augsburg, 1969); and Alister E. McGrath, *Iustitia Dei: A History of the Christian Doctrine of Justification,* 2 vols. (New York: Cambridge University Press, 1986), 1:25-27; 2:17-23.

[19]See my discussion on p. 258, note 74. For my earlier discussion see my *Essentials of Evangelical Theology* (San Francisco: Harper & Row, 1978), 1:188-208.

[20]In his earlier *Commentary on the Sentences* Thomas allowed that prior to faith we can prepare ourselves to receive justification on the basis of our natural ability, without the aid of grace. In his mature work, the *Summa Theologica,* he insisted that we cannot do what lies within us except through the power of grace. See the discussion in McGrath, *Iustitia Dei,* 1:85-87.

[21]For my earlier discussion see pp. 162-67.

[22]See my earlier discussion on pp. 167-70.

[23]Calvin himself held that Christ died for all but that he intercedes at the right hand of God only for the elect. Calvin's successor, Theodore Beza, contended that the atonement is limited to the elect. See R. T. Kendall, *Calvin and English Calvinism to 1649* (Oxford: Oxford University Press, 1979), pp. 13-41.

[24]See Stephen Pfürtner, *Luther and Aquinas on Salvation,* trans. Edward Quinn (New York: Sheed & Ward, 1965); and Otto H. Pesch, "Existential and Sapiential Theology: The Theological Confrontation Between Luther and Thomas Aquinas," in *Catholic Scholars Dialogue with Luther,* ed. Jared Wicks (Chicago: Loyola University Press, 1970), pp. 61-81, esp. 66-67.

[25]See "Canons and Decrees of the Council of Trent," pp. 139-69. Also see *Catechism of the Catholic Church* (United States Catholic Conference, 1994), pp. 357-74. The Eastern Orthodox position is similar to that of Roman Catholicism except that the penalties that the church imposes on the repentant sinner are wholly "without any conciliatory or satisfactory character." See John Karmiris, "Concerning the Sacraments," in *Eastern Orthodox Theology,* ed. Daniel B. Clendenin (Grand Rapids: Baker, 1995), p. 29.

[26]Protestants in whom mystical spirituality is conspicuous include Jakob Boehme, Friedrich Christoph Oetinger, Gottfried Arnold and Gerhard Tersteegen.

[27]On the impact of Neoplatonism on Thomas Aquinas and his predecessors see Paul Rorem, "Procession and Return" in "Thomas Aquinas and His Predecessors," *Princeton Seminary Bulletin* 13, no. 2 (1992):147-63.

[28]Gerald Heard seeks to combine the Neoplatonic schema of emanation with the modern theory of evolution. While he appreciates Christ as a paradigm of authentic spirituality, his emphasis is on works of spiritual purification rather than on divine grace. Because of his syncretistic bent, he could aptly be described as a post-Christian mystic. See his *Creed of Christ* (New York: Harper & Bros., 1940); *Training for the Life of the Spirit* (New York: Harper & Bros., 1941); *A Preface to Prayer* (New York: Harper & Bros., 1944); and *Is God in History?* (New York: Harper & Bros., 1950).

[29]See n. 7 in this chapter.

[30]I owe the illustration of the umbrella for Luther's position to Robert Brinsmead, founding editor of *Present Truth* magazine.

[31]See Alan C. Clifford, *Atonement and Justification: English Evangelical Theology 1640-1790* (Oxford: Clarendon, 1990), pp. 69-94, 240-44.

[32]John Calvin, *The First Epistle of Paul the Apostle to the Corinthians,* trans. John W. Fraser, ed. David W. Torrance and Thomas F. Torrance (Grand Rapids: Eerdmans, 1960), p. 46.

[33]In ecumenical dialogue we as Protestants should frankly acknowledge that justification by works seems to be affirmed by James (Jas 2:14-26), though it is palpably contradicted by Paul (Rom 3:21-28). Although the context clearly indicates that James includes faith in our justification, it is a faith that is fulfilled in works of self-giving service. The faith that justifies is a faith that produces fruit. In the light of the fuller New Testament vision, we need to say that our works of love do not procure or earn our justification but manifest and confirm it. While there are admittedly tensions between James and Paul, the two are not on opposite sides, for their emphases are complementary. James is thinking of justification in the final sense when our words and lives will be judged by Christ, whereas Paul stresses justification as the initial act and ground of Christian faith and life. See the helpful discussion in Bo Reicke, *The Epistles of James, Peter and Jude,* Anchor Bible (Garden City, N.Y.: Doubleday, 1964), pp. 32-35. Also see Clifford, *Atonement and Justification,* pp. 221-39; and R. C. Sproul, *Faith Alone: The Evangelical Doctrine of Justification* (Grand Rapids: Baker, 1995), pp. 160-68.

Chapter 8: Law and Gospel: A Reformed Perspective

[1]Thomas Aquinas, *Summa Theologica* 1-2.106.1.

[2]Pope John Paul II, *The Splendor of Truth (Veritatis Splendor)* (Washington, D.C.: United States Catholic Conference, 1993), no. 24, p. 40.

[3]Martin Luther, "Preface to the Epistle to the Romans," trans. C. M. Jacobs, in *Works of Martin Luther* (Philadelphia: Holman, 1932), 6:457.

[4]Reinhold Niebuhr, *The Nature and Destiny of Man*, 2 vols. (New York: Charles Scribner's Sons, 1951), 2:202.

[5]Quoted in François Wendel, *Calvin*, trans. Philip Mairet (London: Collins, 1963), p. 204. See Calvin, *Institutes* 3.19.2.

[6]For a more extended discussion of Barth's position on law and gospel see Donald G. Bloesch, *Freedom for Obedience* (San Francisco: Harper & Row, 1987), pp. 117-21; and Gerhard O. Forde, *The Law-Gospel Debate* (Minneapolis: Augsburg, 1969), pp. 137-74. Also see Karl Barth, "Gospel and Law" (trans. A. M. Hall), in Barth, *Community, State and Church*, ed. Will Herberg (Garden City, N.Y.: Doubleday Anchor, 1960), pp. 71-100.

[7]See Jacques Ellul, *The Theological Foundation of Law*, trans. Marguerite Wieser (New York: Seabury, 1969).

[8]Karl Barth, *The Göttingen Dogmatics: Instruction in the Christian Religion*, trans. Geoffrey W. Bromiley (Grand Rapids: Eerdmans, 1990), 1:195.

[9]Karl Barth, *The Word of God and the Word of Man*, trans. Douglas Horton (1957; reprint, Gloucester, Mass.: Peter Smith, 1978), p. 264.

[10]See I. John Hesselink, *Calvin's Concept of the Law* (Allison Park, Penn.: Pickwick, 1992), esp. pp. 110-12, 231-34.

[11]See James R. Edwards, *Romans* (Peabody, Mass.: Hendrickson, 1992), pp. 247-50.

[12]This nuance of meaning is brought out in the alternate reading of Rom 10:4 in the NEB: "Christ is the end of the law as a way to righteousness for everyone who has faith." ·

[13]Niebuhr, *Nature and Destiny of Man*, 2:106.

[14]Reinhold Niebuhr, *Christian Realism and Political Problems* (New York: Charles Scribner's Sons, 1953), p. 164.

[15]Karl Barth, *The Epistle to the Romans*, trans. Edwyn C. Hoskyns (1933; reprint, New York: Oxford University Press, 1975), p. 159.

[16]See Heidelberg Catechism, question 86, in *The Creeds of Christendom*, ed. Philip Schaff (1877; reprint, New York: Harper & Bros., 1919), 3:338.

[17]See Bloesch, *Freedom for Obedience*, pp. 150-53.

[18]Barth, *Göttingen Dogmatics*, p. 180.

[19]*The Confessions of St. Augustine*, trans. and ed. John K. Ryan (Garden City, N.Y.: Doubleday Image, 1960), 10.29.40, pp. 255-56; cf. 10.35.56, p. 266.

[20]See *Presbyterians and Human Sexuality 1991* (Louisville: Office of the General Assembly, Presbyterian Church [U.S.A.], 1991). Also see Susan Thistlethwaite, ed., *A Just Peace Church* (New York: United Church Press, 1986).

²¹See M. Eugene Osterhaven, "Covenant," in *Encyclopedia of the Reformed Faith*, ed. Donald K. McKim (Louisville: Westminster/John Knox, 1992), p. 85.

²²Barth, *Community, State and Church*, p. 81.

Chapter 9: The Lordship of Christ in Theological History

¹See Jürgen Moltmann, *On Human Dignity*, trans. M. Douglas Meeks (Philadelphia: Fortress, 1984), pp. 93-96; Ernst Käsemann, "Paul and Early Catholicism," in his *New Testament Questions of Today* (Philadelphia: Fortress, 1969), pp. 236-51; Käsemann, "Ephesians and Acts," in *Studies in Luke-Acts*, ed. L. E. Keck and J. L. Martyn (Nashville: Abingdon, 1966), pp. 288-97; and Käsemann, *Commentary on Romans*, trans. and ed. G. W. Bromiley (Grand Rapids: Eerdmans, 1980), pp. 350-64. Käsemann sees in Ephesians a growing sacramentalism and a marked stress on the cosmic role of Christ, very uncharacteristic of Paul. See the discussion in Paul J. Kobelski, "The Letter to the Ephesians," in *New Jerome Biblical Commentary*, ed. Raymond E. Brown, Joseph A. Fitzmyer and Roland E. Murphy (Englewood Cliffs, N.J.: Prentice Hall, 1990), pp. 884-85; and Markus Barth, *Ephesians 1-3*, Anchor Bible (New York: Doubleday, 1974), pp. 13-21, 32-36.

²Augustine, *The City of God*, trans. Marcus Dods (New York: Modern Library, 1950). Also see Reinhold Niebuhr, "Augustine's Political Realism," in his *Christian Realism and Political Problems* (New York: Charles Scribner's Sons, 1953), pp. 119-46.

³Thomas Aquinas, *Commentary on Saint Paul's Epistle to the Ephesians*, trans. Matthew L. Lamb (Albany: Magi, 1966), p. 80.

⁴Ibid., p. 30. Note: these are the words of Matthew Lamb.

⁵Augustine nevertheless recognized that the state contains much that is of value for human life. See John Neville Figgis, *The Political Aspects of St. Augustine's "City of God"* (1921; reprint, Gloucester, Mass.: Peter Smith, 1963), pp. 51-67.

⁶See W. A. Visser't Hooft, *The Kingship of Christ* (New York: Harper & Bros., 1948), pp. 141-42. See also Ernst Troeltsch, *The Social Teaching of the Christian Churches*, trans. Olive Wyon (1931; reprint, London: Allen & Unwin, 1950), p. 406.

⁷H. Richard Niebuhr, *Christ and Culture* (New York: Harper & Bros., 1951), pp. 143, 146.

⁸Visser't Hooft, *Kingship of Christ*, pp. 54-55.

⁹See John H. Leith, *John Calvin's Doctrine of the Christian Life* (Louisville: Westminster/John Knox, 1989), pp. 160-65.

¹⁰Friedrich Schleiermacher, *The Christian Faith*, ed. H. R. Mackintosh and J. S. Stewart, 2 vols. (New York: Harper & Row, 1963), 2:469.

¹¹Ibid., p. 470.

[12]Visser't Hooft, *Kingship of Christ,* p. 26.

[13]Wilhelm Herrmann, *The Communion of the Christian with God,* trans. J. Sandys Stanton, rev. R. W. Stewart (1906; reprint, Philadelphia: Fortress, 1971), pp. 86-87.

[14]Albrecht Ritschl, *The Christian Doctrine of Justification and Reconciliation,* ed. H. R. Mackintosh and A. B. Macaulay (Clifton, N.J.: Reference Book Publishers, 1966), p. 669.

[15]Reinhold Niebuhr, *Discerning the Signs of the Times* (New York: Charles Scribner's Sons, 1946), p. 96.

[16]Ibid., pp. 105-6.

[17]Reinhold Niebuhr, *Beyond Tragedy* (New York: Charles Scribner's Sons, 1937), p. 277.

[18]Ibid., pp. 191-92.

[19]Niebuhr, *Discerning the Signs of the Times,* p. 134.

[20]Ibid., p. 143.

[21]Karl Barth, *Church Dogmatics,* trans. G. W. Bromiley, ed. G. W. Bromiley and T. F. Torrance, 2d ed. (Edinburgh: T. & T. Clark, 1975), 1(1):47-48; ibid. (1957), 2(2):688-700. Also see his *The Christian Life,* trans. G. W. Bromiley (Grand Rapids: Eerdmans, 1981), pp. 263-65.

[22]Moltmann, *On Human Dignity,* pp. 79-96.

[23]Ibid., p. 94.

[24]Ibid., p. 104.

[25]Ibid., p. 99.

[26]Leading liberation theologians include Gustavo Gutiérrez, Juan Luis Segundo, Jon Sobrino, Ronaldo Muñoz, Hugo Assmann, José Míguez Bonino, José Miranda, Leonardo Boff, Clodovis Boff, Frederick Herzog, Dorothee Sölle and Ismael Garcia. For a brief bibliography see note 15 in chap. 10, p. 294.

[27]Harvey Cox, *Religion in the Secular City: Toward a Postmodern Theology* (New York: Simon & Schuster, 1984), p. 147.

[28]Jon Sobrino, *Christology at the Crossroads,* trans. John Drury (Maryknoll, N.Y.: Orbis, 1978), p. 307.

[29]Matthew Fox, *The Coming of the Cosmic Christ* (San Francisco: Harper & Row, 1988), p. 107.

[30]Note that Revelation proclaims the joint lordship of Son and Father (Rev 11:15; 12:10).

[31]In this view the millennium itself is not something static and finalized but something dynamic and unfolding, having its goal and perfection in the complete subjection of all earthly authorities to the lordship of Jesus Christ.

[32]This is not to deny that on occasion the scope of redemptive history may be curtailed because of the hardness of the human heart. But just as the ocean tide may recede and then come back with even greater force, so God's grace

too cannot be permanently obstructed but will finally have its way even in the midst of unfaith and apostasy.

[33]Clinton Morrison, *The Powers That Be,* Studies in Biblical Theology 1/29 (Naperville, Ill.: Allenson, 1960).

[34]I have serious reservations concerning the efforts of both Christian Reconstructionists to establish a theocratic state governed by Old Testament laws and some Christian coalitionists to build a Christian America. It is one thing to promote Judeo-Christian values in a basically secular culture (a practice I wholeheartedly endorse) and quite another to impose laws that palpably belong to another era or dispensation on a modern pluralistic society. On the one hand, the Bible can be a legitimate resource in shaping our ideas of truth and justice, but it does not furnish a blueprint for a Christian world order that gives a privileged position to the church or the faith community. The state should take care not to impose forms of worship or particular theologies upon its subjects, but it should allow people freedom to practice their religion so long as they respect the rights of others. On the other hand, a state based on Judeo-Christian values should strive to maintain these values and may in some contexts appeal to the Bible to amplify these values, which are rooted in the moral order of the universe and ultimately in the living God himself. On the Christian Reconstructionist movement see Gary DeMar, *The Debate over Christian Reconstruction* (Fort Worth, Tex.: Dominion, 1988); H. Wayne House and Thomas Ice, *Dominion Theology: Blessing or Curse?* (Portland, Ore.: Multnomah, 1988); Bruce Barron, *Heaven on Earth? The Social and Political Agenda of Dominion Theology* (Grand Rapids: Zondervan, 1992); David Smith, *A Handbook of Contemporary Theology* (Wheaton, Ill.: Victor, 1992), pp. 259-72; and Anson Shupe, "The Reconstructionist Movement on the New Christian Right," *Christian Century* 106, no. 28 (1989):880-82.

[35]Visser't Hooft, *Kingship of Christ,* pp. 133-34.

[36]Ibid., p. 134. I would add that people of faith as they fulfill their secular occupations should keep themselves open to the leading of the Spirit as he seeks to implement God's commandment in the social and political spheres of life. This is not arrogating to ourselves royal lordship: it is simply practicing good citizenship for the purpose of maintaining peace and justice in society. Our efforts to fortify justice must not be confounded with the new reality of the kingdom of God, though they may in some circumstances testify to the coming of the kingdom.

Chapter 10: The Finality of Christ

[1]Friedrich Schleiermacher, *On Religion: Speeches to Its Cultured Despisers,* trans. John Oman (New York: Harper & Row, 1958), p. 175.

[2]See Ernst Troeltsch, *The Absoluteness of Christianity and the History of Religions,*

trans. David Reid (Richmond, Va.: John Knox, 1971); and Troeltsch, "The Place of Christianity Among the World Religions," in his *Christian Thought: Its History and Application*, trans. Mary E. Clarke et al., ed. Baron F. von Hügel (1923; reprint, New York: Meridian, 1957), pp. 33-63. Whereas in his earlier work Troeltsch argued for the uniqueness of the Christian experience of God, in his later work he allowed that other religions also have a "naive claim to validity." Here we can discern a move from modernism to postmodernism.

[3]William James, *The Varieties of Religious Experience* (1902; reprint, New York: New American Library, 1958), p. 368. Some of those in the current theology of religions movement also espouse ontological pluralism, e.g., Paul Knitter: "Pluralism seems to be of the very stuff of reality, the way things are, the way they function. . . . There can never be just one of anything." Knitter, *No Other Name?* (Maryknoll, N.Y.: Orbis, 1985), p. 6.

[4]Paul Knitter, "World Religions and the Finality of Christ," *Horizons* 5, no. 2 (1978):153. Note that Knitter believes interfaith dialogue should not revolve around God or Christ but around meeting the human need of deliverance from suffering. See Lesslie Newbigin's criticisms of Knitter in Newbigin, "Religious Pluralism and the Uniqueness of Jesus Christ," in *The Best in Theology*, ed. J. I. Packer (Carol Stream, Ill.: Christianity Today, 1990), p. 269. Also see Newbigin, "Religion for the Marketplace," in *Christian Uniqueness Reconsidered: The Myth of a Pluralistic Theology of Religions*, ed. Gavin D'Costa (Maryknoll, N.Y.: Orbis, 1990), pp. 135-48.

[5]*National Catholic Reporter* 6, no. 24 (1970):7.

[6]Hans Küng, "The World Religions in God's Plan of Salvation," in *Christian Revelation and World Religions*, ed. Joseph Neuner (London: Burns & Oates, 1967), p. 52.

[7]John Hick, *God Has Many Names* (London: Macmillan, 1980), p. 88.

[8]John Hick and Paul Knitter, eds., *The Myth of Christian Uniqueness* (Maryknoll, N.Y.: Orbis, 1987). Also see John Hick, *A Christian Theology of Religions* (Louisville: Westminster/John Knox, 1995).

[9]See James Jeans, *The Mysterious Universe* (1900; reprint, New York: AMS Press, 1976); and Fritjof Capra, *The Tao of Physics* (Boston: New Science Library, 1975).

[10]Theologians who have sought to learn from crisis theology include Thomas F. Torrance, Bernard Ramm, Arthur Cochrane, John Hesselink, Kenneth Hamilton, John Vissers, Michael Horton and Donald Bloesch. All these scholars would identify themselves as evangelical.

[11]See Carl E. Braaten, *No Other Gospel!* (Minneapolis: Fortress, 1992). Braaten follows Tillich in viewing Christ as God's final revelation but not the only revelation. See pp. 65-81.

[12]Alexander Schmemann, *Church, World, Mission: Reflections on Orthodoxy in*

the West (Crestwood, N.Y.: St. Vladimir's Seminary Press, 1979), p. 123.

[13]See John B. Cobb Jr., *Christ in a Pluralistic Age* (Philadelphia: Westminster, 1975). Cobb wishes to affirm the uniqueness of Christianity but also the uniqueness of other religions. See his "Beyond 'Pluralism,'" in *Christian Uniqueness Reconsidered*, ed. Gavin D'Costa (Maryknoll, N.Y.: Orbis, 1990), pp. 81-95.

[14]Paul Tillich, *The Future of Religions* (New York: Harper & Row, 1966), p. 87.

[15]See Alfred T. Hennelly, ed., *Liberation Theology: A Documentary History* (Maryknoll, N.Y.: Orbis, 1990); Leonardo Boff and Clodovis Boff, *Introducing Liberation Theology*, trans. Paul Burns (Maryknoll, N.Y.: Orbis, 1987); Claus Bussmann, *Who Do You Say? Jesus Christ in Latin American Theology*, trans. Robert R. Barr (Maryknoll, N.Y.: Orbis, 1984); José Míguez Bonino, ed., *Faces of Jesus: Latin American Christologies*, trans. Robert Barr (Maryknoll, N.Y.: Orbis, 1983); Dorothee Sölle, *The Window of Vulnerability: A Political Spirituality*, trans. Linda M. Maloney (Minneapolis: Fortress, 1990); Ismael Garcia, *Justice in Latin American Theology of Liberation* (Atlanta: John Knox, 1987); Jon Sobrino, *Spirituality of Liberation: Toward Political Holiness*, trans. Robert R. Barr (Maryknoll, N.Y.: Orbis, 1988); Christopher Rowland and Mark Corner, *Liberating Exegesis: The Challenge of Liberation Theology to Biblical Studies* (Louisville: Westminster/John Knox, 1989); Eleazar S. Fernandez, *Toward a Theology of Struggle* (Maryknoll, N.Y.: Orbis, 1994); Pedro Casaldáliga and José-Maria Vigil, *Political Holiness: A Spirituality of Liberation*, trans. Paul Burns and Francis McDonagh (Maryknoll, N.Y.: Orbis, 1994); Leonardo Boff, *Ecology and Liberation: A New Paradigm*, trans. John Cumming (Maryknoll, N.Y.: Orbis, 1995); Cyris H. S. Moon, *A Korean Minjung Theology* (Maryknoll, N.Y.: Orbis, 1985).

[16]George A. Lindbeck, *The Nature of Doctrine* (Philadelphia: Westminster, 1984), p. 64.

[17]Marcus J. Borg, *Jesus: A New Vision* (San Francisco: Harper & Row, 1987).

[18]Matthew Fox, *The Coming of the Cosmic Christ* (San Francisco: Harper & Row, 1988), p. 145.

[19]Matthew Fox, *Original Blessing* (Santa Fe: Bear, 1983), pp. 201-7.

[20]See Karl Barth, *Church Dogmatics*, trans. G. W. Bromiley, ed. G. W. Bromiley and T. F. Torrance (Edinburgh: T. & T. Clark, 1961), 4(3a):89-97, 114-15, 118, 122, 355-56.

[21]I fully agree with Mark Heim that while we need to respect the humanity of those who adhere to other religions we must not presume that we are all saying the same thing or even something very similar. See Heim, *Is Christ the Only Way?: Christian Faith in a Pluralistic World* (Valley Forge, Penn.: Judson, 1985); and his *Salvations: Truth and Difference in Religion* (Maryknoll, N.Y.: Orbis, 1995). Also see Hendrik Vroom, *No Other Gods: Christian Belief in Dialogue with Buddhism, Hinduism and Islam*, trans. Lucy Jansen (Grand Rapids:

Eerdmans, 1996); and Harold Netland, *Dissonant Voices: Religious Pluralism and the Question of Truth* (Grand Rapids: Eerdmans, 1991). In a review of Heim's *Salvations* Netland charges, perhaps unfairly, that Heim fails to safeguard the exclusivistic claims of Christian faith. Netland also objects to the radical agnosticism of Hick. Harold Netland, "A Review Essay of John Hick's *A Christian Theology of Religions* and S. Mark Heim's *Salvations: Truth and Differences in Religion,*" in *Religious and Theological Studies Fellowship Bulletin,* no. 12 (Sept./Oct. 1996): 17-19.

[22]See Karl Barth, *Church Dogmatics,* trans. G. T. Thomson and Harold Knight, ed. G. W. Bromiley and T. F. Torrance (Edinburgh: T. & T. Clark, 1956), 1(2):280-361.

[23]Hans Küng, *Theology for the Third Millennium: An Ecumenical View,* trans. Peter Heinegg (New York: Doubleday, 1988), pp. 240-56.

[24]Frederick Herzog, *Liberation Theology* (New York: Seabury, 1972), p. 147. Also see his *God-Walk: Liberation Shaping Dogmatics* (Maryknoll, N.Y.: Orbis, 1988). For Herzog's critique of my position see *God-Walk,* pp. 255-56.

[25]Peter Beyerhaus, "The Theology of Salvation in Bangkok," *Christianity Today* 17, no. 13 (1973):17.

[26]See Robert McAfee Brown, *Frontiers for the Church Today* (New York: Oxford University Press, 1973), pp. 42-43.

[27]Cited by Thomas O'Meara, *Romantic Idealism and Roman Catholicism* (Notre Dame, Ind.: University of Notre Dame Press, 1982), p. 20.

[28]See Michael S. Horton, *In the Face of God: The Dangers and Delights of Spiritual Intimacy* (Dallas: Word, 1996), pp. 21-67.

[29]Rosemary Radford Ruether, *Womanguides: Readings Toward a Feminist Theology* (Boston: Beacon, 1985), pp. ix-xii; Ruether, *Sexism and God-Talk* (Boston: Beacon, 1983), pp. 21-22. Daphne Hampson goes even further and calls for a post-Christian feminist theology in her *Theology and Feminism* (Cambridge, Mass.: Basil Blackwell, 1990).

[30]Cited in Stephan A. Hoeller, *The Gnostic Jung and the Seven Sermons to the Dead* (Wheaton, Ill.: Theosophical Publishing House, 1982), p. 194.

[31]Cited in Peter Stuhlmacher, *Historical Criticism and Theological Interpretation of Scripture,* trans. Roy A. Harrisville (Philadelphia: Fortress, 1977), p. 39.

[32]Ibid.

[33]Many feminists also tend to associate patriarchalism with the Jewish ethos, and this accounts for their distrust of Judaism as well as historical Christianity. Susanne Heine warns that "feminist literature, which sweepingly makes 'the Jews' and their allegedly martial God responsible for all women's suffering down the centuries, affords a powerful stimulus to antisemitism." Heine, *Matriarchs, Goddesses and Images of God: A Critique of a Feminist Theology,* trans. John Bowden (Minneapolis: Augsburg, 1989), p. 166 n. 26. Also see Katharina von Kellenbach, *Anti-Judaism in Feminist Religious Writings* (Atlanta:

Scholars Press, 1994).

[34]An egregious example is the *New Century Hymnal* of the United Church of Christ (Cleveland: Pilgrim, 1995). For my critique see Donald G. Bloesch, "Hymns for the Politically Correct," *Christianity Today* 40, no. 8 (1996): 49-50.

[35]"Jews Decry Prayer Book," *Christian Century* 107, no. 1 (1990):10.

[36]Klaus Scholder, *The Churches and the Third Reich,* trans. John Bowden, 2 vols. (Philadelphia: Fortress, 1988), 1:427.

[37]John H. Leith, ed., *Creeds of the Churches* (1963; 3d ed., Atlanta: John Knox, 1982), p. 520.

[38]See Langdon Gilkey, "Plurality and Its Theological Implications," in *Myth of Christian Uniqueness,* pp. 37-50.

[39]See Peter L. Berger, "Different Gospels: The Social Sources of Apostasy," in *American Apostasy: The Triumph of "Other" Gospels,* ed. Richard John Neuhaus (Grand Rapids: Eerdmans, 1989), pp. 1-14.

[40]Richard Blow, "Moronic Convergence," *New Republic* 198, no. 4 (1988):26. Note that the actual wording is that of the author of the article.

Name Index

Subject Index

Scripture Index